AF378311

THE FREELANCE PHOTOGRAPHER'S PROJECT BOOK

THE FREELANCE PHOTOGRAPHER'S PROJECT BOOK

**Edited by John Tracy
& Stewart Gibson**

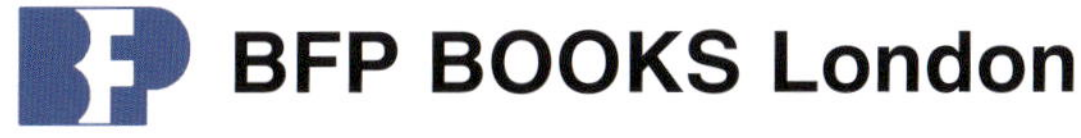

BFP BOOKS London

A catalogue record for this book is available from the British Library

ISBN 0-907297-56-0

All photographs within the book are by the author of the particular project unless otherwise stated.
Cover photographs by (left to right, top) Keith Plant, Angela Hampton, Lesley Crawford, Angela Hampton; (left to right, bottom) Dawn Sumner, Keith Plant

Published BFP Books, the book publishing division of the Bureau of Freelance Photographers, Focus House, 497 Green Lanes, London N13 4BP. Typesetting and page layout by BFP Books. Printed in Great Britain by Butler & Tanner Ltd.

Contents

Approaching the Market

by TRACY HALLETT

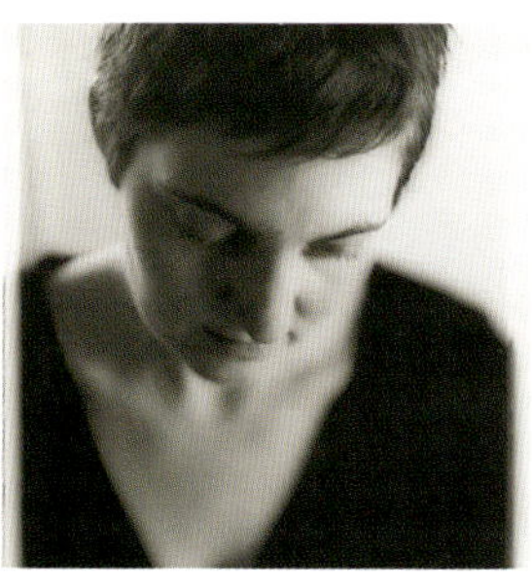

Working for a monthly photographic magazine, as I do, is a mixed blessing. While the opportunity to view hundreds of images every week is an obvious perk, there are days when mountains of poorly composed family snaps and blurry prints of pet dogs threaten to trigger an envelope avalanche in the office.

Though extreme, these examples illustrate a common complaint in the publishing industry: less than 5% of the work received meets the needs of the market. Reasons for rejection range from inappropriate technique to missing contact details and pushy phone calls.

But, despite the seemingly low level of acceptance, freelance photography is not a lottery – success is a simple matter of reducing the competition until the odds fall in your favour.

Next time you're tempted to rush a submission off in the post, bear the following in mind: the editor must satisfy the needs of his/her readership, and you, consequently, must satisfy the needs of the editor. Initially this might seem daunting, but the key to the editor's happiness is within your reach. Make a mental note of the following six steps to satisfaction and you could be well on your way to hitting the jackpot.

Researching the market

Looking at the wealth of magazines available on the newsstands, it's clear that demand for high quality imagery is stronger than ever. The good news is that the majority of this material comes from freelance photographers.

In order to join this collective, you must first identify an appropriate market for your work. Spend a few minutes thinking about your interests other than photography; do you enjoy walking, gardening, angling or boating? Specialising in a field you're passionate about can be a great way of breaking into the market; the competition is less fierce and your "inside knowledge" will prove invaluable if you decide to write articles to accompany your images.

Once you have selected a target publication, get hold of a couple of recent issues

Tracy Hallett currently works on the editorial staff of *Outdoor Photography*, where she is able to combine her passion for images with a love of writing. After receiving a first-class honours degree in Media with Cultural Studies in 1999, Tracy's photographic work has been featured in 18 consumer titles including *The Independent on Sunday Magazine* and *The British Journal of Photography*. In 2002 Tracy's work appeared in The National Portrait Gallery in London. In 2005 a selection of her photographs was published in the book *Viewfinder: 100 Top Locations for Great Travel Photography*, and later that same year a manual on the Canon EOS 300X, which she co-authored and illustrated with colleague James Beattie, was published by the Photographers' Institute Press.

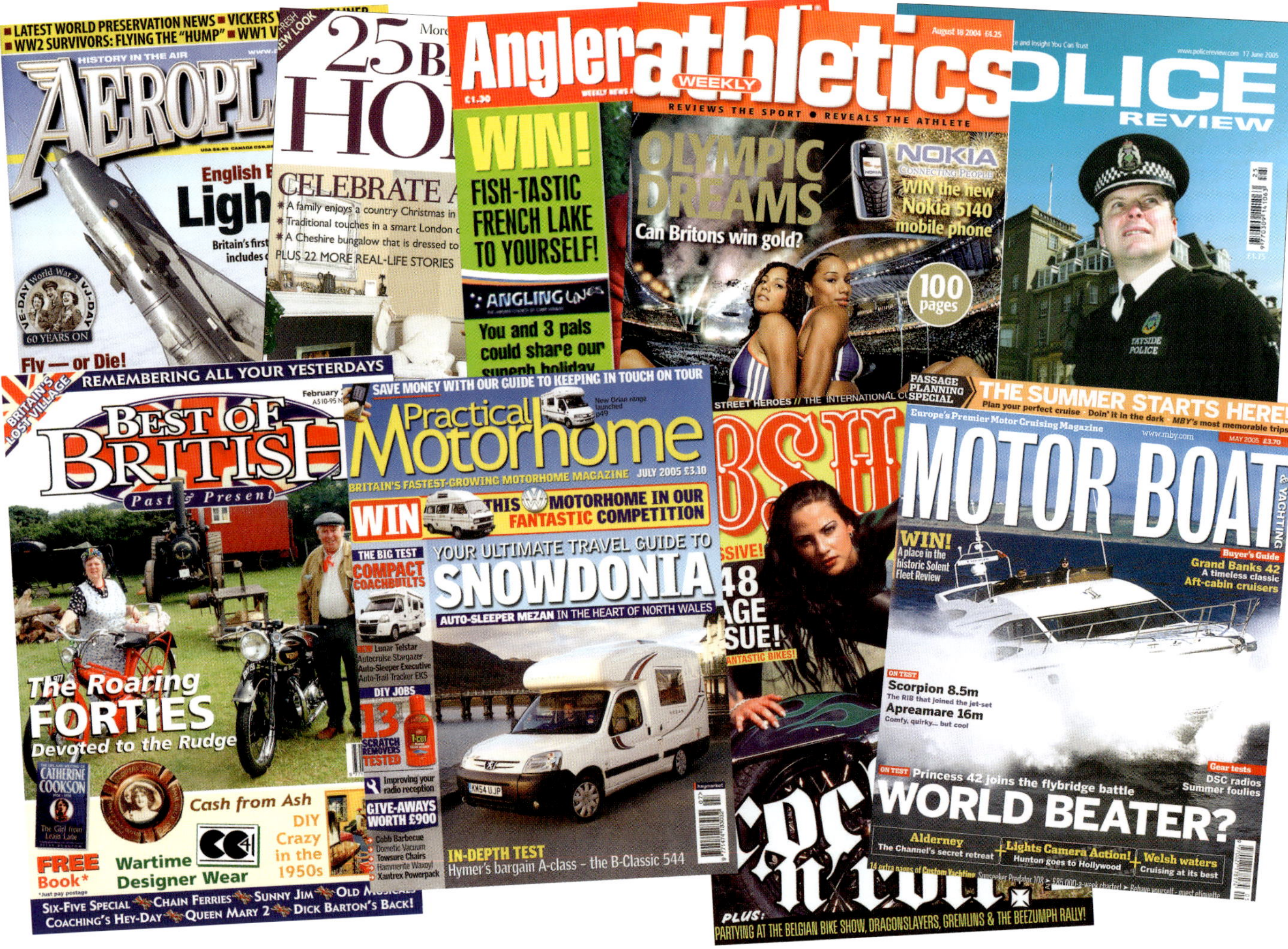

of your chosen title. Rather than buy them you could, as a prospective contributor, ask the magazine itself. But while most editorial staff will happily send out one or two copies, it's good practice to ask whether or not you need to pay for them.

Next, determine the readership of your magazine, by looking at the advertisements. While you can gain an idea of a magazine's audience from its content, it's quicker, and more effective, to let someone else do the legwork for you. Advertisers spend thousands of pounds on research, and a quick scan of the products they promote will enable you to build up a mental picture of the "average" reader. Armed with this information you will be able to tailor your submission to satisfy their needs.

Now turn to the editorial pages. Look at the types of images used, and the names that appear alongside them. Compare these picture credits to the staff list at the front of the magazine – those that don't appear are usually freelance contributions. A wealth of different names means a wealth of opportunities.

Before moving on, check whether or not your chosen title accepts speculative or "on spec" submissions – a quick look in *The Freelance Photographer's Market Handbook* should provide the answer. Finally, if your chosen title publishes guidelines for contributors, send for them – and follow them to the letter.

There are literally thousands of magazines published in the UK today, covering just about every conceivable subject. Virtually all of them offer a market for freelance photography

Editing your submission

Once you have identified, and analysed, a potential market, it's time to take a long, hard look at your photographs. Competition in the freelance world is fierce, and it's simply not enough to produce visually average images. Your photographs need to offer something extra, something that only you can provide.

There are many ways to achieve this "edge". Firstly, if you are an expert in any one particular field, show it in your picture selection. For example, if you shoot plant portraits, select pictures that are more than mere record shots. If a plant is known for its delicate petals, choose images that focus on this feature. Stress your ability to provide full botanical information, and label your images with Latin names.

Alternatively, you might have perfected an unusual photographic technique – synchronised flash for example – try selecting images that illustrate your competence in this area.

Whatever you decide to include in your submission, make each photograph count, and remove any that you are not 100% satisfied with. Never include sub-standard or technically imperfect images just to bump up the numbers; they will dilute the overall quality of your submission.

Finally, consider a magazine's lead-in times. The majority of monthly publications work a good 10 weeks ahead, and your image selection needs to reflect this fact. For example, if you are submitting winter shots, be aware that the editor might be looking to fill their winter issues in early autumn. Alternatively, if your preference is for calendar work, bear in mind that many publishers only accept submissions once a year – it can be helpful to keep a diary of what to send in and when.

Once you are happy with your selection, it's time to convince the editor that what you are offering is exactly what they need.

Writing a query letter

While there is much scope for one-off images – particularly in photography magazines – producing word and picture packages is a much more lucrative way of transforming your creativity into hard cash. The benefits of being able to produce tightly written, informative copy cannot be overstressed.

Once you have formulated an idea for an article, stop writing. While you may be prepared to spend weeks penning elaborate prose, it could be that the editor has recently commissioned a similar article from another source, or that your text is twice the length of the space available. You can save yourself a great deal of time, and heartache, by using the writer's ultimate selling tool: a query letter. Together with your photographs, this will determine whether your work is returned to you with a rejection slip or, ultimately, a cheque.

As with any written proposal, the query letter – which, these days, many editors are happy to receive by e-mail – should be short, businesslike and to the point. The aim of the letter is to whet the editor's appetite before offering a brief, but enticing, outline of the proposed article, leaving them hungry for more.

A word of warning though – never offer anything that you can't deliver. Nothing will destroy your reputation faster than failing to fulfil your promises.

Make sure that your query is addressed to the editor by name, which of course should be correctly splelt.

Presentation and packaging

As soon as a submission arrives in the editorial office – even before the envelope is opened – it is judged. Recycled Jiffy bags and photographs sandwiched between old cereal packets do not create good first impressions. If you want to be treated as a professional, present your pictures with the same care and attention you exercised when taking them.

Digital images should be saved in TIFF or JPEG format. Some editors are happy to receive low resolution images by e-mail, but be sure to check this point first. Generally you should avoid sending final images via e-mail, unless requested to do so – an editor will not thank you for crashing their computer while struggling to open a 50MB file. Send a CD containing low-res images and a sheet of corresponding thumbnail shots to begin with; high-res versions can always be posted later.

If submitting transparencies, they should be mounted (but not glass-mounted) and labelled clearly with full contact details, preferably on the bottom. Each should be marked with a unique reference number, and presented in clear plastic sheets with pockets. These sheets should then be placed between two pieces of card, secured with elastic bands, and slotted into a padded envelope.

If you are sending prints, ideally they should be roughly 8x10in in size.

Don't forget that all images should be accompanied by brief captions – the information you provide will depend on the market you're supplying, but it's useful to follow the old writers' adage of who, what, why, where and when. For example: *A young family launch a floating candle in praise of water spirits at Loy Krathong festival, Thailand 2005.*

Whether sending digital files, transparencies or prints, if you would like your work returned be sure to enclose a self-addressed envelope (SAE) with adequate postage.

Next, insure your work against consequential loss – ask at the Post Office. This way, should your photographs become damaged or lost in the post, you are entitled to claim loss of future earnings.

Finally, be sure to keep accurate records of what you have sent, and the outcome of each submission.

Following up a proposal

Patience is an essential virtue for a freelance photographer. Editorial offices are often understaffed, so it can take time before your submission receives attention from a member of the team.

It is common practice to be sent a note acknowledging the safe receipt of your work, but if you're worried about your package, Royal Mail can trace Special or Recorded Delivery items. Once you know that your photographs have been delivered, try and forget about them for a while. If, however, you are still awaiting news after about six weeks, it's quite acceptable to ring and ask whether the magazine intends to use your submission.

When phoning with an enquiry, remain professional and businesslike at all times – never demand feedback or chastise the editor for not getting in touch. If you would like your work returned at this stage then say so, but keep your request polite – establishing a good relationship with the editor is paramount to securing future commissions.

Whatever you do, never turn up at an editorial office without an appointment – editorial staff rarely have time to receive visitors and your intrusion could be considered a real nuisance. Similarly, avoid phoning the day a magazine goes to press. If you are unsure of the exact date, phone the switchboard first to check the most convenient time to make contact. Having chosen your moment carefully, a quick chat with the editor should confirm whether or not your submission has been successful.

Rejection and success

Rejection, though disappointing, is rarely personal. In an ideal world each unsuccessful submission would be returned with a detailed critique offering reasons for its unsuitability and suggesting areas for improvement. Sadly, lack of time and resources prevents such a response, and it's often up to you to ascertain why your proposal has been turned down.

Have you researched the target market thoroughly? Edited your photographs tightly? Written an enticing query letter? Provided professional packaging? Remained polite and courteous at all times?

If the answer to all of these questions is yes, then don't be dispirited, the final decision could ultimately have been based on personal taste – and there's not a lot you can do about that!

If, on the other hand, your submission has been a success, give yourself a pat on the back. If it's an article deliver the finished piece promptly, and attend to any suggestions from editorial staff immediately and without complaint. Once your submission appears in print, look at the images the editor has selected, and compare any text against your original copy. Take note of any major alterations – this information will allow you to make future submissions even more irresistible.

Finally, and most importantly, consider the main reason why so many potential freelance contributions remain unpublished: because they stay tucked away in a drawer or cupboard at home. There is one sure-fire way of increasing your chances by 100% – send in your photographs.

Selling family photos

by ANGELA HAMPTON

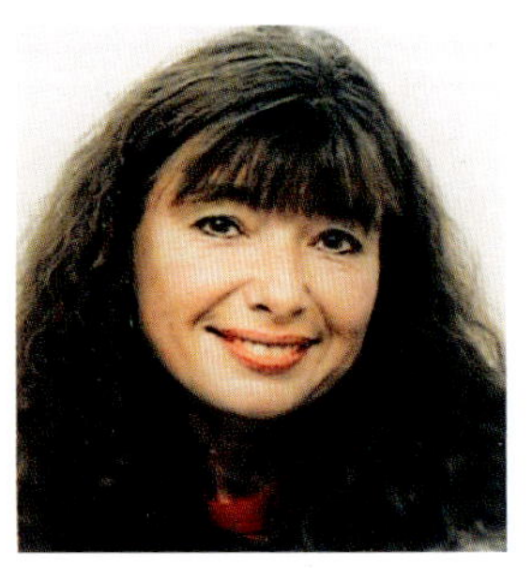

It's always a good idea to specialise in a subject you enjoy most, and if it's people, then you're on to a real winner, because the scope for lifestyle pictures is unlimited. Current magazines and books reflect just how much publishers need images of people doing ordinary things. So if you have family members who are willing to pose for you, you're at a distinct advantage as it's such an obvious place to start.

Common everyday activities are things readers identify with, no matter how mundane, be it brushing teeth, reading a book, going to the doctor, hairdresser or dentist, shopping, buying a car or a house, doing homework, looking stressed, pursuing a hobby, fixing the washing machine, arguing with a difficult teenager.

Wherever there's an opportunity to take your camera, take it. If you don't, you can guarantee that when a client comes along and asks you for a shot like a family boarding a plane, you'll have just flown back, and you'll be kicking yourself for not having captured it. A sale from such a popular request like that can recoup the cost of your holiday!

So whether you're on the beach, dining in a burger bar, or attending a parent and toddler group, take the camera. These topics sell – over and over again.

Natural models are best

Don't worry about what your family models look like. Adults will usually make the excuse "I'm not photogenic", so reassure them that this is not as important as looking natural. Once you've studied a range of images used in the media, you'll learn that not all models look like they've just fallen off a catwalk. No-one's going to use a wafer-thin celebrity look-alike for an article on obesity! The market needs all shapes, ages and sizes.

Later on though, if clients want to continue using you, you'd be wise to expand your modelling pool.

Where makeup needs to be worn, the effect should be natural but professional looking. Your subjects should wear neutral clothes that will not date the pictures. Fashions are ever-changing and it sometimes seems that youngsters are changing

Angela Hampton was born in Sheffield and moved to the United States in 1982 where she discovered and improved her talent for photography. In 1987 she returned to England and gave birth to Charlotte. Like most parents, she photographed every milestone. In 1988, she had her second child, Maya, and began to socialise frequently with other parents, camera always in hand ready to capture the antics of babies and toddlers. In time, no friend or family member escaped her camera lens. To finance this expensive hobby, she chose a career to fit around family, writing and illustrating human interest stories for magazines. These images, added to her growing collection of family life pictures, evolved into a specialist stock library which by 1999, totalled over 50,000 images. Angela has successfully marketed these around the world, as sole photographer and through collaborations with other agencies.

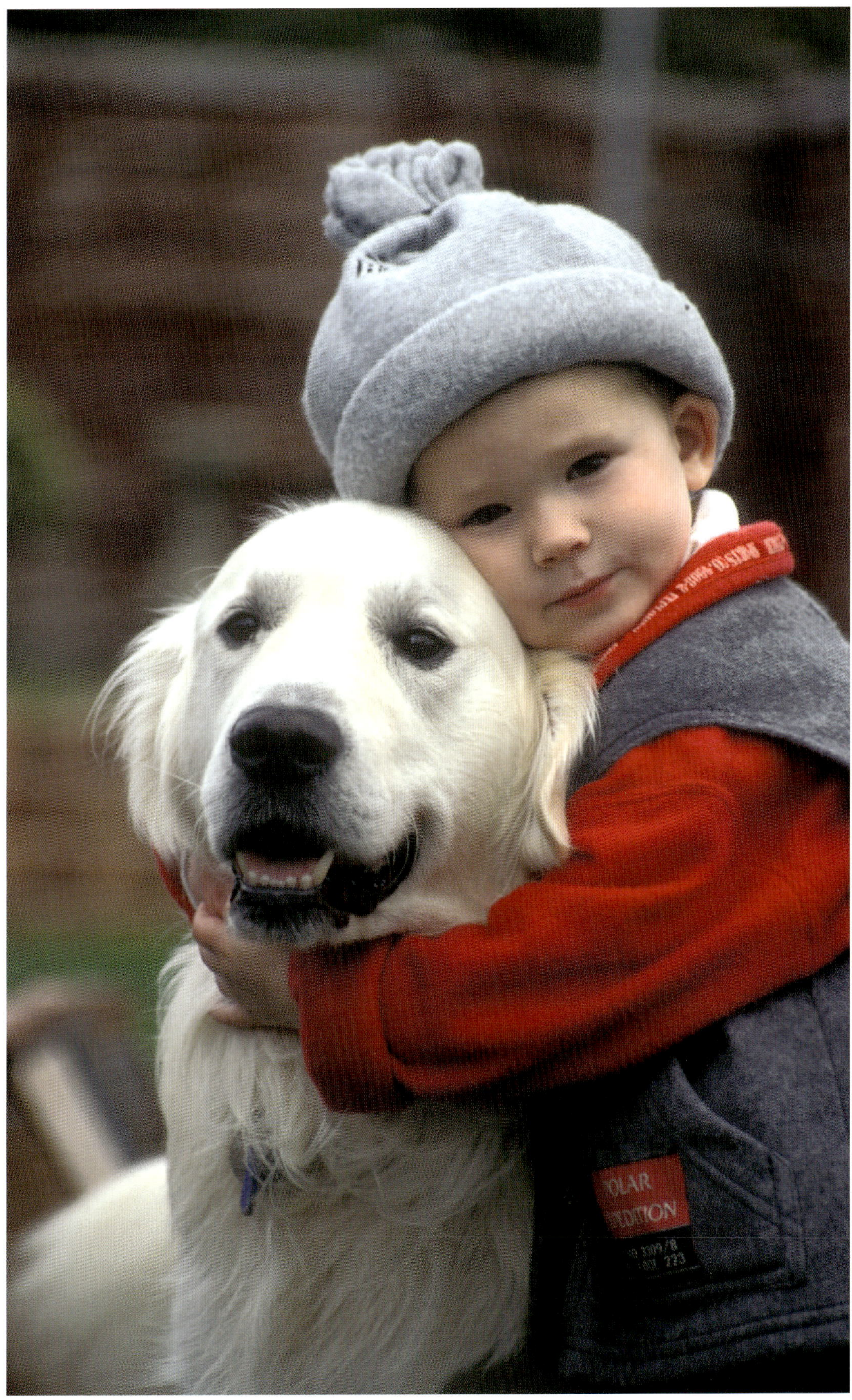

The author's best-selling image, earning over £2,000 to date through the RSPCA Photolibrary

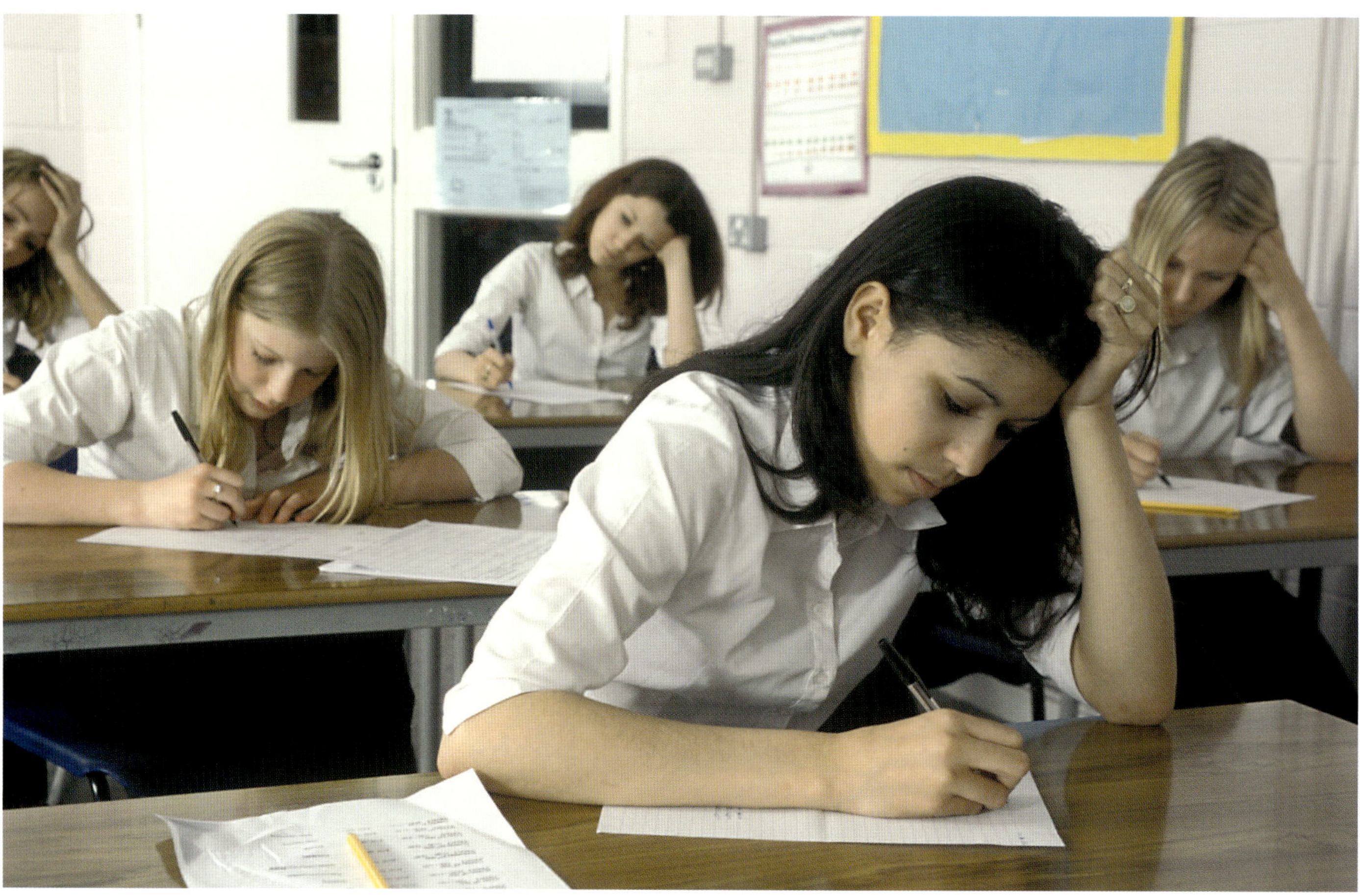

their wardrobes every week! Picture buyers will reject an image if a hairstyle or a prop like a mobile phone looks "*so* last year!"

You'll need to take generic shots that can illustrate multiple topics. For example, someone looking sad could be used to illustrate depressed, bereaved, going through a divorce, or having a medical problem.

"We're not interested in pretty pictures", says Loisjoy Thurstun of Bubbles – a Suffolk based picture library specialising in people. "With kids, we require useful subjects that involve not just milestones in their lives, but all the stages of development, including those relating to education and even times when the children are sick. We get asked for these pictures daily and we are only willing to consider taking on photographers who can fill these needs."

Knowing your market

Whether you're aiming to use an agent to sell your work, establish your own collection, or do a combination of both, you'll need to do some preparatory work. Shooting for your own amusement now takes a low profile and a serious look at what the industry wants takes its place.

Investigate what's out there already. Browse a few websites and be sure you can achieve the same standards. Visit a bookshop and peek through literature on family subjects, such as pregnancy guides, health encyclopaedias, caring for pets, etc.

Study the photo credits to see where the pictures came from. Some editors source most of their pictures from stock picture agencies; others may commission an individual photographer. Authors may

This image of teenage girls in a classroom is a regular seller. It frequently sells, through the Bubbles picture library, to national newspapers, regularly earning up to £180 for each usage

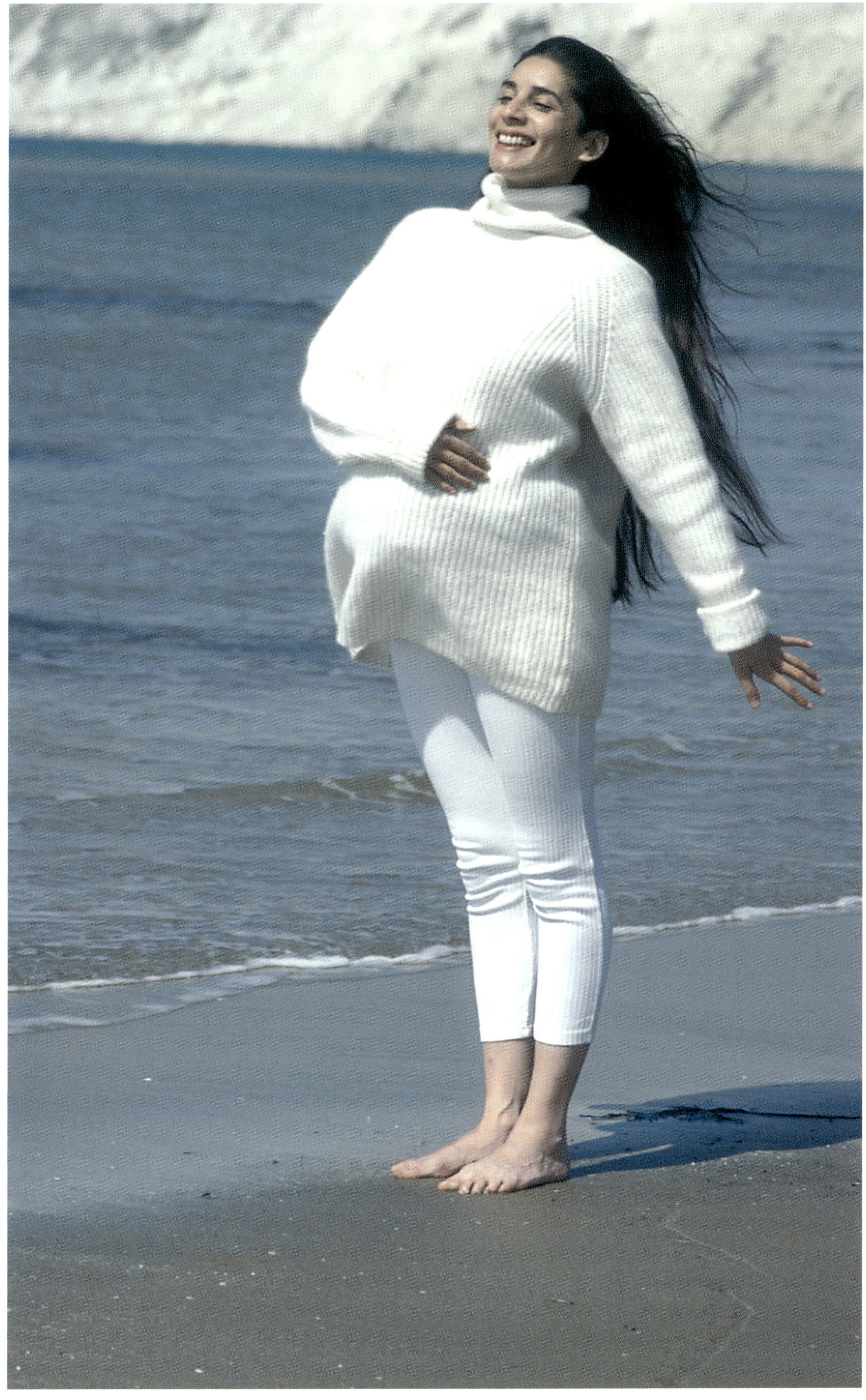

Another regular seller through the Bubbles picture library, this image is often picked up when an editor or picture buyer is looking for a photo to illustrate the joys of pregnancy

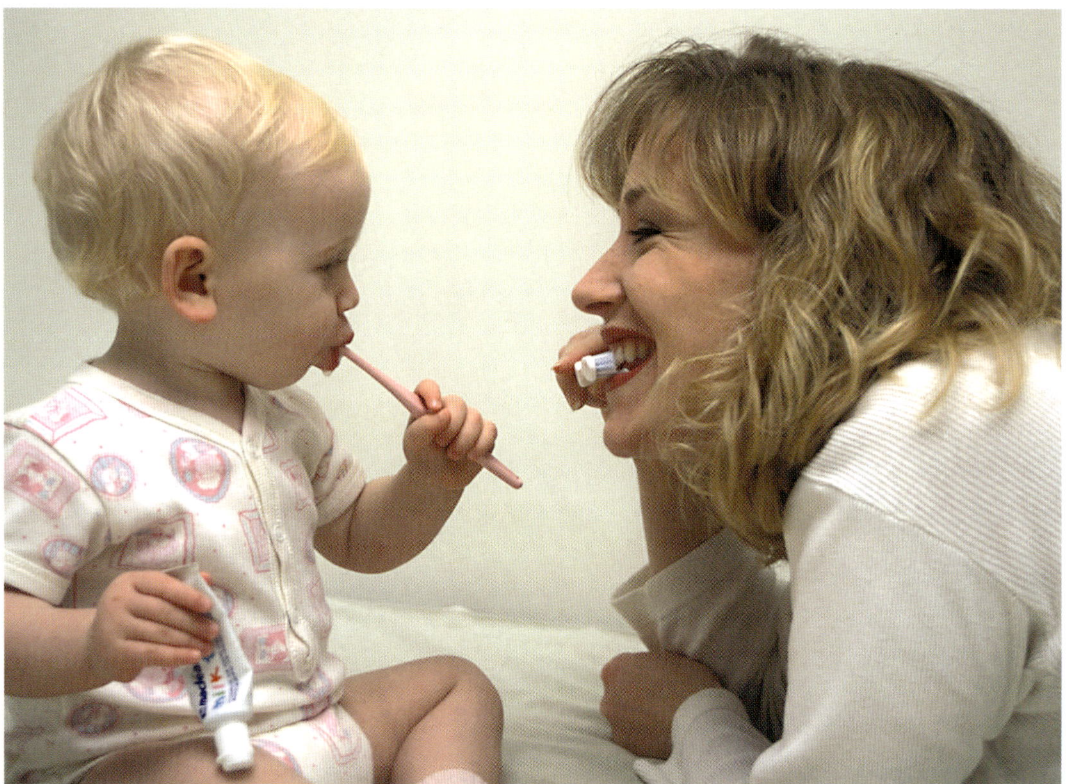

write and illustrate their own books, or in-house employees may be used.

Next, scrutinise newspapers and magazines. Cut out and keep pictures that inspire you. Make a checklist: What are the subject headings? Who got the picture credits – a stock agency, an individual, or a royalty free company? You'll find that month by month, the same subjects crop up again and again, with familiar credits. What style of imagery is used? Is it literal or more creative?

Newsagents' shelves are packed with magazines, so to avoid being overwhelmed, start with one subject. It might be women's interests, or babies. However, if you want to earn good returns, it's not enough to be a specialist in only one.

For infant subjects, pick up parenting titles like *Practical Parenting*. This sort of research is something you need to do quite often, because magazines frequently revamp their style as editors with different ideas come and go.

Practical Parenting is a good example of this: its style of imagery has altered dramatically over the years, from very literal images to the impressionistic. Once upon a time, a crying baby would be photographed as the eye saw it – a realistic picture of a mother soothing her tearful child, focused from nose tip to infinity. Today, you might get one teardrop in focus with a fuzzy image of baby's face and a mother implied by a blurred object in the background.

Trends come and go, so contrary to the old advice to keep only your best shots and toss the rest, it can be a mistake to edit too early. It's not such a bad idea to store your rejects in a separate place in case they come into fashion later.

Every magazine has its own ideas about what carries a strong visual message, as will you. Editors take a shine to something innovative if it suits their style. Your aim is to sell, so go with the flow; if they adopt a light, dreamy feel, offer it; if it's

The type of picture that is often used by parenting magazines to illustrate aspects of child care and learning

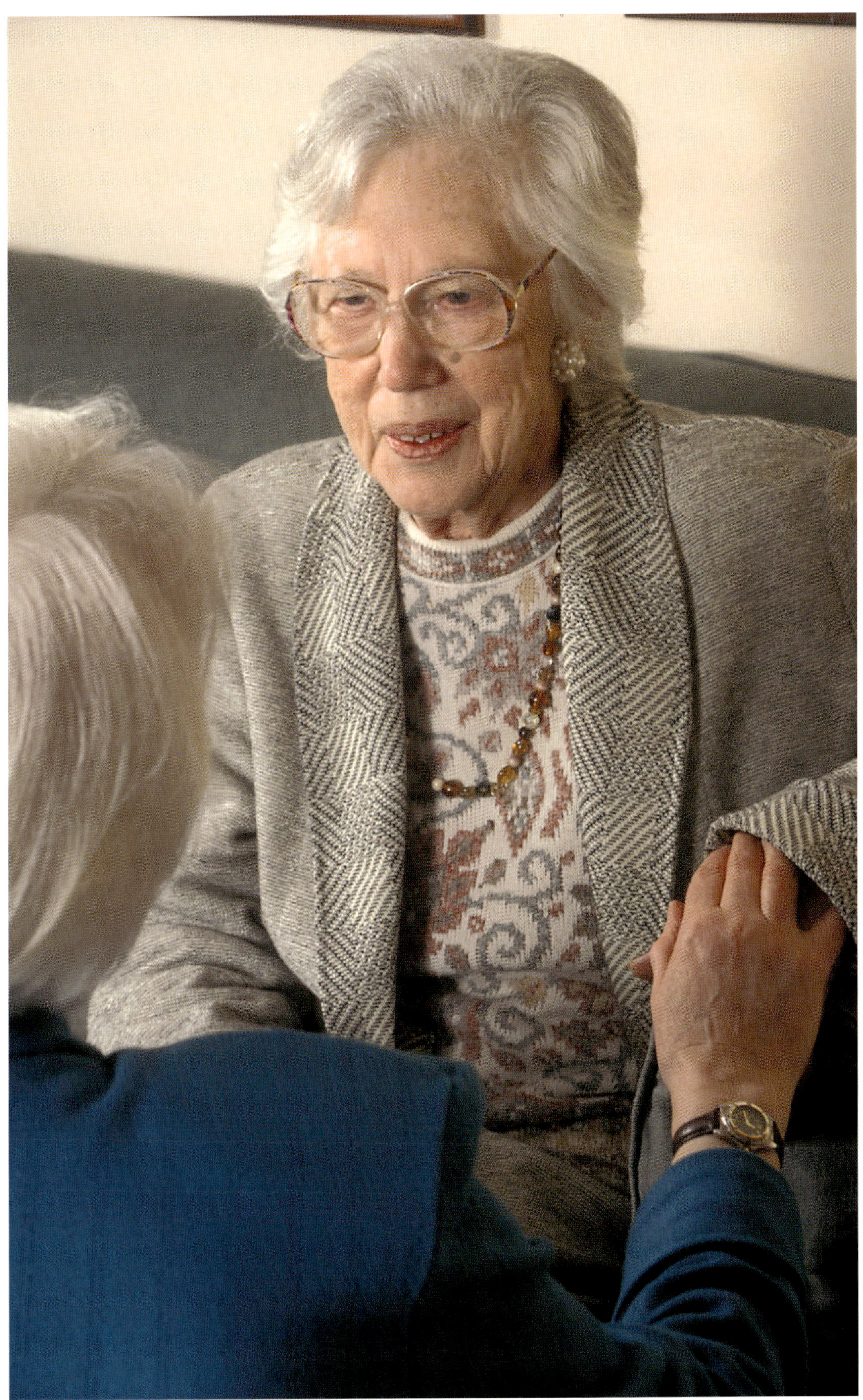

It's not just pictures of the young that sell. This image has been used a number of times, to illustrate aging and other aspects of being a "senior citizen" in today's world

sharp and vibrant, send that. Each time you take a photo, think laterally, with more than one publication in mind, and more than one caption.

A showcase for your work

Once you have a stunning portfolio of several hundred images under your belt and are confident they're saleable, you'll be ready to announce the launch of your business. You'll need a long list of potential clients, which you'll find through source books or on the Internet.

For your own showcase, a website is essential, for this is where picture researchers go. Try to make personal contact first, then direct them to your website. It's impossible to compete with the giant agencies who are set up to sell millions of stock images on-line, but you don't have to sell on-line; researchers will telephone you or e-mail their requests if they think you've got what they're looking for. But they need to know that you are there, so put *yourself* in the picture and *keep* yourself in the picture.

"Keep up with fresh material and hit as many people as you can with newsletters," advises Shelley Noronha of Glass Onion Pictures, an independent picture research company in Sussex. "I get bombarded with e-mails on a monthly basis. Some photographers contact me every week. I recommend that you home in on what you do best and get every aspect covered. I'd certainly make time to see someone personally if I thought they had something useful to offer."

Shelley points out that it's no use setting your fees too high. In such a competitive market, photographic agencies are tying up nifty deals with publishers.

"I can't go into deals with photogra-phers where there are constraints," says Shelley. "We work within a budget with publishers. If we set a reproduction fee of, say, £70 per picture, we can't suddenly pay a commission rate of £300 for a day's work for a single image."

Sometimes editors would rather change the copy than pay for the hassle of obtaining a difficult picture!

Expanding your opportunities

In my view, you'll optimise sales if you both sell your own pictures directly and lodge some with either one big stock agency, or several smaller agencies worldwide. With the first type of agency, you're a small fish in a big ocean; with the latter option, a big fish in lots of small oceans. Both have their advantages.

Some agencies want exclusive rights to your pictures, but you can request to have this clause removed if you feel you can't rely on one agency alone. But don't alienate an agent by sending identical images to others. It gets confusing when a researcher goes to different libraries and gets the same pictures from all of them!

An agent usually takes 50 percent commission from sales, but it's worth every penny because you get more exposure while the commercial side of business, like finding clients and having to be a salesperson, is all done for you. Agencies, however, will only be willing to accept you if they know they can sell your work, and if you make regular submissions.

Note that the pictures you send to agencies will have to be model released.

As you continue your journey into marketing, you can make sales beyond your own frontier, all over the world. However, styles vary from country to country, and the

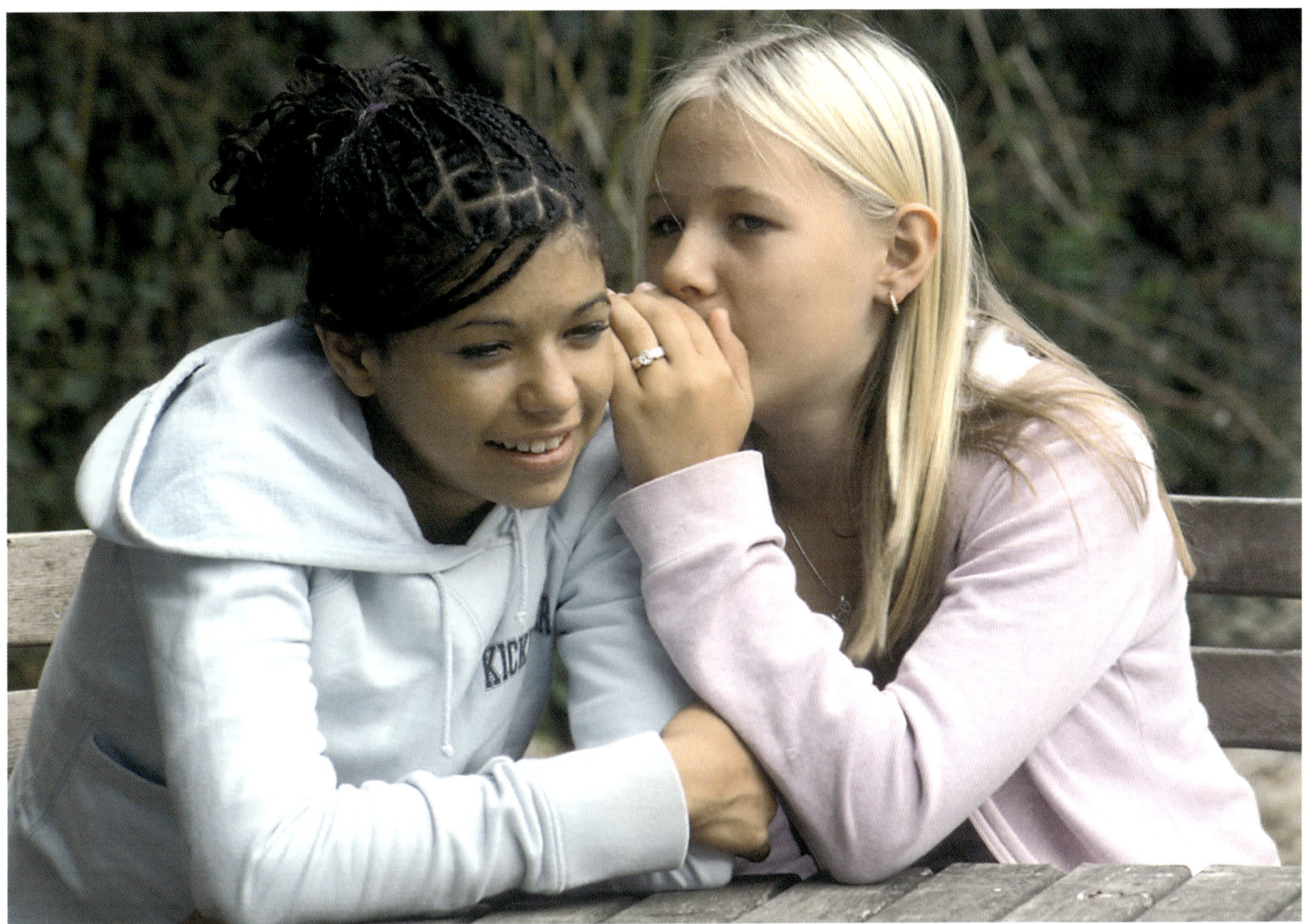

saying that one man's trash is another man's treasure certainly applies to the publishing trade. Some continental magazines, for example, use pictures that our editors would snub. Here's what Denise Hager of Catchlight Visual Services, an agency in Holland, has to say:

"I'm not interested in polished pictures generally. When the first thing I see is a portrait of a beautiful person and the eyes are asking 'Am I beautiful enough to be in your magazine,' then I'm sorry, I want to see something of the inside, too, real life people – pictures that give you a feeling like you understand."

Her cover girls are ordinary young women who usually have no modelling experience. They could be your wife, your sister or your daughter. What they do have, says Denise, is a face that makes you say, "I want to be friends with you".

Small can be beautiful

Surprisingly, researchers don't always find what they want in the big picture libraries. They might come to you as a last resort and hey presto – you have that obscure image they've been tearing their hair out over. You have to be resourceful though, by offering to shoot anything they can't find elsewhere. It often means sticking your neck out, but it's reassuring for buyers to know there's someone out there who will come to the rescue. And it's more stock to

Sharing secrets: another regular seller, which editors have used to illustrate various aspects of teenage life

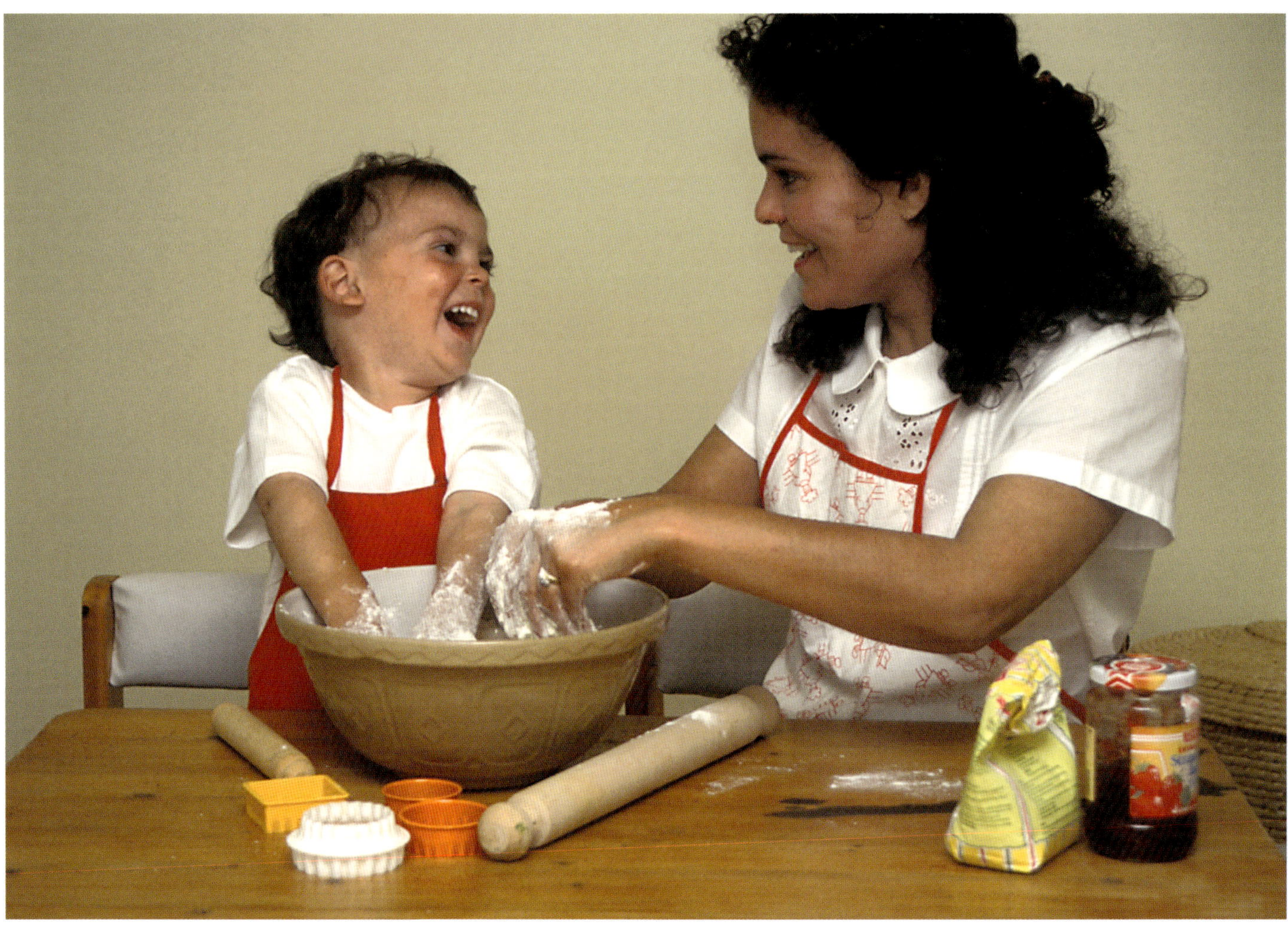

Helping mummy: a good shot that parenting and other magazines have used to illustrate various aspects of family life

add to your collection.

Be realistic about what you can and can't do, but try not to refuse a request. The first years of my photographic career were frantic. I went out with a portfolio of only 200 images and fooled clients into thinking I was a big concern because my 200 images contained an impressive range of subject matter. When picture requests came flooding in on the basis of that presentation, I'd say yes to every one, rush out and shoot the pictures, then charge off to the processors and deliver them to the publisher within 48 hours (with today's technology of course, they can be downloaded and transmitted the same day).

My own family were my life-line, my on-the-spot models, and I was lucky to live in an environment which had every amenity a stone's throw away – shops, schools, beaches, countryside, sports centres, and a bright apartment for working in. In five years I had a collection of over 30,000 images, mostly of my family and friends. This is how my picture library grew into over 50,000 images, with a network of clients and several agents worldwide.

The first years are tough and it may take a long time to get a return on your investment. Putting yourself in the picture is something you may literally have to do on occasion, if you need a model at a moment's notice! Putting yourself in the picture with clients is something you will *always* have to do if you are to become a successful freelance.

Selling outdoor photos

by JON SPARKS

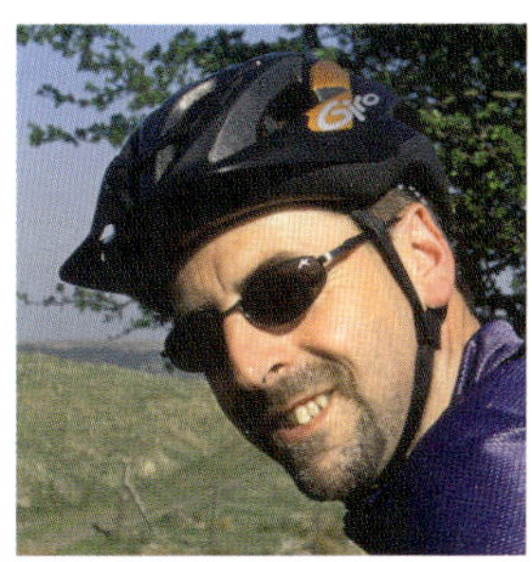

Jon Sparks is an award-winning photographer and writer specialising in landscape and outdoor subjects, and has 13 books to his name. These include several books of photographs as well as guidebooks for walkers, climbers and cyclists and the well-received *Outdoor Photography.* Jon is based in the historic city of Lancaster, in sight of the Lake District Fells, and has travelled and photographed in Pakistan, Morocco, New Zealand, Australia and Canada, as well as most countries in Europe. He supplies images directly from his own library and is also represented by Corbis and Alamy.

The great outdoors, and the things people do in the outdoors, are great subjects for the photographer, and there is a great market for this material. However, there are a lot of talented photographers already in this market, so it isn't an easy one to crack. It helps if you already have a love of the outdoors, as sooner or later you will need to develop a range of outdoor skills to accompany your photographic ones.

You also need to apply the general principles of sound freelancing: know the market and supply what it needs – with, of course, some fine-tuning to this particular marketplace.

Know the market

Do you haunt the shelves of your local W H Smith? It's usually time well spent. But to see all the specialist titles you may need to haunt specialist outdoor shops too. Anyway, keep in touch with the leading titles and be aware of the kinds of images they are using *now*. This is your immediate competition, and you need to be able to do at least as well. Ideally, in some way or other, you need to do better.

However, there is something this exercise doesn't tell you – at least not directly. It doesn't tell you what kinds of images the magazines would be using if only they could get them. Figure this out and you're ahead of the game. If you're really familiar with the field, you may be able to spot the gaps. And sometimes editors will actually tell you what they're short of – for instance through the BFP's *Market Newsletter* and *Market Handbook*.

For example, Dan Joyce at *Cycle* magazine says: "We never get enough good touring shots. There are photographers who specialise in road racing or mountain biking, but none who specialise in touring or commuting cycling."

What's true for cycling is equally true for many other activities. Established professionals in the field tend to concentrate on the glamorous side of an activity, while the bread-and-butter stuff can be relatively neglected even though it is exactly what many readers are interested in.

Better than the rest

Whether you're focusing on the glamorous or the everyday, the standard of photography in most outdoor magazines is already

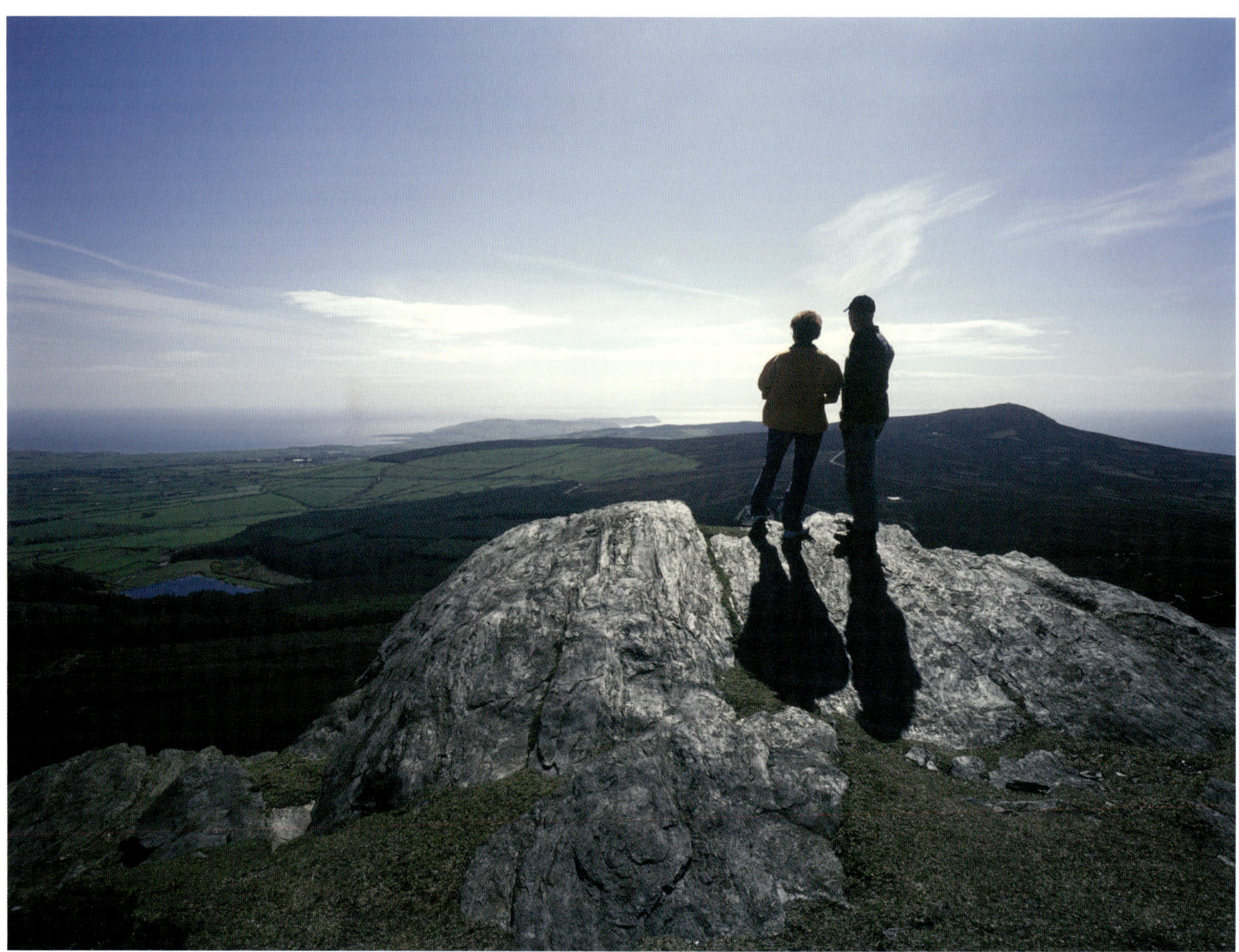

high. You won't impress anyone just because your shots are sharp and correctly exposed – though it should go without saying that you never submit anything that isn't. But you really need to stand out in some other way.

Standing out may mean finding a genuinely new angle on a familiar subject. Radical approaches probably go down better in areas like mountain-biking or snowboarding – where magazines already feature creative use of blur, mixed flash and daylight, or differential focusing effects – than hill-walking or cycle-touring.

But you don't necessarily have to be radical, just try harder. Long-serving out-door magazine editor Geoff Birtles says, "the biggest problem is people actually taking the trouble to be in the right place, with the right lens with the right lighting."

Another way to lead the competition is to find new subjects. There is always potential, even in familiar territory like UK walking. The Countryside and Rights of Way Act has opened up areas never previously accessible to walkers. Topicality may arise from walking festivals or new long-distance paths and National Trails. Stay alert for such opportunities and editors will appreciate you over competitors who stick to well-worn subjects like the Pennine Way.

This shot of Striding Edge on Helwellyn has been used for a book cover. It could work equally well for a magazine spread

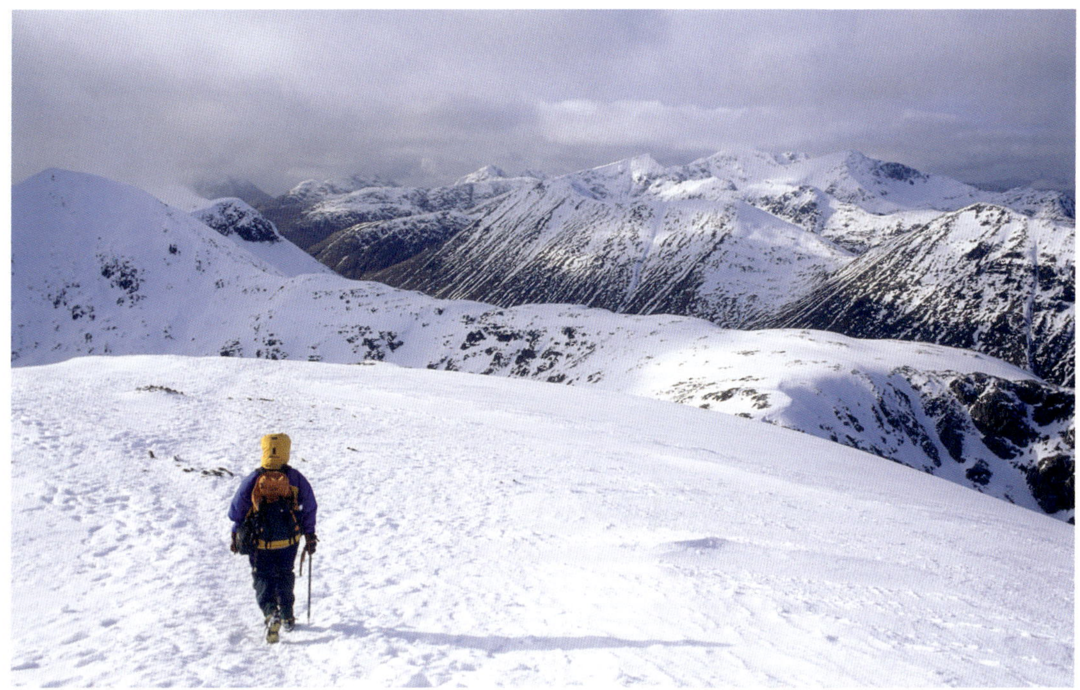

Be specific

Outdoor magazines nearly always want specific subjects. Generic shots may sell to other markets: climbing and mountaineering are frequently used in advertising to suggest "teamwork" or "achievement", for instance. A strong generic shot may work as a cover – it depends if the magazine likes to link its cover to a story inside. Some titles do have scope for a few pages of evocative or inspirational shots. But while specific locations are vital, there is relatively little scope for pure landscape shots in most outdoor magazines, except as part of a package to illustrate a feature on an area.

When a walking magazine wants a shot of Beinn Alligin, it's no good sending them one of Liathach. Climbing magazines frequently need shots not just of a specific crag but of a specific route on that crag. You should be sure that you have correctly identified it (asking the climbers is usually a good start!). Get these details wrong and, no matter how good your images are, you'll alienate editors.

As a rule, shots with people in are the mainstay, preferably people actively engaged in the relevant activity. The "figure in the landscape" shot is a great standby. Sometimes they will happen opportunist-ically, sometimes you have to wait, and sometimes you have to be pro-active and ask someone to take a particular line or stop in a particular spot. Close-up shots are harder to get right and often need to be set up rather than merely taken. They can also date all too quickly.

There is also steady demand for what we might call "specific generic" shots; not simply "walking" but reading a compass or GPS, packing a rucksack, eating on the trail. Again, it's important to be aware of what is new and topical, and what will make a shot look dated or just plain wrong. Clothing or gear needs to be reasonably contemporary, and it certainly shouldn't be obviously out of date.

Attention to detail really counts. As Dan Joyce of *Cycle* comments: "Things like helmets worn incorrectly can render useless an otherwise good shot".

Stob Dearg, Buachaeille Etive Mor, Glencoe, Scotland. Walking on Scotland's mountains in winter conditions does demand competence in the use of ice-axe and crampons

Photographic skills & outdoor skills

It should be evident by now that being a competent photographer is not enough. In fact a lot of outdoor photography is technically straightforward. However, to be in the right place at the right time, and to avoid howlers like the helmet worn incorrectly, you need solid background knowledge of the activity you're covering. Even this will only take you so far. You can photograph football without being an active player, as long as you have a good grasp of the game. But in outdoor pursuits there is often no substitute for direct involvement.

For a start, being in the right place at the right time may involve rather more than a few stops up the Northern Line. It's difficult to do much walking photography without being a walker yourself, and there is simply no way to photograph high-altitude mountaineering without climbing to altitude. Making this distinction between activities where you can shoot from the sidelines, and those where you really have to be a participant, helps you clarify which you can reasonably target, either because you don't need specialist skills, or because you already have or can acquire them.

Shooting from the sidelines can work, and often in areas you might not expect. A surprising amount of rock-climbing – as distinct from mountaineering – photography, for example, is done from the ground. Many of the hardest climbs are found on low, accessible crags, while the sub-sport of bouldering takes it to an even smaller scale. Dan Joyce's plea for more pictures of commuter cycling suggests another opportunity.

Mountain-biking, on the other hand, is a good example where even the sidelines may be out of reach unless you ride yourself. Many of the growing number of purpose-built trails are barred to walkers for safety reasons. Elsewhere, most riding is on bridle-ways, legally accessible only on foot, on horseback and by bike. But on foot you haven't a chance of keeping up with your subjects. In fact, if you don't want to annoy them with lots of hanging around, you need to be at least as fit and competent as they are so you can get ahead of them at key points. And while you can keep your camera gear fairly simple, you will still need to carry more than they will.

The right gear

Photography for outdoor magazines does not, by and large, require anything exceptional in the way of camera gear. Image quality demands will nearly always be satisfied by a decent SLR, film or digital.

There are two key criteria. On the one hand, the gear needs to be light enough to carry, perhaps on difficult terrain, perhaps throughout a long day or over a multi-day expedition. On the other, it must be reliable and rugged enough to cope with occasional knocks and – in Britain at least – more than occasional poor weather. Some activities will involve exposure to more rigorous cond-itions, such as very low temperatures or immersion in water.

When saving weight is really critical, as in high-standard mountaineering, many experts swear by a top-notch 35mm compact or rangefinder: the Ricoh GR-1 series has many adherents. Extended use in low temperatures is still pushing the limits for most digital gear.

For easier subjects like walking or cycle-touring, I've found a digital SLR and a couple of lenses to be ideal. Personally I want my lens range to stretch as far on the wide-angle side as possible, to cover landscape and "figure in landscape" shots, and I'll accept the corollary of a relatively modest telephoto capability. This can be augmented by careful cropping (using good interpolation software where necessary) at the subsequent processing stage.

For mountain-biking, however, I have stuck with film and my trusty Nikon FM2. It's lighter than any digital SLR yet made, but more importantly, it's built like a tank – and there's a lot less to go wrong anyway! I'm a lot more confident that it will survive a tumble, which with my level of skill on the bike is always possible.

What you carry is only half the battle; the other is how you carry it. The classic photographer's shoulder bag is annoying even for simple path-walking and downright dangerous in more rugged terrain. If you've a lot to carry a dedicated backpack is ideal: LowePro is probably the best-known supplier. If you've a lot of non-photographic gear to carry, a standard rucksack may be your only choice, with camera gear stowed in pouches inside.

None of these offer really rapid access to your gear. However, carrying the camera on a neck-strap is often impractical. A dedicated pouch on waist-belt or chest harness protects the camera and keeps hands free. The waist-belt gives a lower centre of gravity, which is ideal when balance is important (climbing, cycling, skiing), though in some cases the chest harness makes the camera less vulnerable to direct impact in a fall.

Camera support is always desirable but often means extra weight. Practice handholding, and be prepared to improvise. Walls, rocks and trees give something to brace against and an ultra-light mesh stuffsack can turn spare hats and gloves into an effective "bean-bag".

If you're skiing, or you walk with poles, you can support the camera very effectively by linking the wrist-straps. This is quicker and more flexible than relying on the tripod bush built in to some walking poles.

Sometimes there is no substitute for a tripod. Geoff Birtles says, "I've begged people for long-lens photos for years, but mostly they're too lazy to carry a tripod and without a tripod there is no depth of field on 300 to 500mm. With a tripod there is so much creative photography available."

As ever, an inadequate tripod is worse than useless. Carbon-fibre is expensive but gives the best combination of weight and rigidity.

Challenge and reward

Photographing for outdoor magazines, with its frequent demand for outdoor skills in addition to photographic ones, is undoubtedly challenging, but with the challenge come immense rewards.

Because the outdoor photographer is so often a participant rather than a mere spectator, images have a directness and sense of involvement that is satisfying for the photographer as well as appealing to the viewer. Outdoor photography also means doing exciting things in inspiring places. It calls for persistence, imagination and a willingness to embrace new skills, and even then it almost certainly won't make you rich. But I can't think of a better way to earn a crust.

Selling wildlife photos

by MIKE READ

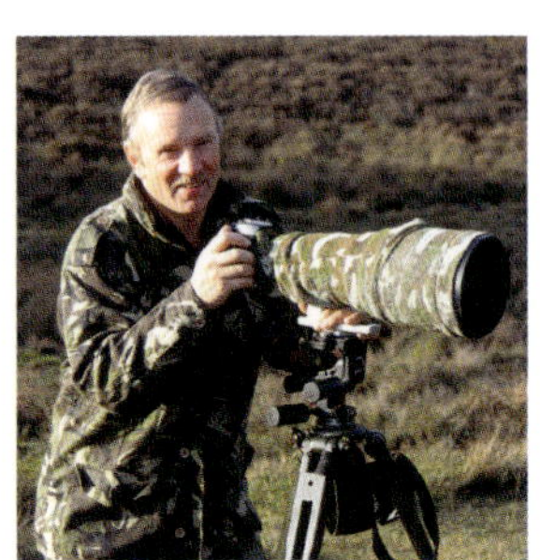

Mike Read has been working as a professional nature and landscape photographer for over 20 years and has travelled widely to build up an extensive library of stunning images. As a photographer and as a writer, he has contributed to a wide range of wildlife, photography and other magazines and has written or co-authored several books including _The Robin, The Barn Owl, New Forest Moods_ and _Red Kite Country_. Mike sells his photography through a number of photographic agencies as well as supplying work directly to various outlets himself. His stock library consists of over 80,000 images and this is still expanding.

Though there are many outlets for nature and wildlife photography, finding them is often the problem. And as with all markets, getting the right image in the right place at the right time is what it is all about.

Before we consider the markets more fully, let's think about the practical side of things. Working in a specialist field like wildlife requires long lenses and other expensive equipment. But it also requires a lot of thought regarding subject matter and your approach to photography.

Most importantly, there is a huge moral obligation to be borne by nature photographers. The welfare of the subject and its habitat must always be of primary consideration. Disturbance of a hungry, tired, displaced, rare migrant bird could prevent it from feeding or resting and lead to its death; visiting ground-dwelling wader nests may leave a scent trail that a fox will follow to steal the eggs; and so on.

Then there are legal considerations. In Britain many birds are given extra legal protection during the breeding season and a licence is required to photograph rare species at the nest or with dependent young. This includes species like the barn owl, kingfisher and many of the birds of prey.

All British reptiles and plants are protected by law; it is illegal to put up a hide too close to a badger sett, and disturbance of bats, dormice and shrews could lead to a huge fine or even a prison sentence!

Failure to observe these points could give you a bad reputation. Word spreads rapidly in this field of work and your ability to make sales would be severely hampered by any adverse reputation.

While the legalities quoted above refer to Britain, throughout the EU and the rest of the world there may be equally stringent legal obligations that should be checked before you travel.

Getting started

Often the starting place for nature/wildlife photographers is their interest in a certain subject, such as my own specialist subject, birds. It may begin with occasional record shots, but then, following a degree of success, the interest deepens and what was

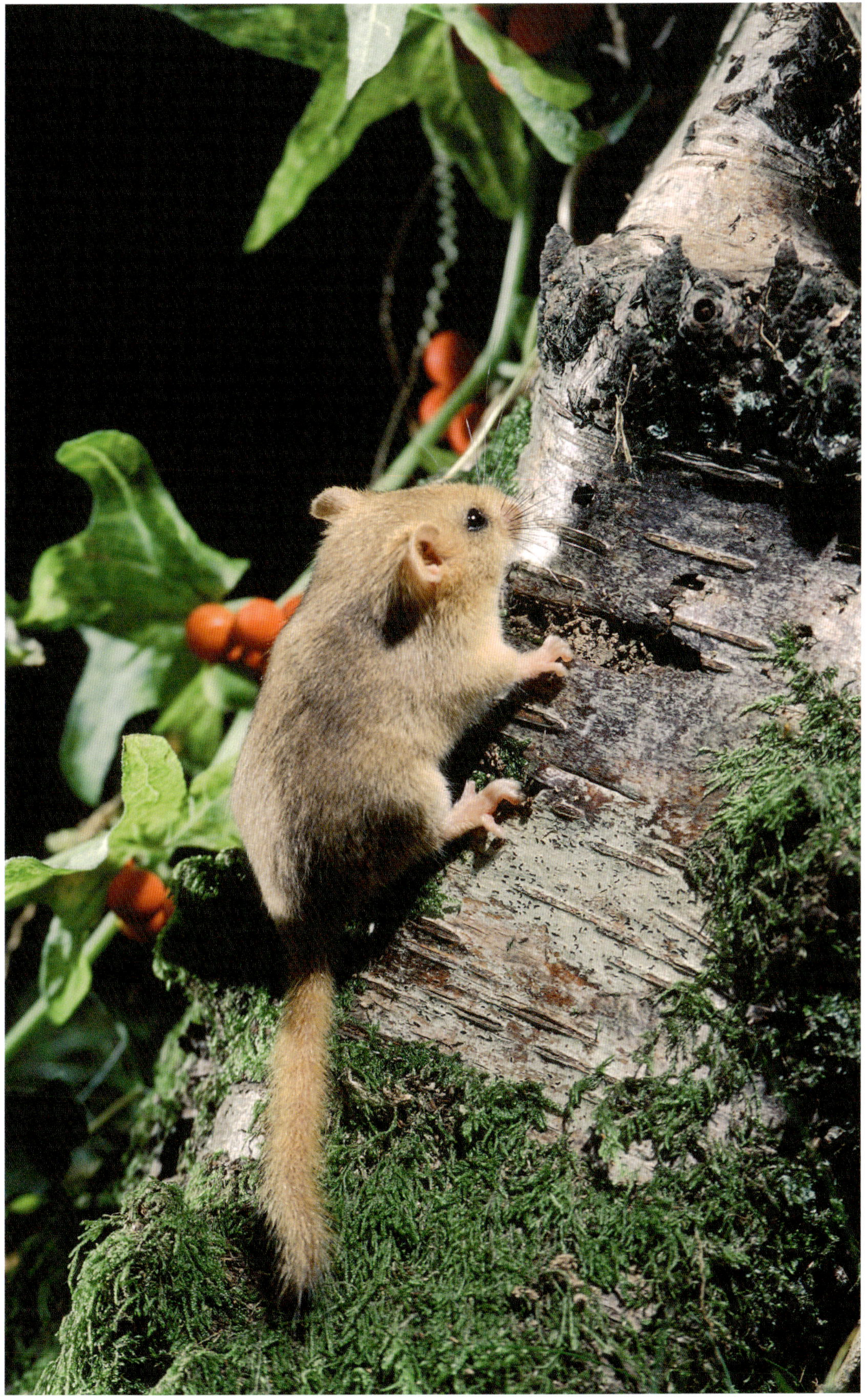

Dormice are rare and difficult to photograph in the wild and a licence from English Nature is required to do so. Thankfully there are captive breeding programmes in operation and this animal was part of such a programme

once a hobby develops into a busy sideline or even a full-time job.

This is a good way to start – ease into it. I have heard of people who, having just purchased a camera and a "round-the-world" air ticket, write to agents and publishers seeking commissions despite a total lack of experience or knowledge of the market requirements! The chances of their enquiry receiving more than a couple of seconds consideration by a busy editor is minimal. There is no substitute for a sound knowledge of the market and proving, with excellent work, that you are capable of producing exactly what is required.

So does this dictate that you almost require a proven track record in wildlife photography before you start? Well, not exactly. If you can put some words with your pictures, you can begin by approaching local and/or small circulation magazines with an illustrated article on your favourite location or species. Within this market generally, a words and pictures approach does help considerably and increases the chances of acceptance.

Some of these markets don't have much of a budget for freelance contributions, but even as a starting point, don't offer anything for free. It instantly lowers the value of your work and if you want a fee from the same publication for a subsequent article you will probably be refused.

So check the magazine to assess style, then contact the editor to see if he/she likes your idea and to ascertain fees. If everything sounds OK, send in your images with a covering letter.

The magazine market

Many birding magazines publish pictures of rarities, so all you really need here is one good image to make a sale. Images that illustrate animal behaviour, both typical and unusual, should also find a ready market. However, if you want to see more of your work published, you will eventually need hundreds of relevant images that can illustrate magazine features as they come up.

Some magazines hold stocks of various photographers' work and will begin with these when seeking images for a particular issue. Only after doing this will they then circulate to their favoured photographers a list of their other requirements. To get on this list you should be able to send images immediately. You will need the ability to dip into your stocks, pull out the appropriate species, behaviour and/or location shots and mail them off straight away. Remember that these are the final pictures needed for the next issue of the magazine and the editor will have a fast approaching deadline.

Other wildlife-related magazines take a different approach to finding their images. Rather than hold photographers' stocks themselves, they let others do that for them – specialist picture agencies. The magazine will circulate a list to the various specialist agencies or search the agency websites.

These magazines rarely come to individual photographers unless they know you as a specialist on a certain species or location that they are featuring. And they will only know about your specialisation from seeing previously published work, from your publicity information, or from searching the Internet for a particular picture.

Promoting yourself

The best form of publicity by far is to have work regularly published and to receive a credit line every time you do so. A photographer's credit is a legal requirement and

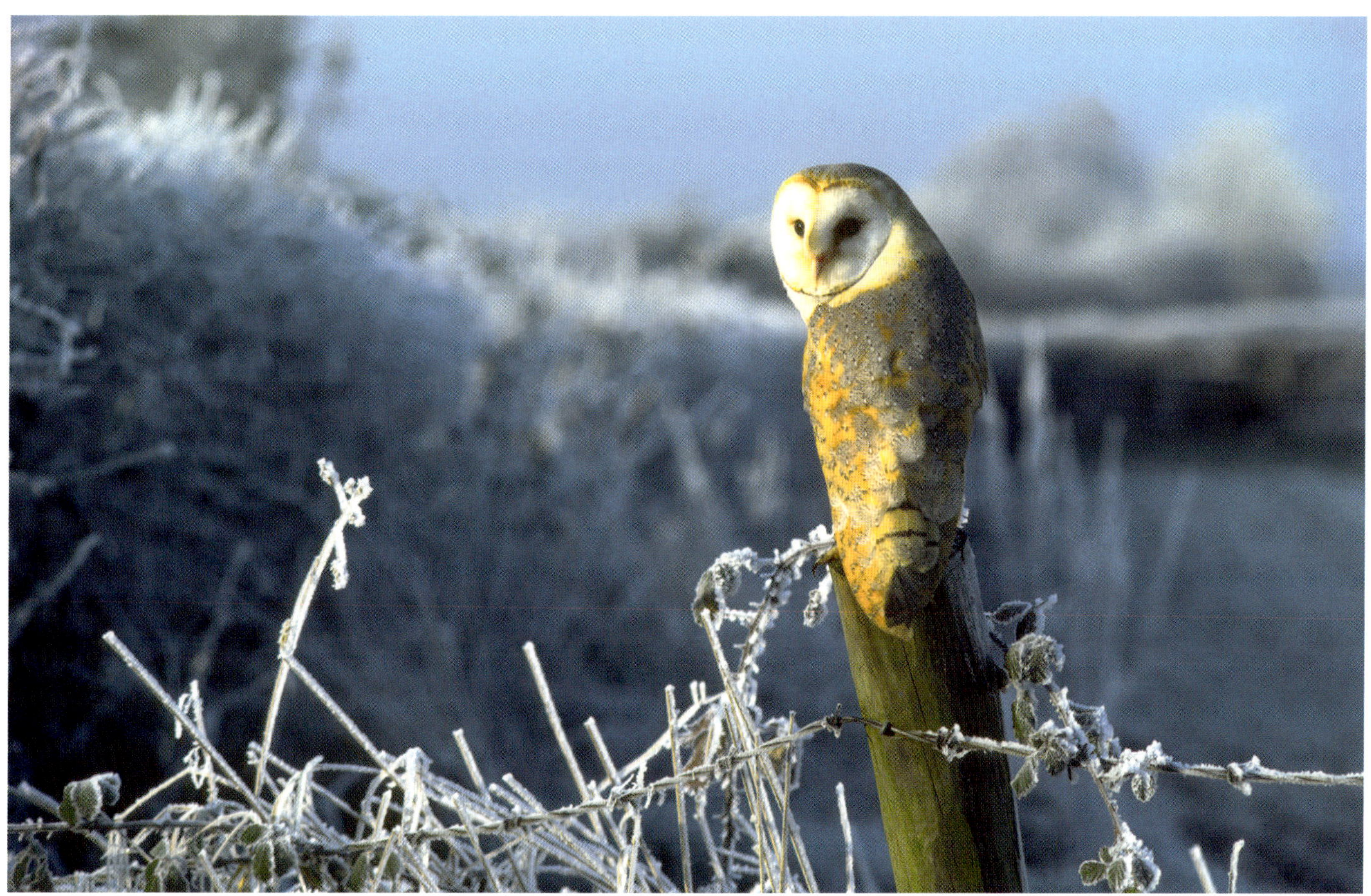

most publishers will oblige. However, sometimes you may need to emphasise the fact that you would like a credit. In some publications no credit lines are given, but in that case increased fees should reflect this.

Other forms of publicity can be an occasional letter or printed card detailing your stocks and sent to various editors, picture researchers and anyone else you can think of who might use wildlife photos!

Alternatively, e-mails sent to the same people might do the trick. But when taking either of these approaches, bear in mind all the junk mail that comes through your letterbox or all the spam that is e-mailed to you. You therefore need something that will catch the eye immediately or your mailing will end up in the bin very quickly. It also needs to be brief, to the point and visual.

Remember it is photography you are trying to sell.

But don't make the mistake of a huge e-mail with lots of picture attached. Send perhaps just one image with a link to pages on a website.

This latter approach means you will need your own website with the ability for new pages to be displayed. Many companies exist who offer site-making and hosting facilities. Equally, with the software available today, it is possible to do it yourself if you are competent on the computer.

Whichever approach you take, your site must be able to be found by the various search engines, not only under your own name and/or trading name but also by the various species and locations your website displays or that are contained within your stocks.

This image of a barn owl has been published in a book, a calendar, a greetings card and several magazines

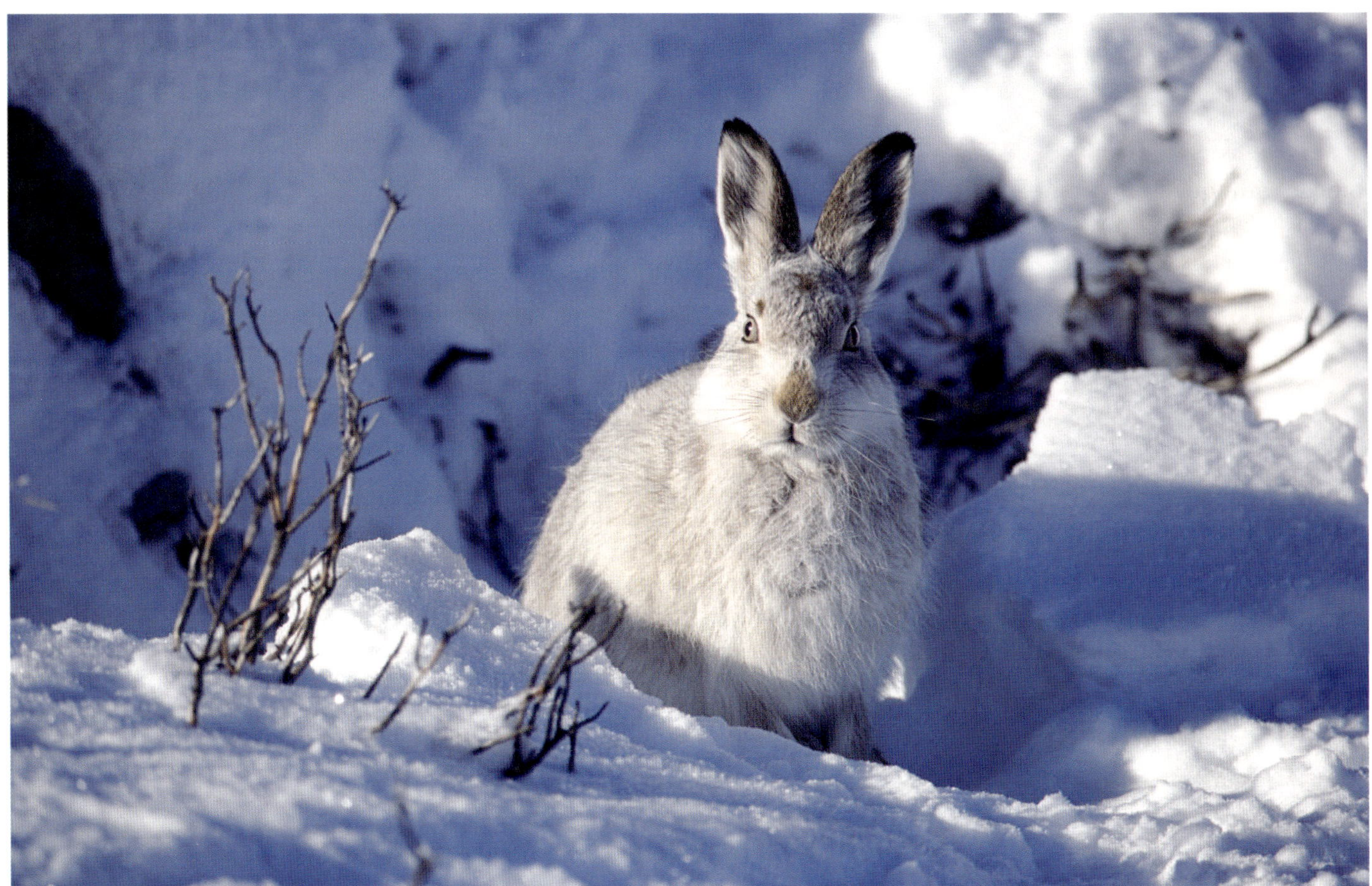

Wildlife is a hugely popular subject and a good website can bring enquiries from all parts of the globe, but at the same time you have to appreciate that you are competing for the picture seekers time with thousands, perhaps millions, of other photographers worldwide. What makes your site stand out from the rest?

Specialist picture agencies

Selling via agencies is significant method of making sales in this field. There are a number of excellent specialist nature photo libraries and some have huge quantities of images.

As stated earlier, agencies are often the first port of call for many picture researchers and art editors. They are also much used by book publishers, who may need dozens or even hundreds of images for individual projects.

So if you have substantial stocks with an agent you can expect a reasonable degree of financial return. Regular submissions to your agent will help increase your sales, but note that some agencies expect as many as 200–500 images as an initial submission and a regular supply of new pictures from you annually.

However, a couple of things are worth bearing in mind.

Firstly, images placed with an agent must be regarded as a long-term investment. Book publishers, for instance, seek pictures up to a year before the agency receives any form of payment. As a consequence, most agents require your pictures to be with them for a minimum 3–5 year period.

Normally found on Scottish mountain tops during the summer, mountain hares are forced lower by adverse winter weather

Secondly, agencies reckon that the average return is £1 per year for each image lodged with them.

So it really is a numbers game – combined with quality and uniqueness! You may have hundreds or even thousands of images with an agent and only a handful might make sales. Study what has sold and then supply more pictures in a similar vein. If possible, chat to other library contributors to try to find out what they are selling.

Once in a while, an advertising agency may make use of your work. If this happens, your agent will be more likely to negotiate an impressive fee on your behalf. Some nature images have earned over £10,000 in this market, but you need to be very lucky or very good to get this type of remuneration.

Advertising agencies and design companies also sometimes produce promotional material such as calendars for their clients, which brings us to another big market for wildlife material.

Cards and calendars

Cards and calendars need to have a very broad appeal in order to sell in quantity in a very competitive marketplace. The subject matter needs to attract people of all types or ages, and bird, mammal and flower photography certainly comes into this category.

As with all potential market types, check the BFP's own *Freelance Photographer's Market Handbook*. However, not all potential outlets are listed so keep checking every calendar or photographic greetings card that you see. You need to check for style and content as well as the company contact details.

If you honestly feel you can compete with previously published work, give them a call to ascertain their needs. Be brief and thank them for their time – whatever their reaction. Learn from each phone call you make or response you receive and you will make progress. If you cannot compete with, or better, what is already being used in this market, go away and take more images until you can.

Small businesses often purchase "ready made" calendars with their own company name overprinted. It provides them with year-long cheap advertising, but obviously the calendar needs to have a broad appeal for this form of advertising to be effective and wildlife often fits the bill.

You may even consider publishing your own greetings cards and/or calendars. But to get a satisfactory and competitive price you often need to have a minimum print run of 2,500, so unless you know that you can sell that quantity in a short space of time this is not to be taken on lightly. Calendars need to be sold before the preceding year-end, and having stocks taking up space in your garage (or wherever) for year after year is entirely vanity publishing – and consider how much time selling that stock will take away from your photography. Which would you rather be doing?

To sum up, wildlife photography must be regarded as a long-term business, but words and pictures combined will start to establish your "track record".

Most importantly, enjoy the experience of taking the images. This is a wonderful branch of the picture business to be in – providing you don't want to get rich quick!

Selling country photos

by SIMON EVERETT

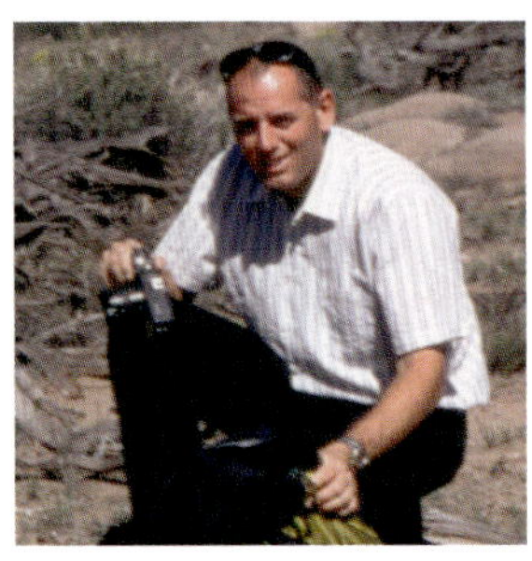

Simon Everett has been a regular, contributing photographer to countryside publications for over 20 years. His broad depth of knowledge has been gained from an HND in agriculture and through participating in country sports from the time he could walk.
A real countryman, he has successfully made photography his full time career.

In many ways the country and countryside market is one of the easiest subject areas in which to find sales. There is such a wealth of diversity of subjects available, and there are so many magazine titles covering every conceivable aspect found within the countryside, that any competent freelance should be able to find a market for their pictures without too much trouble.

One of the joys of the British countryside is that it is not only domestic markets that require input – the European and American markets also offer good opportunities for the heritage and tradition found in our diverse rural areas.

Know your subject

As with every other subject, it helps to know something about what you are actually photographing, especially in specialist country pastimes such as angling, equestrian, hunting, shooting, and even walking.

Those people who participate in the subject, or regularly photograph it, will produce the best pictures, because of their empathy with what is going on.

If you have an ambition to photograph for a particular magazine title, you should, as has been made clear in previous projects, take time to study the style and content. Look at the magazine and dissect the subject matter. There will be a pattern that they work to and this will give you the information as to what to shoot. You will make more sales by knowing in advance what kind of pictures the editor is looking for.

The countryside is very conservative and so too are the titles associated with it. This has created an anomaly in that many of the countryside magazines still like to receive transparencies rather than digital files. And many still prefer medium format, although they will accept 35mm.

The way the majority of the offices work means they are not equipped to find digital images once the initial feature has been run. For front covers, for instance, transparencies are pulled out of the initial job and put in a file marked "possible covers". When they are searching for a cover it is to this sheet of transparencies that they go, and by simply holding the sheet up choose the cover shot there and then, in about 30 seconds. Digital images on a disc

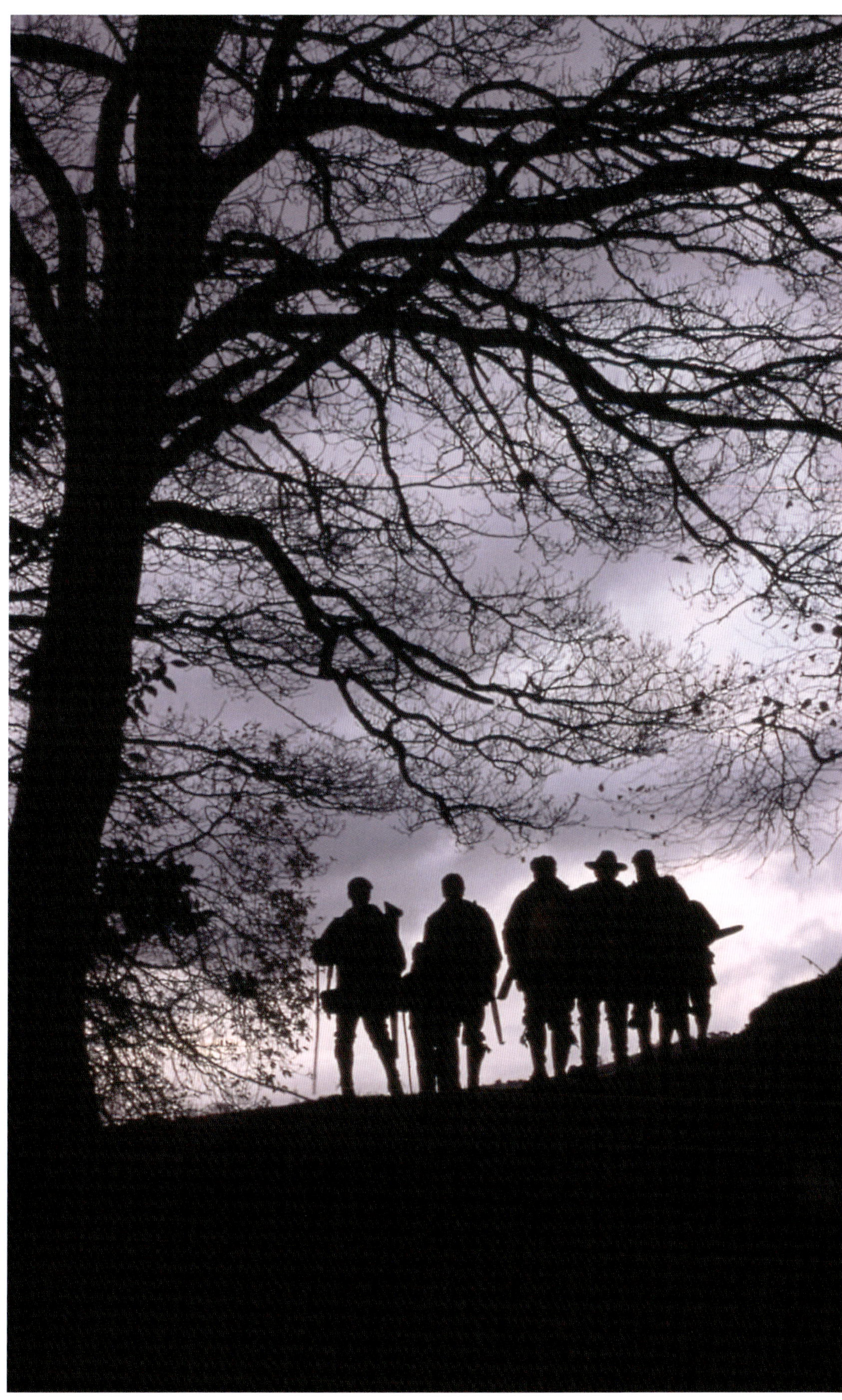

Silhouettes work brilliantly as stock sellers. This picture of a shooting party has sold several times to illustrate different aspects of shooting. Keep your eyes open for pictures that can be used in different editorial contexts and you will increase your sales potential

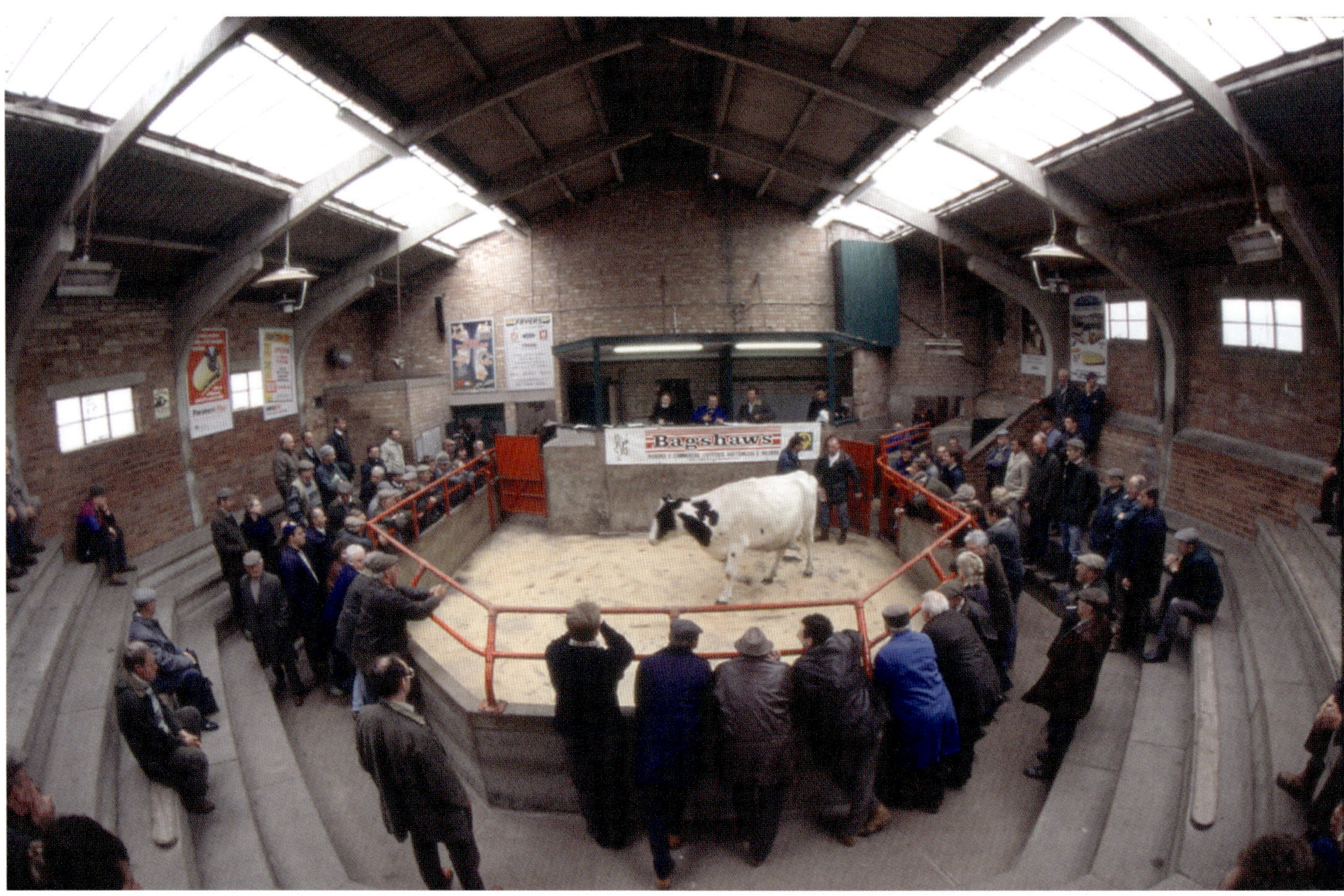

stand very little chance of being re-used at a later date.

For this reason I still shoot transparencies for the countryside market, and probably shall do for some years to come.

County magazines

County magazines offer a good starting point for the aspiring freelance. Many of these – and some of the larger counties have more than one – offer good outlets for the stand-alone picture as well as for photo essays or feature illustrations.

Front covers are probably the best example of stand-alone picture use, and all of these magazines need good, bright images of local scenes. My local example is *Derbyshire Life* and like all magazines they require upright images for their covers.

But like many other county magazines they also publish an annual calendar, in landscape format. So when I am out with an idea to shoot for a front cover, I also keep my eyes open for landscape format pictures that could be of use for the calendar. By choosing a slightly different viewpoint of the same subject I have, on occasions, managed to obtain a front cover and calendar shot from just one location visit.

If there is a local festival or custom these could be covered in depth and offer an opportunity for a photographer to show what they can do. Remember, though, magazines do like to vary their content, so it is probably best not to cover an event that was covered only last year.

The countryside comes to town every month. This cattle market was photographed with a fisheye lens to provide a different view. It has been published several times in country magazines

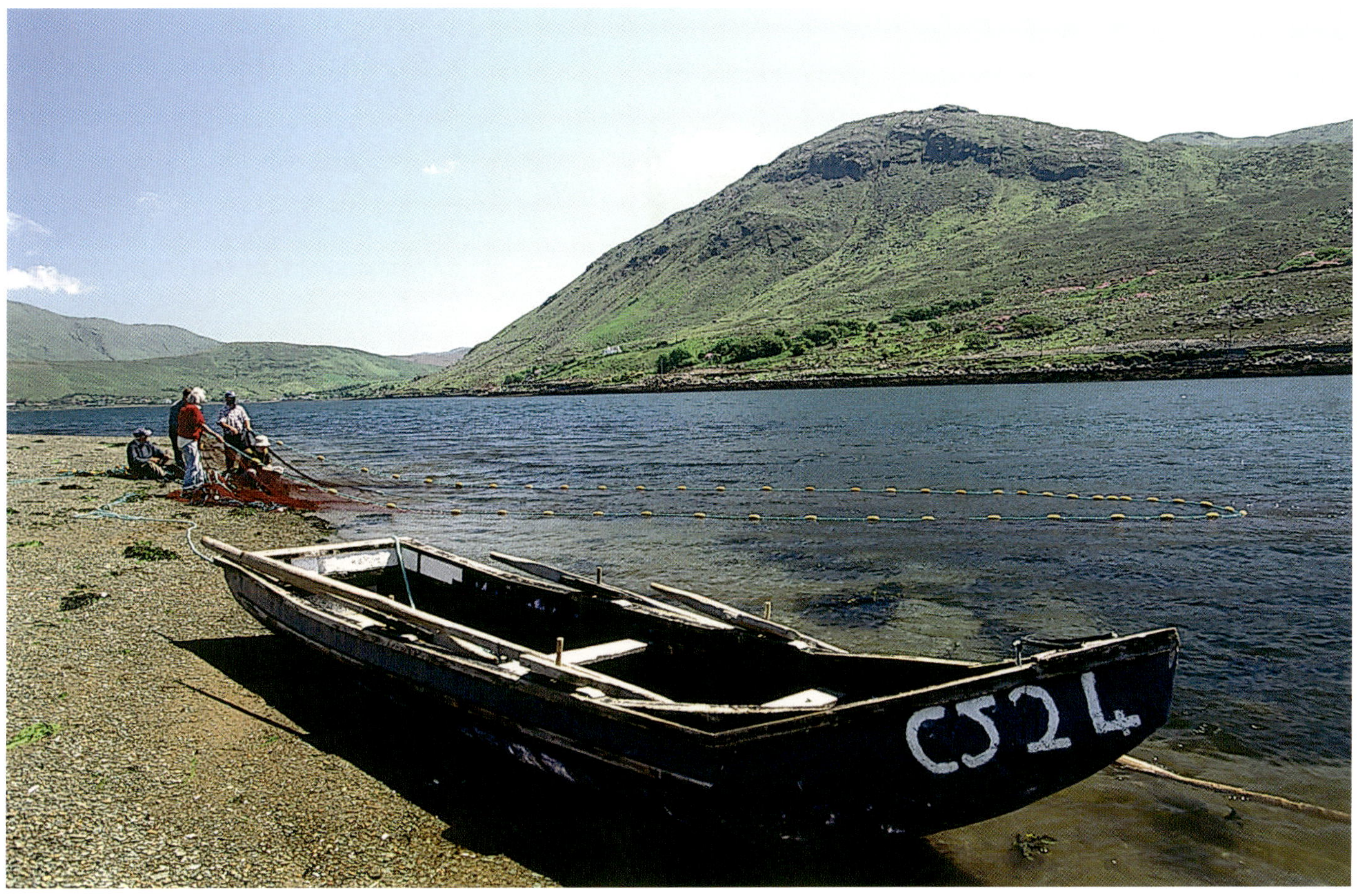

Another possibility is to offer to produce classic portraits of leading local figures for a series on local personalities. The Lord Lieutenant would be a good place to start. Then there are local artists, sculptors, musicians, sporting celebrities, up and coming youngsters.

You will be able to think of other topics, perhaps a tour of the country houses or museums within the magazine's area.

Thinking laterally

It is always worth widening your options – it increases the chances of a sale and by shooting several frames of each subject you can expand your chances even further by sending the pictures to more than one outlet. Well-known locations shot in good light will also be of interest to a wider market, such as national magazines, guide books, calendars or postcards.

You should remember that the countryside is seasonal and that magazines must, by necessity, work some months ahead. Late snow in February, for example, obviously looks out of place published in a magazine with a May cover date, yet in early March this is the issue being worked on!

So as a photographer very often one is shooting images for use in the following year, so don't be impatient and expect an immediate use. Stock can be held for years before being used, then suddenly it becomes the picture of the moment. And last year's failures can always be re-submitted.

Salmon netsmen in Ireland. Traditional pastimes or ways of life are often covered in countryside magazines, and images like this can prove good sellers

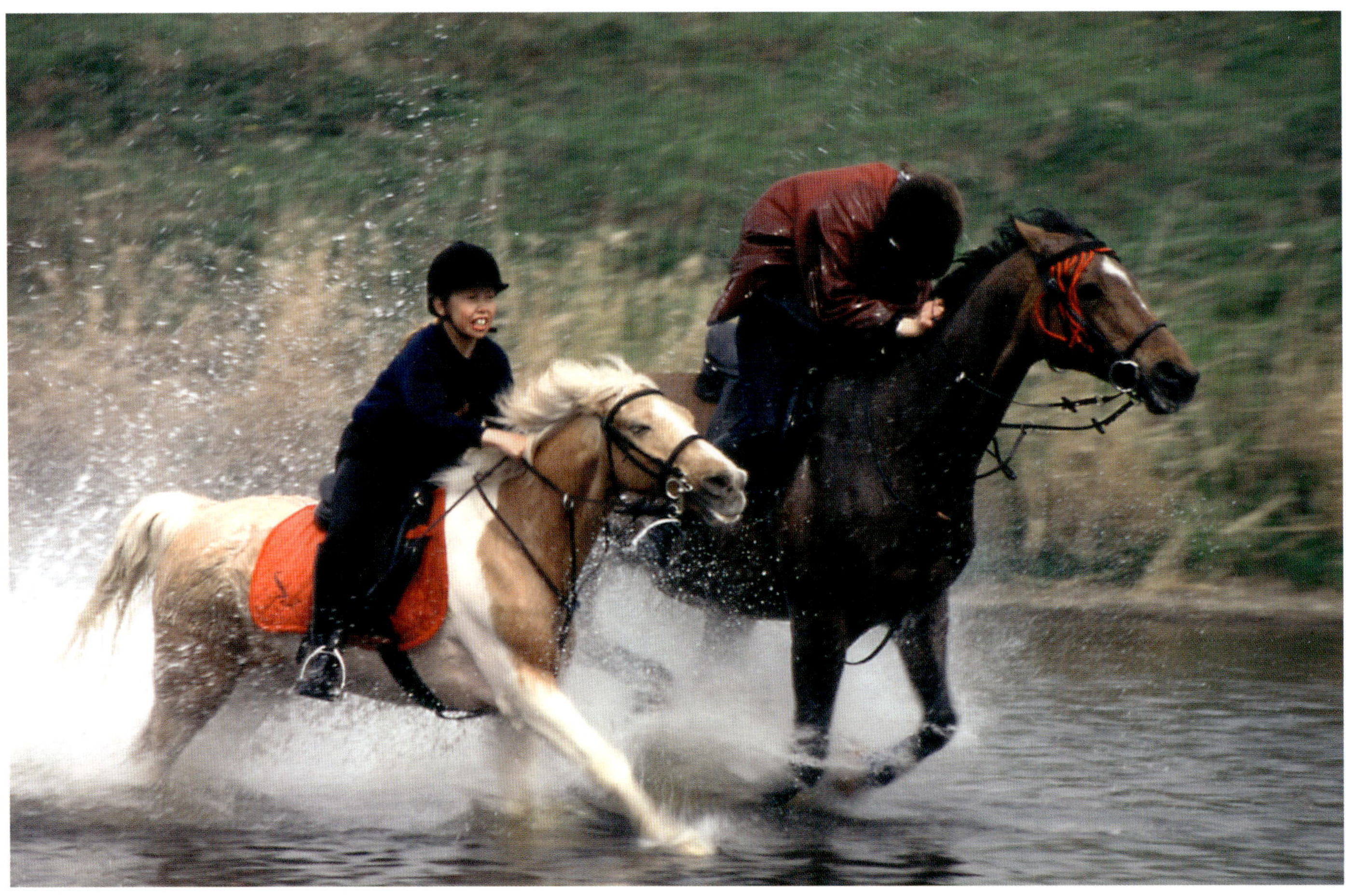

Country sports

Country sports have been big news for the past few years and the upsurge of interest all this publicity has generated has expanded the opportunities available to the freelance.

The irony is that hunting has never enjoyed so much popularity as it has since the law to criminalise those who participate was passed, and it looks set to be a big seller for some time to come. The other country sports have also seen a big surge of interest and shooting is one of the fastest growing sports in Britain.

Good pictures of anything to do with the countryside have a wide appeal to editors in more general publications too.

Angling is Britain's largest participant pastime and angling magazines are always on the lookout for good photography. Pictures of angling venues are a good seller; if you are somewhere there are anglers, then there are pictures that will sell. As with most countryside topics those photographers who know something about fishing will produce the best pictures.

Pretty general scenics can be enhanced by the inclusion of an angler, but then taken again without the angler. By working the scene you could possibly end up with a cover shot, a full-page opener for a feature or a contents-page filler.

To tackle this market (pun intended!) it helps to get into the water and get involved with the action, even with coarse fishing which requires the quietest approach of all. This is best achieved with a pair of waders and the cooperation of the angler. Not

This action shot was used as a double-page-spread opener to a feature

many anglers will be very happy at the thought of you wading about in the swim they are trying to fish!

Very few good pictures of angling subjects are taken by happy coincidence; most are thought out in advance and set up carefully. Boat fishing pictures, for example, require the use of a second boat to shoot from. Many angling venues are more than willing to help out by providing a boat, provided they know in advance and that the pictures have a definite destination, but they will not supply you with facilities just on the off-chance that a picture may get used. Arrangements need to be made, normally by one of the editorial team, for a visit to produce a feature.

Equestrian subjects are another enduring source of work for many freelances. There are many openings within this branch of countryside activities, including specialist titles dealing with just one aspect of equestrian sport.

Dressage and polo are two that immediately spring to mind, but these are both very technical and the people looking at the pictures will spot a mistake immediately. The newcomer is unlikely to get work from these markets unless they have an in-depth knowledge of the subject and can show their competence with an impressive portfolio.

Show jumping is more difficult and access passes at the major events will be limited in number and issued to regular, known photographers.

Three-day eventing though, is where the freelance can obtain excellent pictures with which to impress an image hungry picture desk. The cross-country events are open to the public; a little reconnaissance of the spectacular jumps will pay dividends, and long lenses are not needed.

Once established in a niche, specialised photographers can gain something of a stranglehold on that market. I have been the official photographer of The National Coursing Club since 1988 and as such have enjoyed privileged access to the coursing field not available to other photographers, not even the national papers (much to their dismay!).

There is no reason why anyone cannot carve a similar niche in another subject and from that expand into other countryside topics.

Don't forget the detail

Specialised titles are always picture hungry. That does not mean they will publish anything – whatever you shoot needs to be properly composed and well lit. But small details that are usually overlooked can make excellent fillers for a page designer.

Close ups of small items or important little elements will help to illustrate a point. One of my best little sellers is of the red tail tape on a horse. It is only ever used small, but the odd £20 here and there has been well worth the ten frames I shot of it.

Macro details reveal facets of a subject that the eye doesn't usually see and it is this revelation that makes these pictures so saleable.

Just because many of these magazines are specialised titles does not mean they do not appreciate good photography for photography's sake. Indeed, I would say that they will welcome such submissions with open arms.

Much of the photography they rely upon is from participants who happen to use a camera. There are very few photographers going out of their way to produce pure, high-quality photographs of the countryside, other than landscapes and wildlife, yet there is a wealth of material just waiting to be captured for anyone dedicated enough to put in the time to do so.

Selling garden photos

by ANNE GREEN-ARMYTAGE

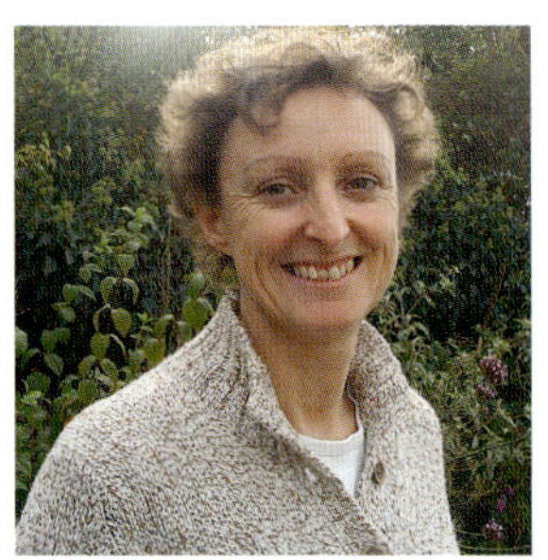

Anne Green-Armytage started taking photographs at the age of seven and turned professional in the 1970s, before changing direction to take a computer science degree and become a software consultant in the City of London. After the birth of her first daughter, she rediscovered photography and feature writing as a way of regaining control over her working life. She is now a professional freelance specialising in plants and gardens and her work is published regularly in a wide range of books and magazines.

Can you get out of bed really early in the morning? Because that's one of the prime requirements for being a successful garden photographer. If the gardens and plants that you shoot don't look their absolute best, your pictures simply will not sell.

Lighting can make or break any image, and garden photographers, like landscape photographers, are at the mercy of the prevailing natural conditions. Bright sunlight is very harsh and during the summer, when the sun is directly overhead, it's about as harsh as it can get. In the early morning or late afternoon the sun is lower in the sky, the light is softer and warmer, and the shadows aren't so intense, so these are much better times for a photographer to venture into the garden.

However, afternoon shooting carries with it the risk that plants will be looking jaded and wilting from a day's exposure to the sun, so I favour the early morning. Add in travelling time to your garden of choice, and you could be looking at a 4am start – or earlier.

Environmental factors

Different weather conditions also affect the quality of light. Mist and fog give an air of mystery, while a sprinkling of summer rain or dew can add freshness and softness to an image. These are the sort of elements that can make an image much more saleable.

Don't limit yourself to the summer season either: autumn brings warm golden sunshine and wonderful opportunities for photographing leaf colour, and of course frost and snow will change the character of a garden completely.

Be warned, though – garden photography is a fairly stationary activity so you'll need your thermals and at least two pairs of socks or your feet will freeze solid. It may be for this reason that winter shots are always in demand with editors – it takes real dedication to stand in sub-zero temperatures for several hours.

The wind is a garden photographer's Enemy Number One. It often picks up as the day progresses, dropping again at sunset, so shooting stock in the middle of the day can be a slow and frustrating experience. As with the rest of the weather, the

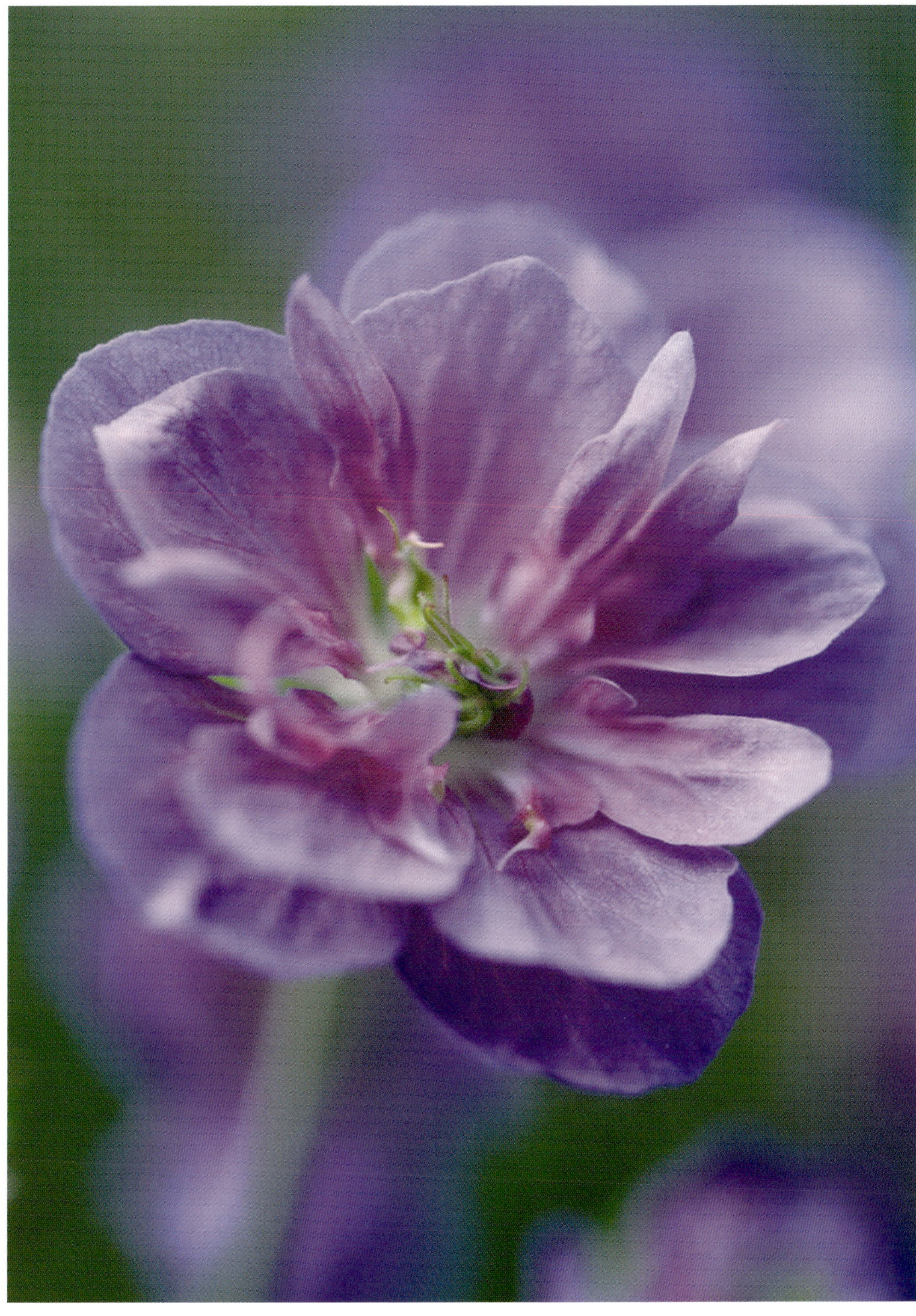

Geranium pratense "Plenum Violaceum". Add impact by filling the frame and using a large aperture to isolate the subject from the background

wind is totally out of the photographer's control, and the only successful strategy I've ever found is to try to avoid working when the wind is high.

If you're serious about selling garden photography, checking the weather forecast on the Internet will soon become a daily habit.

For plant portraiture, the time of day is not so critical, and probably the most con-

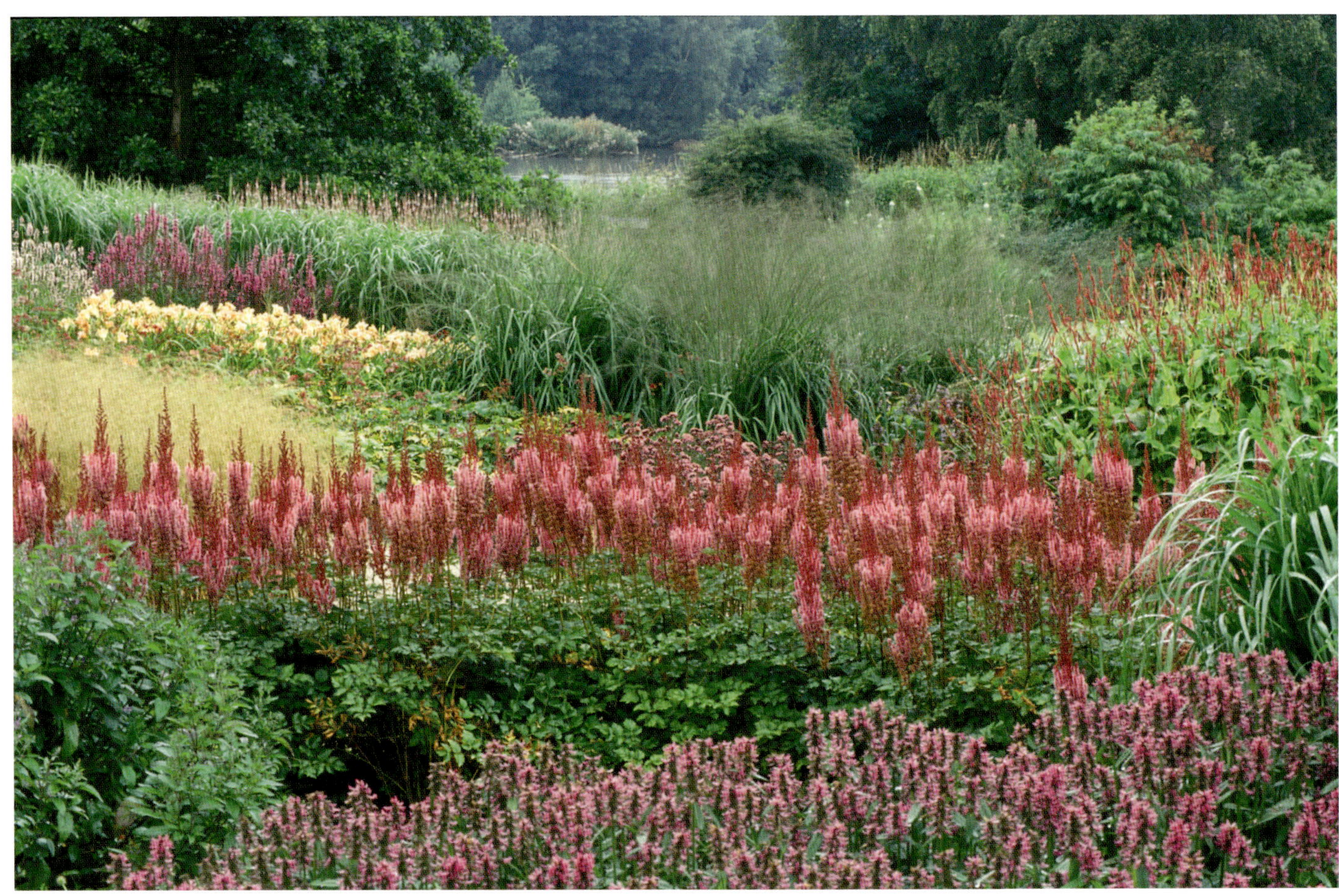

sistently flattering light for a plant close-up is high, thin cloud, which gives diffuse and almost shadowless lighting.

Equipment and techniques

Occasionally you can turn a good plant portrait into a great one by using contre-jour, or back-lighting. It serves to pick out delicate detail – gossamer-fine hairs on a flower stalk, or the grains of pollen on a stamen – and adds depth and interest. Contre-jour translates literally as "against the day", so you will need a lens hood to avoid flare.

A reflector is another essential piece of kit for close-up work, as many plants have nodding flowers with detail on the under-sides. I use a double-sided gold/white collapsible reflector because it's very light and folds away to almost nothing. The gold side warms up shadows, while the white side retains colour integrity, particularly important in white flowers.

The range of lenses used in garden and plant photography is similar to that of most photographers, including a wide-angle lens for views, particularly in small gardens where access is restricted by space, and a telephoto or zoom for detail that may be out of reach.

In addition, for the kind of extreme-close-up plant portraits which are currently popular with magazine and book editors, a macro lens is indispensable.

When using a macro, be aware that as you move closer to a subject, the depth of

The use of a telephoto lens has had a foreshortening effect, making planting appear denser

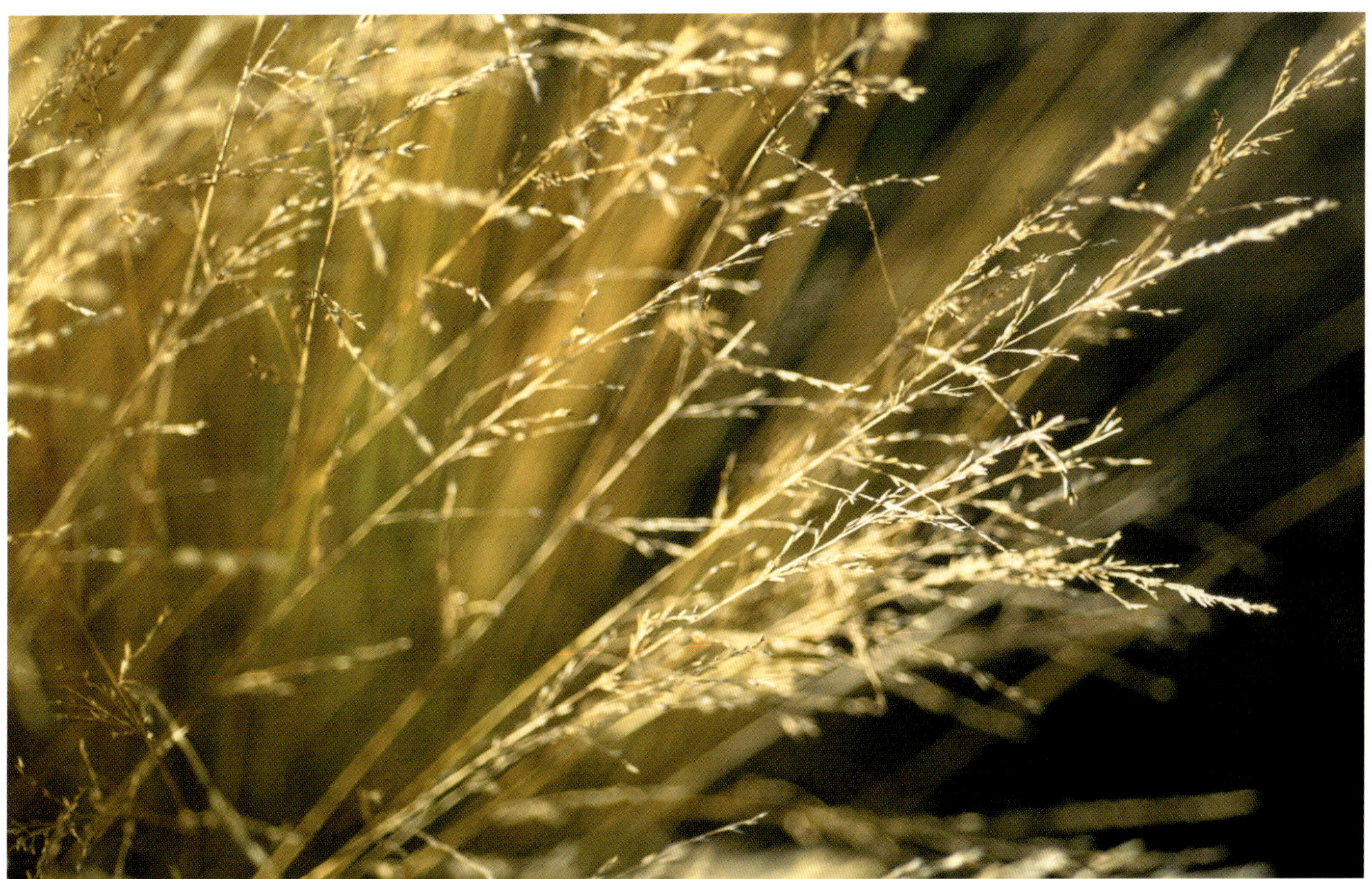

field decreases significantly. To capture a close-up image which is acceptably in focus may mean an aperture of f32 or higher and a correspondingly slow shutter speed. Another reason to avoid the wind.

In general, it's useful to remember that the smaller the focal length of your lens, the greater the inherent depth of field. In other words, a view taken at f16 with a wide-angle lens will have more in focus than the same view, also at f16, with a standard lens, which in turn will have more in focus than the same view with a telephoto lens. A side effect of this is that with a telephoto, objects will appear closer together, or foreshortened.

This characteristic can be put to use in a number of garden situations. For example, if a flower border has promising elements but is showing too much bare earth between plants, by shooting from a distance with a long lens you can pull the plants together and create the impression of denser planting.

Elements of composition

Composition is critical in all photography, and garden pictures are no exception. To me, composition means taking the time to look properly: at shape, colour and form. It means trying to see things afresh, to look from different angles and in different ways. This is a compelling reason for always using a tripod, which forces you to slow down, look harder and frame up your subject more carefully.

Using a tripod also gives you time to see exactly what you're taking, and to notice

Autumn light has produced a pleasing study of these Deschampsia cespitosa "Goldtau" ("Golden Dew")

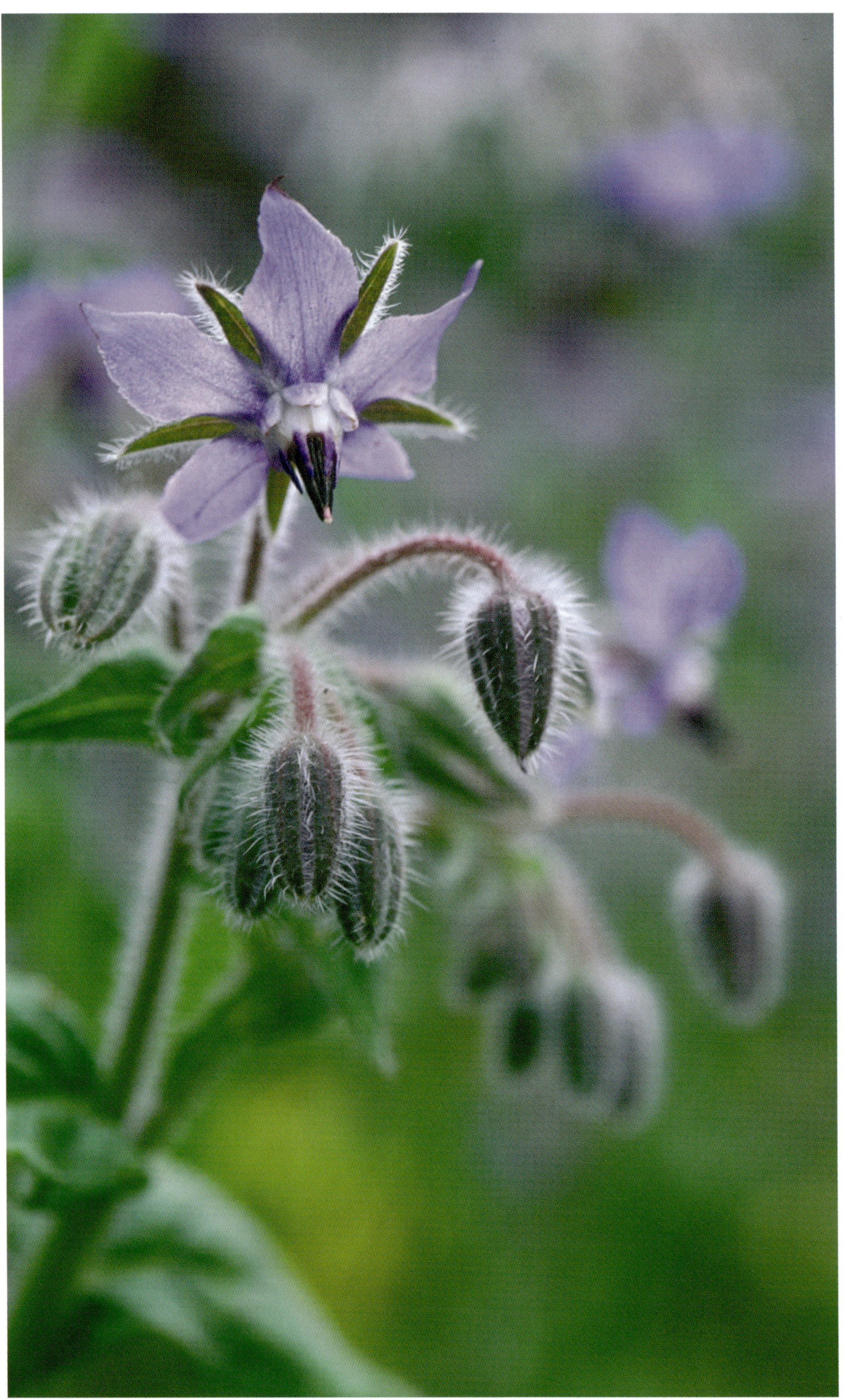

Borago officinalis, borage. Backlighting plus the use of a large aperture has captured this plant at its best

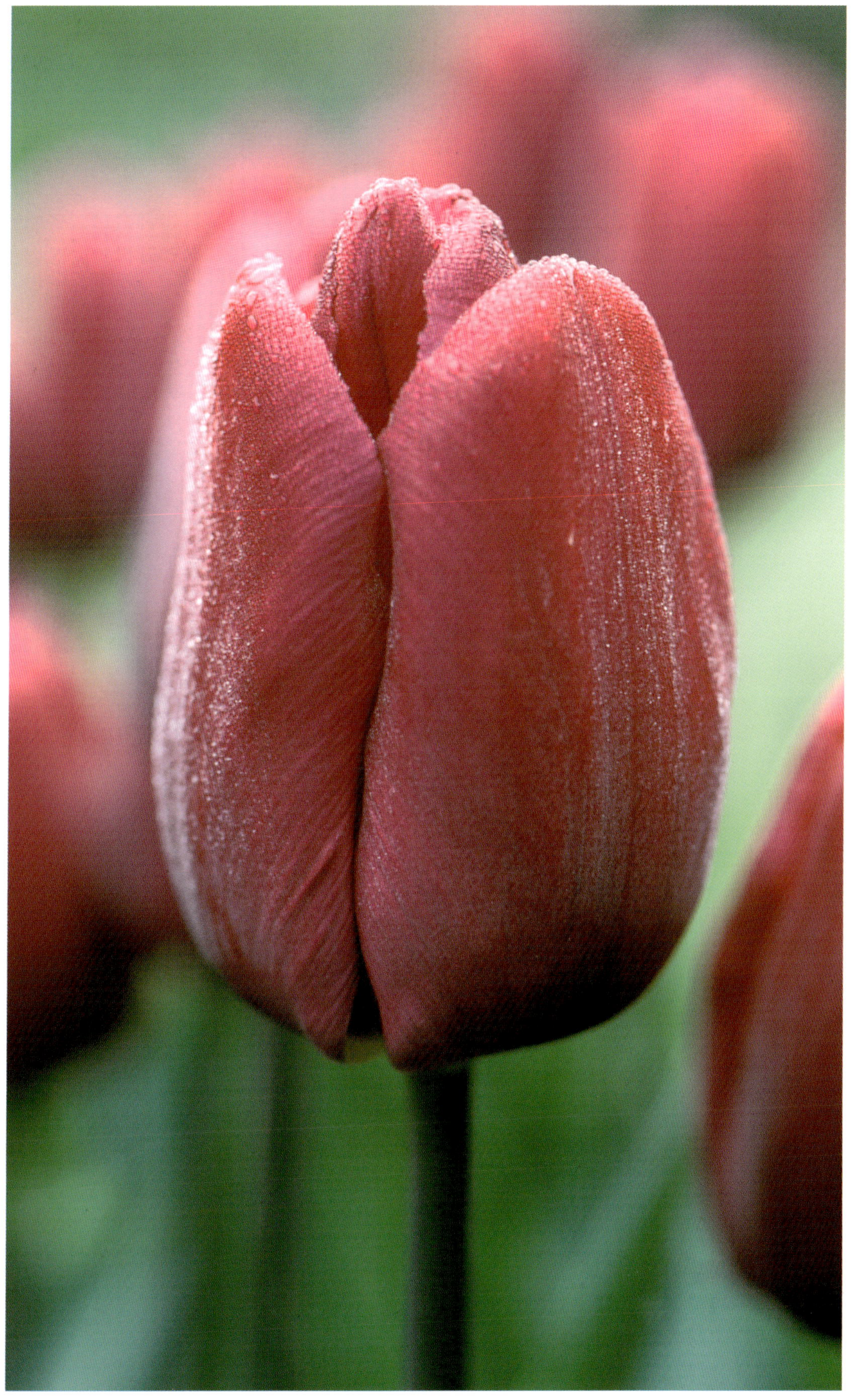

Tulipa "Purple Prince". Dew adds atmosphere to this image and, again, the use of a large aperture renders the background out of focus, thus isolating the subject from its surroundings

that wispy piece of grass in the foreground waving in front of the lens, or the dog poo at the far right.

It is really important to "garden" your pictures: dead flower-heads or diseased leaves, canes, forests of labels – your eye filters these out when you look at a garden in real life, but in a published picture they leap off the page.

Clearly, if you are in someone else's garden, you need to obtain permission before you change or remove anything, but most gardeners are more than willing, provided you religiously return labels and canes to their original positions afterwards. And they are usually quite entertained by the sight of you helping out with the weeding!

When composing a view which includes a man-made structure, make sure that your verticals are truly vertical, and your horizontals are truly horizontal, particularly when using a wide-angle lens, which will emphasise any distortion. Archways and obelisks that imitate the Leaning Tower of Pisa aren't normally very comfortable on the eye – unless of course you've shot it that way deliberately.

Structures will, however, usually create a good focal point in a picture, in much the same way as they will to the garden itself. Focal point structures can include topiary, garden furniture, urns and statuary: all these add impact and appeal to the composition of the picture. Even a simple flowerpot can be enough to draw the image together.

Colour, texture and form are clearly crucial in the composition of a planting combination, although if the garden you're photographing is well planted, the bulk of the work will have been done for you. Look for contrasting foliage shape and texture as well as flower colour, and be aware that anything red will draw the viewer's eye, whether or not that is your intention.

Equally, you can add interest to a picture by making straight lines, such as plant stems or pathways, cross the picture diagonally rather than straight on. A diagonal will always add movement, particularly if it goes from bottom left to top right. This is the way your eyes instinctively read a picture, so a diagonal in this direction has the effect of leading the eye on through.

Finally, when photographing a plant portrait, fill the frame with your subject and keep the background uncluttered. For a garden view maximum depth of field is usually desirable, but for a plant close-up, it is often better to use a wider aperture to isolate the plant from the background. This gives it more impact, and makes the background less distracting.

In fact, attention to background is almost as crucial as attention to subject, as a busy background can ruin an otherwise winning image.

Marketing essentials

Capturing your image is the fun half of the equation, but presenting and selling the final result is just as important and takes a completely different set of skills. Naturally a knowledge and enthusiasm for plants and gardening is a real advantage, especially because a critical requirement in this market is accurate captioning, using both botanical and common names where applicable.

Also, always try to include a garden credit on images that are recognisably of a particular garden. And if possible, get the garden owner's permission for a range of use in advance, so that you don't have to call them every time you want to submit a picture of their garden for publication.

Although the images are legally your copyright, a gardener, quite justifiably, sees his or her garden as their domain, and may be upset if images are used without their consent or without due credit.

Computer literacy is also a prerequisite: as well as many happy hours spent in Photoshop, you will need administrative software to provide labelling, image tracking (which pictures are with which client, history of use, etc) and accounting facilities. In addition, a good telephone manner is essential, not only for approaching potential clients, but also for approaching possible gardens or nurseries, particularly if you want them to let you in at 5:30am!

When you do sell an image, try not to mind what happens to it in its final incarnation on the printed page – I have occasionally had pictures appearing upside-down, or with the wrong caption attached. If you want to work for that publication again, it's best to suffer in silence. Banking the cheque usually helps.

A competitive market

At the time of writing the editorial market for garden pictures in the UK is heavily saturated and competition is fierce. So if you want to break into this field, you need to do some serious market research: look at newsstands and bookshops to see what is already out there, and take note of the various house styles.

Ask lots of questions and get feedback; find out what kind of pictures the market is currently seeking, and provide them. To take an extreme example, if the current need is for a set of pictures of a minimalist urban roof-garden, there is no point in submitting a large, cottage-style country garden.

Don't be afraid to be persistent – research has shown that on average it takes nine contacts with a client before they are likely to commit to buying anything! On the other hand, be patient – if a picture editor has told you that the publication will need a month to deliberate on your latest submission, then wait five weeks before you chase it.

If they are still working with film, then send transparencies and be aware that Velvia is the industry standard in this field.

Talk to the people you are hoping to sell to – the art directors, the picture editors, and if you are writing the words as well, the feature editors. Remember that people buy from people, and it will help enormously if you can build a rapport with a potential client.

If you can put words to a feature to make it more appealing, do so. If you can't, consider finding a writing partner. Talk to your favourite editors and try and find out what is currently required.

Then set your alarm, get your thermals on, and get shooting.

Selling boating photos

by SIMON EVERETT

The boating market is very diverse. Each sector of the market has titles devoted to a particular specialisation and that is the key to opening this particular door – it is the fragmentation of the boating market that provides more opportunities for the freelance.

Motor boating titles are not interested in sailing boats. Inland waterway titles do not want to know about high speed cruising and they are only interested in waterway navigation, not coastal. An activity like rowing has its own specialist magazine.

The sailing titles split themselves into further categories, from those covering dinghy sailing to those for large yachts. Then there are the classic and traditional boating magazines.

The canal and inland waterway titles probably offer the aspiring freelance the easiest opportunities. They don't pay the same rates as the big yachting titles, but then you don't need to charter a helicopter or have access to a big RIB (Rigid Inflatable Boat) in order to get good photographs! For anyone willing to put in the legwork, the canal system offers marvellous walks and accessibility to all canal boating activities from the towpath.

Planning your pictures

As with any other market, the best pictures are taken after some thought and planning. Sometimes you can just happen upon a good picture, but you wouldn't make your living from them.

If you are tackling the canal boat market, study small scale maps to find interesting features and there you will find your pictures. And remember that it isn't just in rural locations that you will find excellent picture opportunities – Birmingham has more miles of canal than Venice.

The industrial heritage alongside the canals in towns and cities provides interesting material. With good lighting and composition these urban landscapes can be made into stunning visuals to arouse the interest of any picture editor. Indeed, these are far more likely to be noticed among the hordes of countryside scenes that arrive every month.

The classic and traditional boat market is another small but dedicated one. The history of our island nation lies in our boatbuilding skills and it is this side of boating that these magazines are devoted to. Find an interesting facet locally and the chances are that you can make

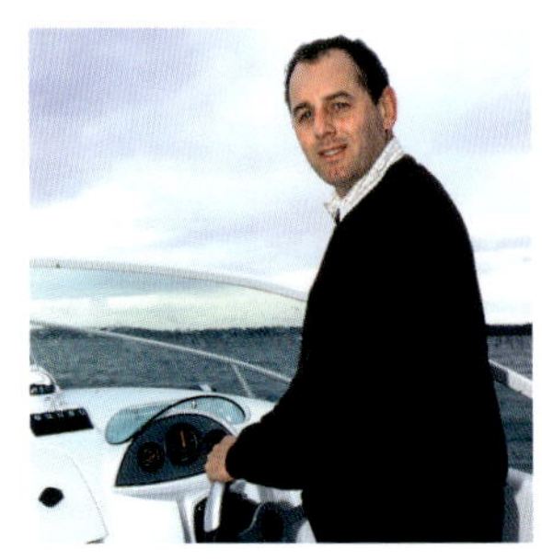

Simon Everett has been a full time professional freelance since 1989. He has been a regular, commissioned, photographer for many boating and yachting titles in the UK, Europe and the United States for the past 20 years.
His knowledge comes from a lifetime of boating beginning when he had his first boat at the age of six. He spent two years as club bosun for the Royal Western Yacht Club in Plymouth and has competed successfully in both sailing and offshore powerboat races.
Simon was a founder member of the Classic Motor Boat Association of Great Britain and is the proud owner of a unique classic powerboat which he takes to rallies all over Europe and sometimes uses as his own photography boat!

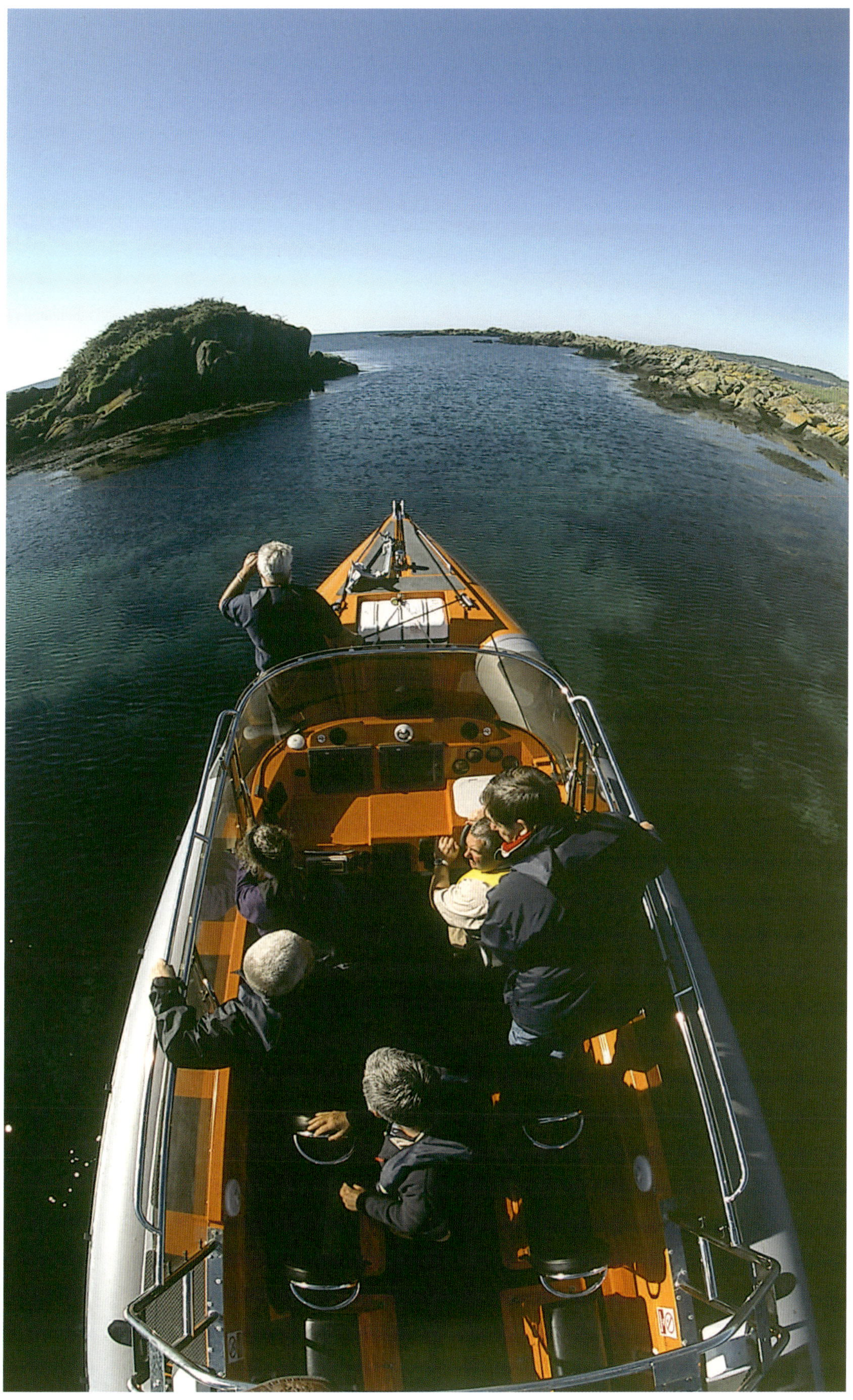

This shot, which was taken with a fisheye lens, produced a successful cover image. The area of blue sky at the top facilitated the overprinting of the magazine's title logo

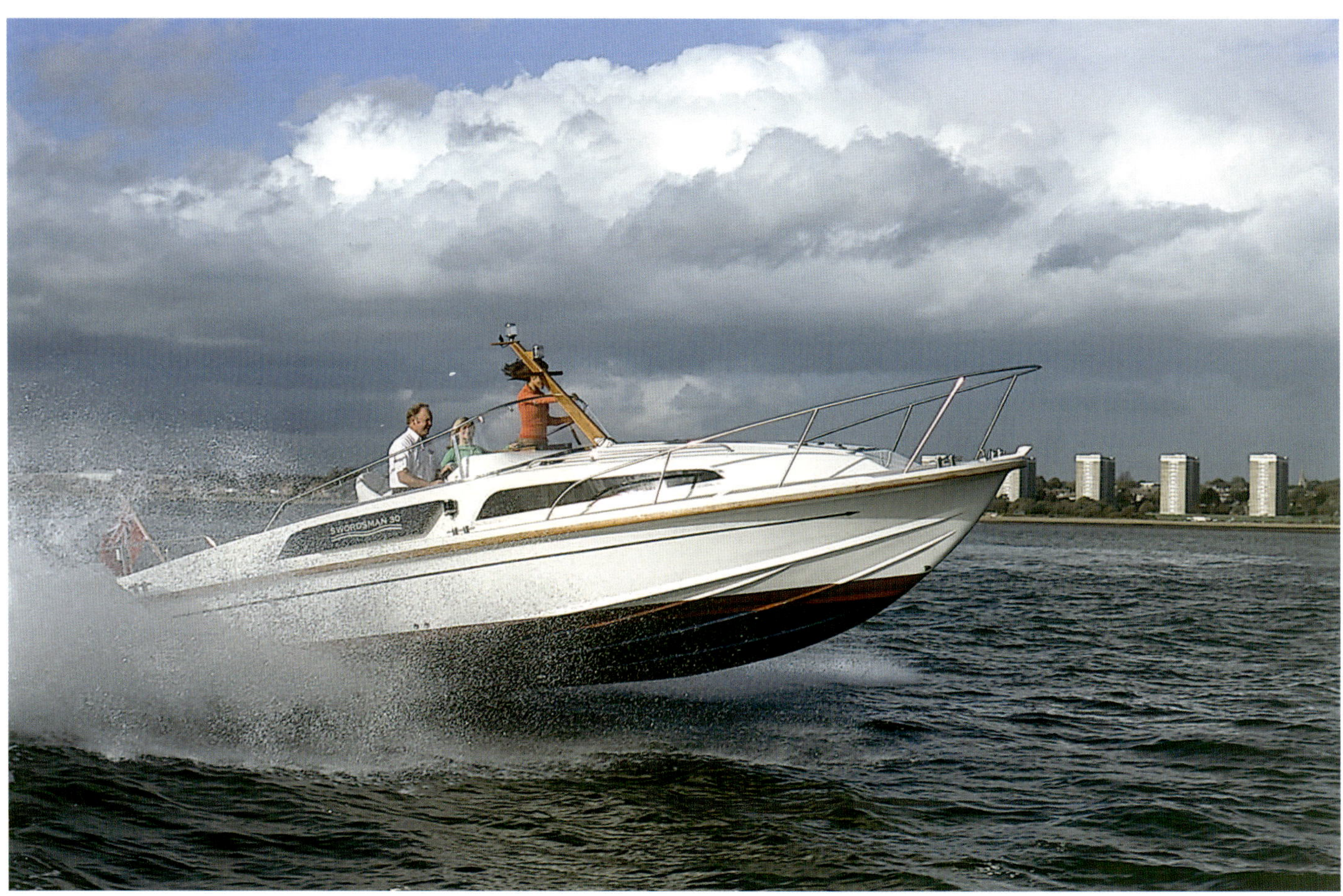

a sale, especially if you can provide a step-by-step pictorial record of a rebuild or restoration.

Perhaps there is a human interest angle about a traditional sailmaker or boat builder. These classic titles sell nostalgia and this type of material is their bread and butter.

Sometimes a really stunning image of one of these subjects will be used as a large, stand-alone picture with a detailed caption. To be successful here stay away from the obvious – it has been done to death. If you can find a little hidden gem somewhere, an editor will treat it as Manna from Heaven.

The mainstream market

For the broader boating market, where the competition is fierce, most material is com-missioned up front. We will deal with com-missioned work later on, but there are some speculative opportunities for those with an eye to the subject.

Single picture uses will come not so much from the boats themselves but more from the infrastructure that surrounds them. Here I am thinking of pretty harbour scenes, lighthouses, buoyage, tide races or any unusual incidents that you might come across.

A picture of a boat on blue water is hard-ly likely to arouse much interest. Close up pictures of the people on board doing things will be of more interest and have a wider appeal to a more general market too.

Fast action and dramatic pictures of powerboats leaping off big waves are what the picture editor of the powerboating titles

This shot was one of a series taken for a boat test for a boating magazine. It was also subsequently used by the boat builder for advertising purposes

is looking for. They must be pin sharp, well lit and fully framed.

Boating photography has its own set of peculiarities due to the environment in which one is working. The first hurdle, like most subjects, is one of access. But here it is more difficult to just walk up to your subject. In fact this trick hasn't, as far as I am aware, been performed for a couple of thousand years!

By definition most boat photography is done from on board, the air, or another boat. Sometimes it is possible to get good photographs from a vantage point on land, perhaps from the end of a pier or breakwater, but this is rare.

To break into the boating market, start by looking at the titles you would really like to work for. Study them intently, assess their content and decide how you could get photographs which would appeal to that editor.

The importance of content

In this market it is not just the picture that is important – the content is also vital. A pretty picture of a boat is much like any other, unless the boat or the crew are of special interest. There must be a reason within the picture for the editor to want to publish it. The picture has to say something or illustrate a current issue.

Armed with this information you are well on your way to success. Pretty pictures are, however, useful for your portfolio and that is the most important tool you have for getting work. Your portfolio should consist of as wide a variety of work as possible, ranging from graphic abstract pictures, through close ups, to fast action and seascapes. You have to show that you are versatile and can work in any situation.

Of course if you do have access to a light aircraft or a friend with a seagoing boat it would be well worth taking the opportunity to shoot some pictures for your portfolio.

As a newcomer you need to supply images which stand out from everything else that has been submitted. You have to gain the interest of the production team with photographs that make them look twice. So how do you go about it?

Events are always of interest, especially off-beat ones that the mainstream photographers don't attend. There is little point in going to one of the boat shows and expecting to sell something from it; these events will be covered by magazine staff. A better idea would be to attend an interesting owners' club rally or join a boat for a spectacular voyage. These ideas are far more likely to arouse interest from an editor, especially if they are based away from the main south coast centres and can offer spectacular scenery.

And here's a tip. By noting the names of the boats you shoot it is possible to track down the owners, who then may well be interested in buying a large print for their personal use. For many marine specialists this approach provides a large proportion of their sales.

Getting commissions

Armed with your portfolio you should make an appointment to see the editor, or picture editor, of the magazine you are aiming at. At this informal meeting your work will be discussed, but so too will your experience, your availability, your geographical location and the rates you expect to be paid.

Boating magazines do not have big budgets and in comparison to some markets their rates are quite modest. You must be realistic to stand a chance of being taken seriously and accept their published page rate with good grace. If it does not meet with your expectations then you must decide whether you still wish to work for that title, or try somewhere else.

If an editor tries to extract story ideas from you as a newcomer, do not provide any detail. The idea will often be noted down and then given to one of their regular photographers to produce the pictures. I learned this lesson the hard way with a car magazine. It holds true for any title.

This may seem unfair, but if an interior designer phoned you out of the blue with ideas for a makeover of your house, would you tell them to go ahead straightaway? No, I thought not. You would want to see some kind of track record. This is precisely why regular photographers get the bulk of the work. It is because they can be relied upon to come back with a good set of pictures from any shoot they are sent on.

When a magazine has set up a boat test on a particular day, perhaps together with an advertising deal based around the pagination of the feature, they simply cannot afford to take the risk of using an unknown photographer. Regardless of the weather on the day you have to come back with publishable photographs, not excuses.

Practical issues

Shooting boats from the air is an expensive business, so it stands to reason that helicopter duty will be assigned to recognised professionals who are used to hanging out of the door with a couple of cameras strapped around their neck.

A less costly way of approaching boats on the water is to shoot from another boat. A large RIB is the preferred conveyance as they are fast, stable and manoeuvrable. They are, however, very wet and keeping your gear dry

becomes a challenge.

So too is the business of shooting an object that is moving rapidly in three dimensions from a platform that is itself also moving rapidly in three dimensions. It takes practise to be able to stand on the deck of a moving RIB with the camera to your eye and still be able to keep your feet without holding on.

On one shoot I had to lie on the foredeck of an offshore raceboat doing 80 mph at sea. I wanted a wide angle shot looking back towards the driver and navigator with the white wake stretching out astern. The deck was totally bare so I only had a rope that we put around the bow to rest my feet on. If I had fallen off my wife would have been a very wealthy woman! Sometimes you just have to take risks to get the shot.

Salt water wreaks havoc with modern camera electrics. There are proprietary camera protection systems available which keep your camera and lens dry, bit I find them a real fiddle with wet, cold fingers. A heavy duty polythene bag and a couple of rubber bands work just as well and it doesn't take ten minutes to change the lens. On fine days I am just careful to keep the gear away from spray.

Gaffer tape over the joints and vulnerable areas also helps to protect the camera gear from water ingress. Top flight professional cameras are very robust and well sealed but it still pays to take some extra precautions.

A question of focus

Autofocus is not so important because a good helmsman will keep you in a shooting position, so the plane of focus remains fairly static.

One of the old masters of yachting photography used to let his little dinghy be run

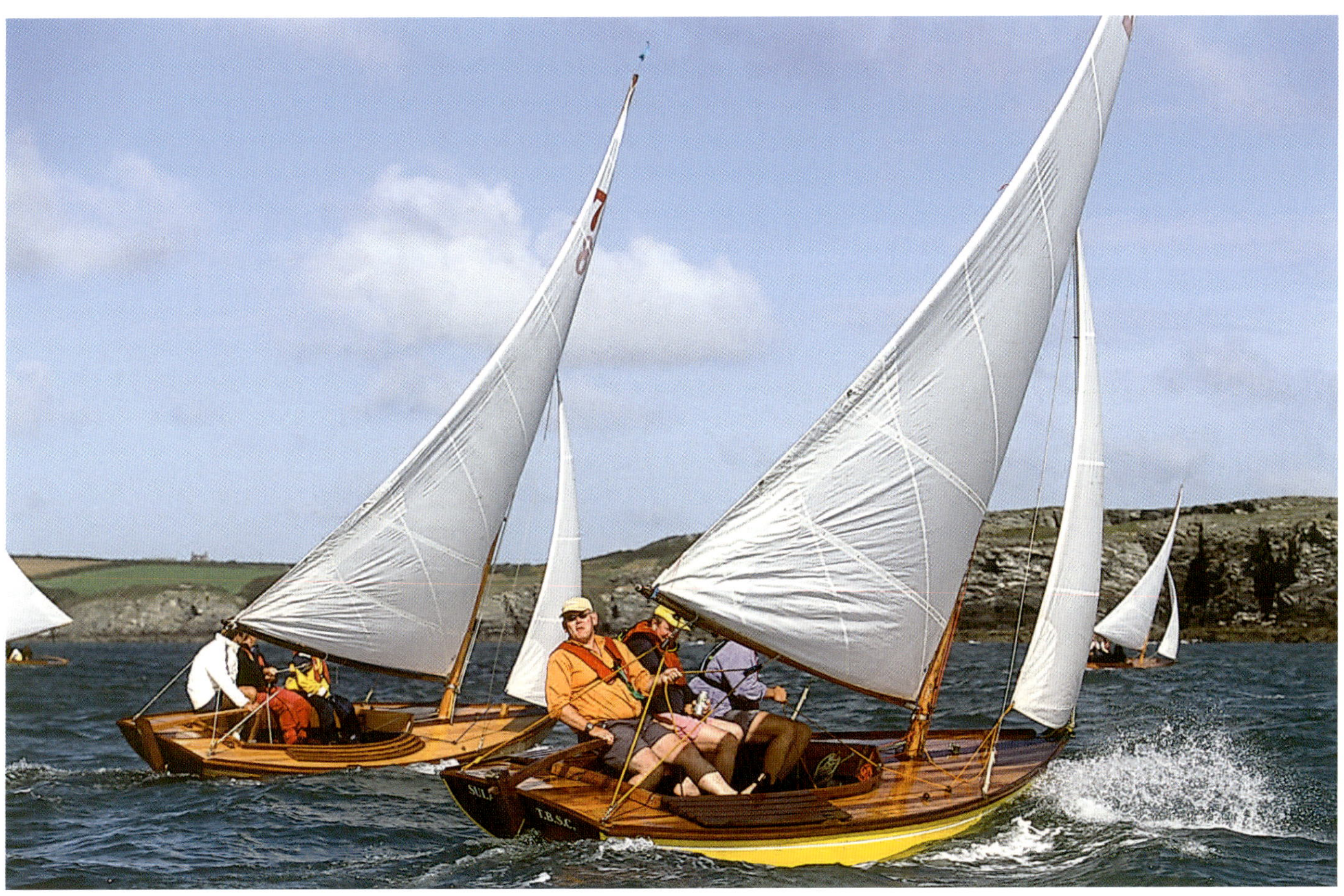

down by the approaching yacht. The little rubber boat would bounce off and be carried away by the bow wave, but the action pictures he created in this way were simply stunning. Fortunately modern RIBs are capable of running close to the target boat, making the job less hazardous!

In rough conditions using autofocus can be really tricky. As the boats are moving about you will find the camera focusing on the sea and sky as you lurch about in the waves. In these conditions I switch to manual focus and wait for the moment when the photography boat is either at the top or bottom of a wave. There is then a moment when the boat remains steady.

It stands to reason that fast shutter speeds are a must in rough water to cancel out the sudden and unexpected movement of the boats.

There is no need for really long lenses to get great boating shots that will sell. The usual system is to use two cameras fitted with a short zoom and a telephoto zoom. The workhorse lenses for most boating photographers are the 28-70 and 80-200 zooms. This combination covers most situations.

For specialist pictures, like shooting from the top of the mast of a yacht for instance, an ultra-wide zoom or even a fisheye can produce drama above the norm. It is a case of seeing the picture, then going about the task of taking it.

As with every other subject, good pictures will always find a market if you take the time and trouble to search them out.

Sailing hard in a stiff breeze. This picture was used as part of a feature in Classic Boat *magazine. Like other pictures taken at the same time, it also sold to the owners of the various boats*

Selling to photo mags

by RACHEL STEWART

There has never been a better time to be a successful contributor to the photographic press, as there are now dozens of photography magazines published each month, not only in the UK but around the world in other English-speaking countries such as the USA and Australia. Unlike many other types of magazine, there is an open global market for the type of material the photo press regularly seeks.

These magazines are broken up into three main types: general photography, digital photography and professional photography. It is mainly the first two that have an insatiable demand for high-quality freelance contributions. But to be a successful photography magazine freelance, you need to be aware of exactly what is available and what type of material they use, so ideally you should subscribe to as many different types of photo magazine as you can afford.

You can also find out what photography magazines are available around the world through the various market handbooks that are published each year. *The Freelance Photographer's Market Handbook* covers the UK, but if you are interested in US titles you should also get hold of the American equivalent called *Photographer's Market*.

There are many information websites on the Internet where you can find lists of the dozens of photography magazines published around the world, usually with links to each magazine's own website where you can download contributor's guidelines and even subscribe online.

Making your work stand out

Photo magazine editors are sent hundreds of top-quality images each week from both amateur and professional photographers from around the globe, so your photographs must be able to stand out amongst a huge number of submissions. Images must be visually stunning with very strong composition, colour, impact and lighting if they are to grab the editor's attention.

Before you send in your images, analyse recent issues of the magazines you wish to submit your photographs to. Study the style of photographs that appear in the magazine – they do not all favour the same type

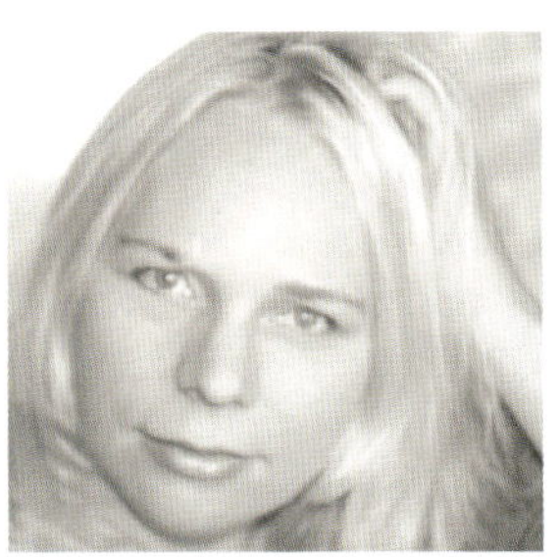

Rachel Stewart was born in Nelson, New Zealand, and first became involved with photography and journalism when only 15 years old, as a reporter and photographer for her high school newspaper. In 1997 she moved to London to further her career in the music industry working as a journalist and photographer for global dance music magazines *DMA* and *Mixology*. Two years later, Rachel moved to Australia. After five years working as a freelance photographer and journalist for a variety of magazines including *Australian Photography* and *Photography International*, Rachel is back in London with her husband and two young children. As well as supplying images to a variety of magazines and stock libraries, she has recently set up her own photography company which specialises in children's lifestyle portraits and stock images.

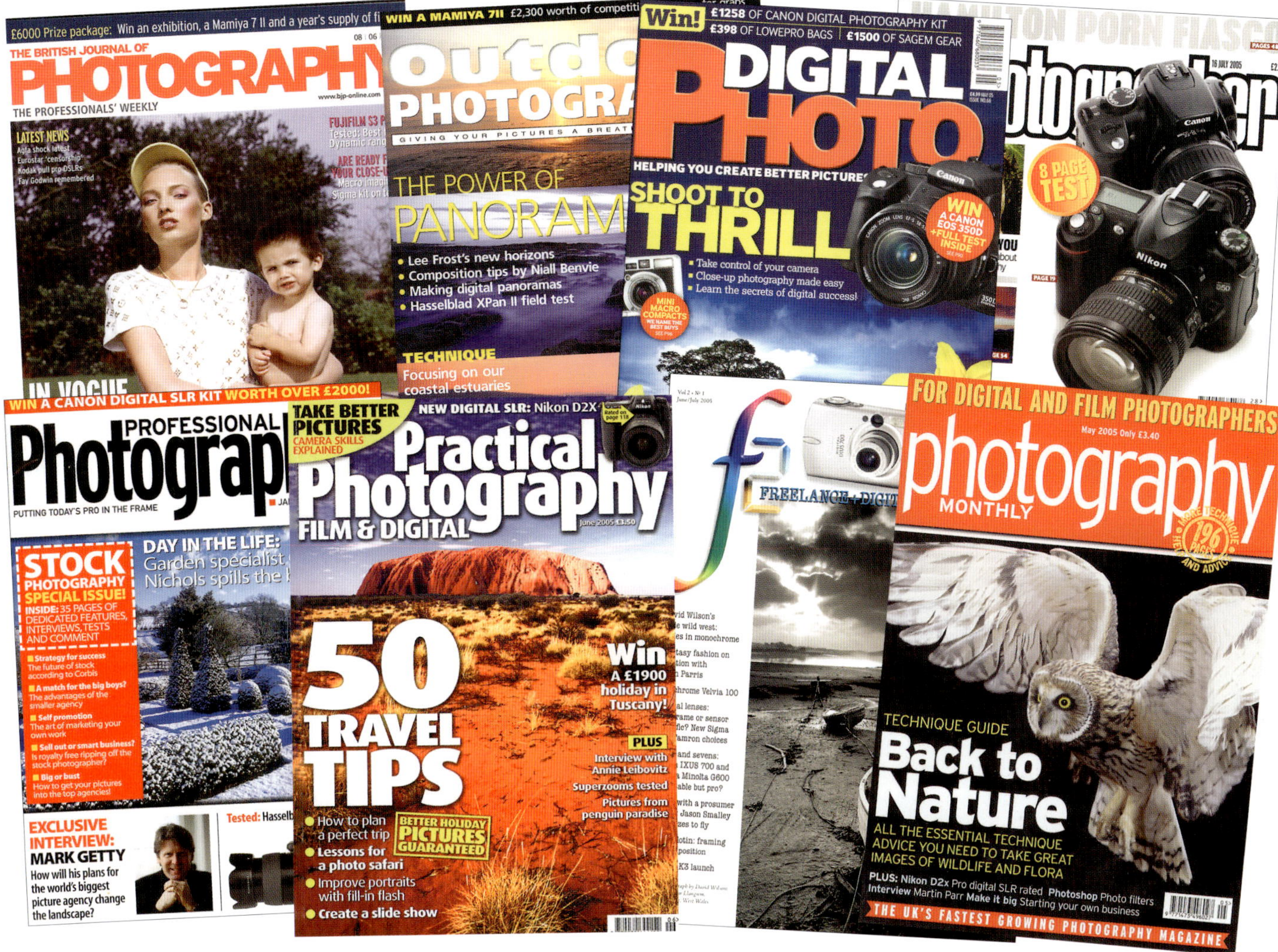

There is a wide range of photographic magazines published in the UK, all of them offering a potential market for the freelance and aspiring freelance photographer

of material. It's no use submitting images you think are fantastic if they are totally inappropriate to the magazine you are thinking of sending them to, as they will be returned to you immediately.

Having assessed your chosen markets, contact the editor of each magazine you are interested in submitting material to by letter or by e-mail, giving them a little background information about yourself including details of any images you have had published before and the areas of photography you specialise in.

Before sending off a submission, ask each editor if they would like an initial portfolio of twenty or so of your best images covering various photographic sub-jects, or a selection of themed material such as landscapes, botanical or nature shots.

If you are unable to get hold of the editor, check the magazine's website as many feature a list of images wanted. You won't go wrong sending images that the magazine actually needs for future issues.

Photo magazines like to use a lot of seasonal material, but be aware that they have long lead-in times so it's no use sending winter-themed shots at Christmas time as the articles and photographs would have been planned months earlier. If you want to submit seasonal images then find out from the editor how many months in advance they are required.

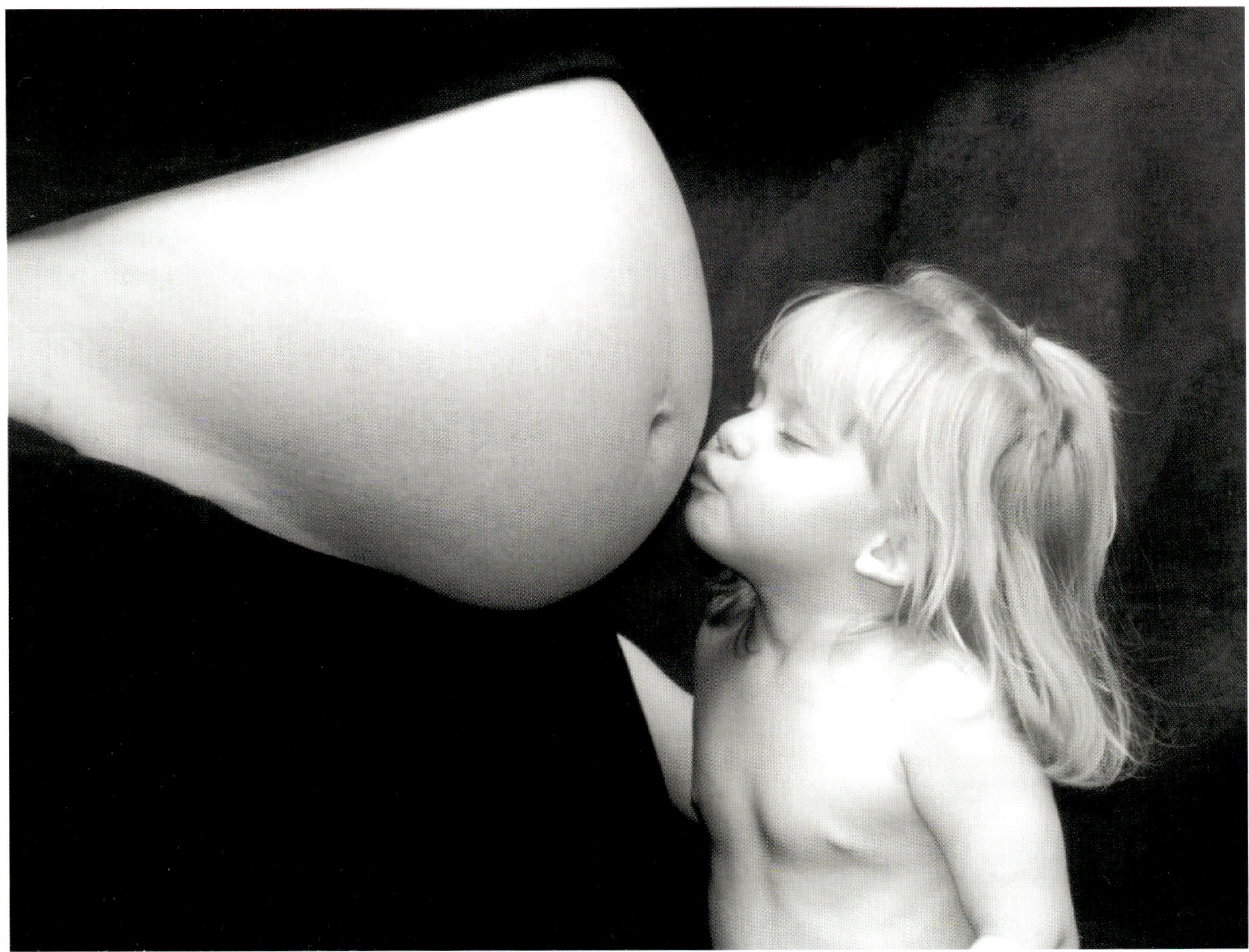

Finding the easiest route

Perhaps the easiest way to get your images into the pages of your favourite photography publication is to submit your images for the magazine's "Readers Portfolio" section. Each month most magazines feature up to a dozen pages of readers' images with a variety of incentives for images used, including cash payments or prizes such as digital cameras, printers and slide films.

Read through the submission requirements for each magazine and then send off your best images in the format required. Your selection of images can either be themed, or a variety of subjects which showcase your talent.

Another good option for the less experienced contributor is to begin with competitions. If you look through all the photography magazines you will find a number of photo competitions in almost every issue with highly desirable prizes such as digital SLR cameras, medium format cameras, holidays and top of the range printers.

As the saying goes, "you've got to be in to win", so read the rules of each competition thoroughly and enter your best image each month. If you're lucky, you may well find a letter in the post a month or so later saying that you are a major competition winner.

This shot of the author's daughter Emma kissing her mother's heavily pregnant tummy has not only appeared in photographic magazines, but has also sold to parenting titles

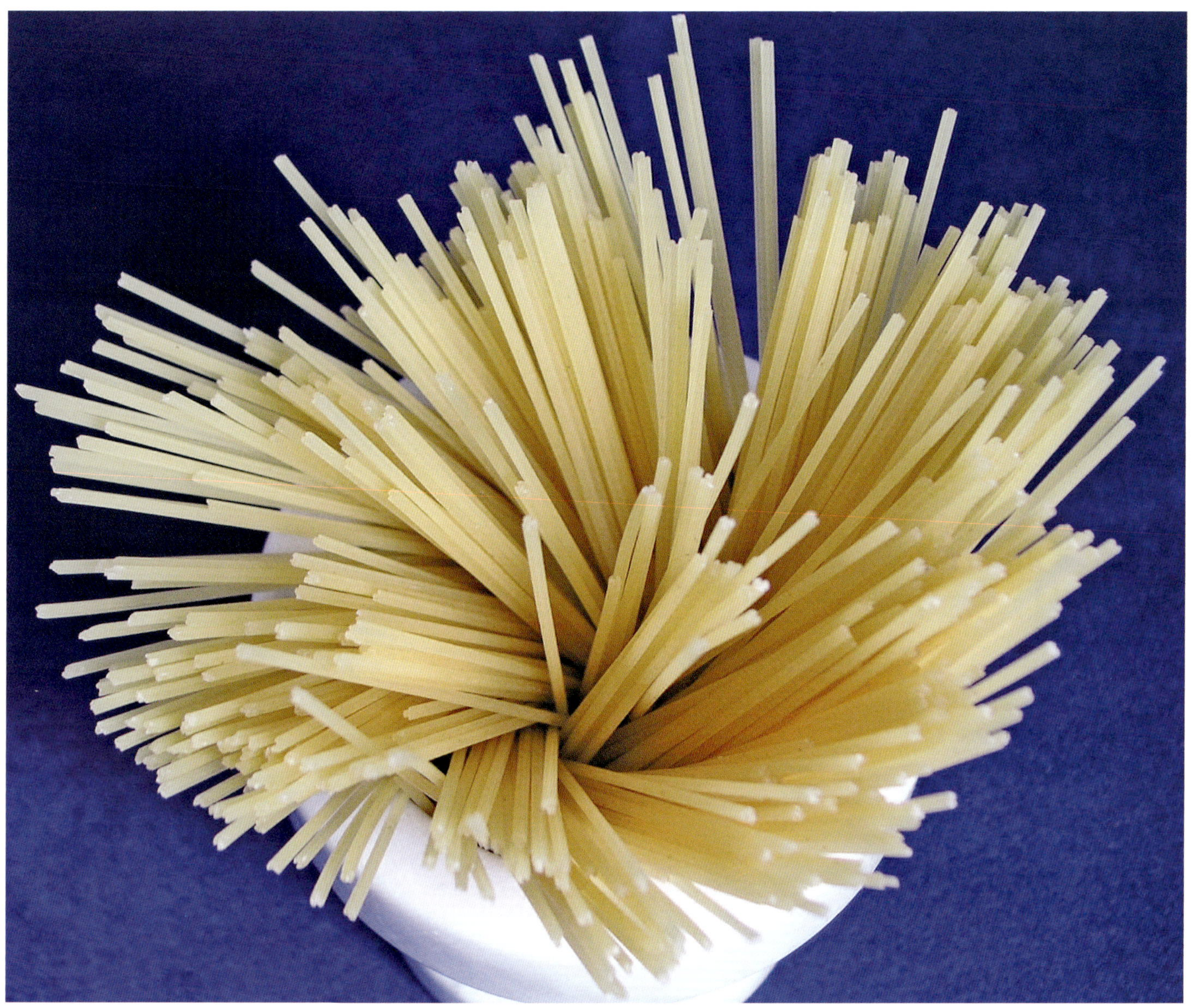

This studio shot of pasta was used to illustrate an article on food photography

When entering a competition, check the closing date so you know how much time you have to get your entry ready, and always allow a week for your entry to get to the magazine.

Find out what formats are accepted in each competition, as some digital magazines will only accept e-mailed entries, while other titles won't accept digital files and may only want 35mm slides or large prints. Clearly, if you send your entries in the wrong format then your chances of winning will be zero.

Most competitions have a theme, so study this carefully and think about how you will interpret it. For your image to make it to the final round of a competition, it must be original, technically perfect (pin-sharp focus and flawless composition).

I subscribed to photography magazines in the UK for over a year before I entered my first competition, so you can imagine how thrilled I was when I won the first contest I entered. Most competitions have thousands of entries each month, but providing your image fits the bill of what is asked for, your chances of winning are as good as the next photographer.

Once you start seeing your winning images in a national magazine your confidence will increase tenfold, and there's nothing like seeing your work in print to promote your photography.

Adding words to your pictures

Your chances of becoming a regular contributor to photography magazines are greatly increased if you offer editors complete "words and pictures" packages instead of simply images by themselves. To do this you must be an excellent all-rounder with great photography and good writing skills.

To attract the attention of these editors and their readers you have to be able to create lively and interesting articles combined with striking, professional-quality images. You are competing with experienced contributors who know how to give these markets exactly what they want. Succeeding as a freelance photographic writer means bringing out a vibrant personality in your writing and showing a unique style in your images to set you apart from others.

Have a good look at the various styles of photographs in your collection. If you have twenty or so publication-quality shots of a particular subject, then go ahead and write an article talking about how your images came about and the steps needed to take successful images of that particular subject.

Read the columns and "step-by-step" articles in your favourite photography magazines to get an idea of how they are put together and study articles written by a number of different writers to see how their individual styles differ.

Before submitting any articles to a magazine, contact the editor with your ideas. They will let you know if the magazine is written entirely in-house or if they offer work to freelance contributors, and will ask you to send examples of your work in order to assess your writing style.

Editors are known to keep hold of articles for up to two years before they decide to use them, so if you have not heard back from an editor a month after sending something, contact them and ask if they plan to keep the article on file for future use. Of course if they do, you won't be able to submit that particular article to any other photography magazines.

If your submission gets returned to you unused, try submitting it to a different title. If there is no market for it, file it away in a safe place for a few months while keeping an eye on the styles of the various magazines. The needs of editors are constantly changing as magazine formats change frequently in this field, so a few months later there may actually be a need for your article.

Do keep in regular contact with editors about their needs, as they may have a gap in the market that you can fill with one of your article and photograph packages.

Formats and Photoshop

Each photographic magazine has a different requirement when it comes to submitting images. All UK titles will accept digital submissions, transparencies or prints.

Make sure you also include a separate photo index sheet that gives detailed additional information about each image submitted. For this particular market, unlike all others, you will need to include full details on the camera, lenses and filters used, film

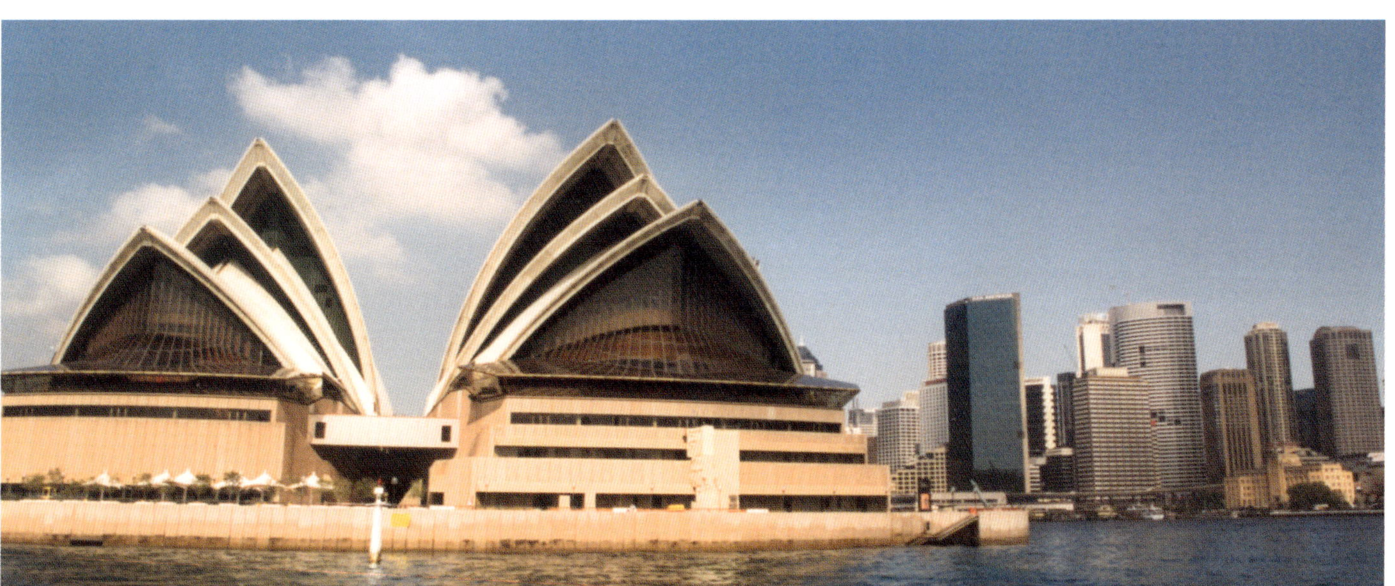

type (if applicable) and speed, exposure details and whether or not a tripod was used.

If you want to submit digital files, find out from the magazine editor exactly what formats and file sizes are preferred before you put your images on CD-ROM.

In this market it will help greatly to have a good knowledge of computer photo enhancing software packages such as Photoshop or Paint Shop Pro, as there is a currently a very high demand for "before-and-after" digitally-enhanced images, especially in the many digital photography magazines.

A great software package to learn on is the basic Photoshop Elements, as it has the main features of Photoshop CS but without the hefty price tag attached. There are a number of very good books available today that explain how to use Photoshop and many photography magazines now include a free CD or DVD each month with "step-by-step" digital enhancement guides.

This photograph of the Sydney Opera House and city skyline, was used to illustrate an article on architectural photography in Australian Photography

Selling to local papers

by DAVE WOODS

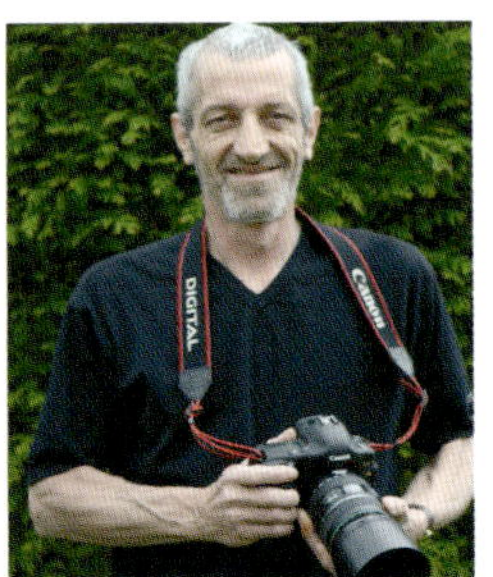

Local newspapers are an obvious outlet for the freelance photographer. Although fees are generally low, if you can supply two or three local papers with half a dozen pictures each week a reasonable income can be earned.

What do you need to get started? Apart from an interest in local life and that obsessive enthusiasm for their craft that all serious photographers have, you will need a reliable camera and preferably a spare body, a reliable car, a telephone and Internet connection.

Broadband is almost a must. One of my local papers accepts JPEG files as small as 150Kb, though their reproduction often leaves a lot to be desired. I take my shots on a 6.3 million pixel camera set at its highest quality level and send the pictures at 30% of their original size, which gives a file size of around 650Kb. E-mailing a 650kb JPEG takes about four minutes with dial-up but only about ten seconds with broadband. When you're sending half a dozen urgent pictures the time saving is considerable.

So then how do you approach the market? In my case I answered an advertisement in the *Brecon & Radnor Express* for a community reporter in my town. These advertisements appear from time to time in most local papers, but rather than waiting for this sort of opportunity to arise a phone call to all of the editors in your area may reap rewards.

Having got a regular column writing local news stories I started submitting pictures to illustrate my articles. It wasn't long before the editor was asking me to photograph anything the paper required. Although most papers have at least one staff photographer, that person can't be everywhere at once and at certain times, such as bank holidays, there is always scope for the freelance.

I made sure that I was at every major event in the locality, such as the town carnival and remembrance services – basically any event that was newsworthy. And I made sure I had the pictures on the editor's desk as soon as possible after the event.

Finding the news

OK, so you've got the kit you need and you've got an editor interested. What is

Dave Woods has been supplying photographs for local newspapers in mid-Wales for almost 20 years as well as selling to other markets such as tourist authorities, magazines and postcard publishers. As well as news photographs, Dave shoots sports photographs every weekend for the *Becon & Radnor Express.* His photos have also appeared in the (Powys) *County Times, Mid-Wales Journal, Cambrian News, Heart of Wales Chronicle* and *Shropshire Star.* Dave also devotes some time helping to run a unique mid-Wales community photo library, cambrian-images.co.uk

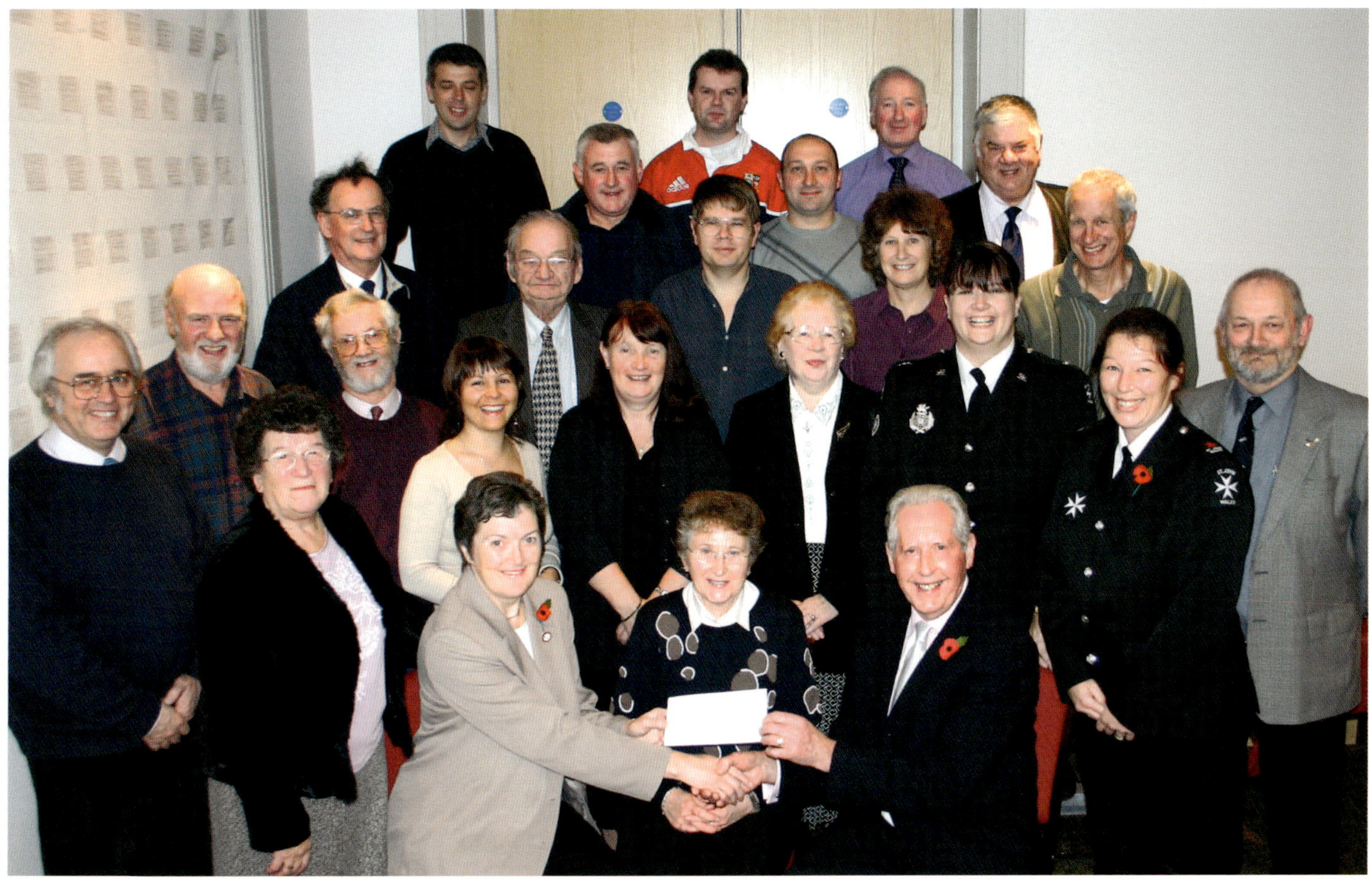

news and how do you find it? Remember that local papers use local interest stories for the bulk of their content, with only the occasional really "hard news" story.

A good starting point is your local community, town or parish council. Your local council will meet once a month and these meetings are open to the public. Most will have an area reserved for the press. Everything from local events and fundraising activities to planning applications is discussed at these meetings, suggesting plenty of photo opportunities.

The council will itself generate several opportunities such as the yearly election of a new chairman/mayor or the award of council funding to voluntary groups. Our town council make an award to the best-kept garden in the town, yet another photo opportunity each year. The Mayor and other councillors will each have their own priorities and concerns and as you get to know them even more opportunities will present themselves.

After a short while every organisation in town will be phoning you to let you know of a presentation, open day or awards ceremony taking place, especially after another local organisation has made the front page!

If you want to capture images of disasters, famine and war then obviously the local paper isn't your best bet. Pictures of, for example, a road traffic accident may be newsworthy but they aren't necessarily what your paper will be looking for.

You may cover the occasional flood or fire, but you must be sensitive as the fire you're busy photographing is often someone's home or place of work and the situa-

An ability to organise groups of people is an important skill when shooting for local newspapers. Always take several shots to ensure that there is at least one where everyone is looking at the camera

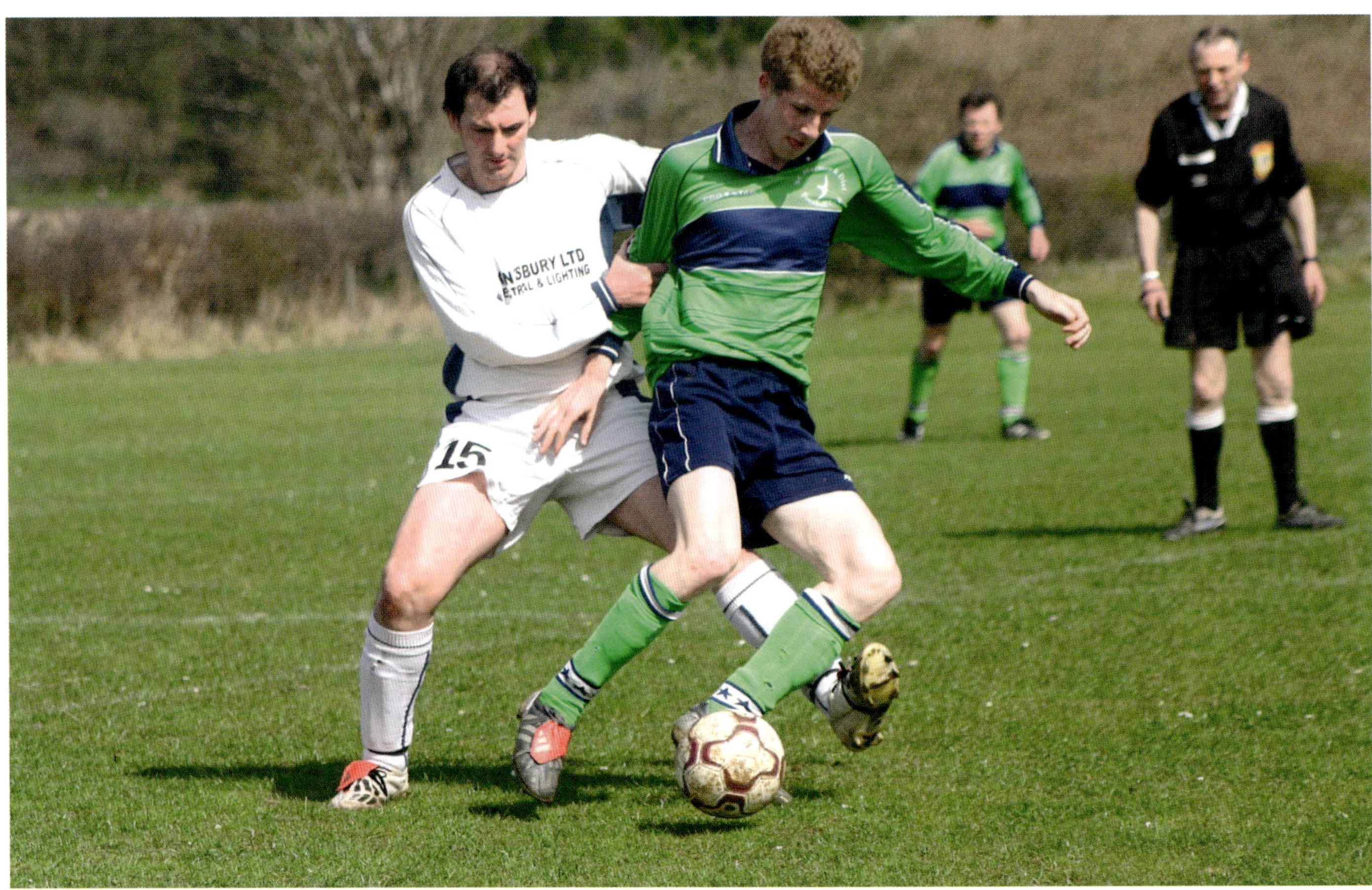

tion is upsetting enough without you exploiting their misfortune. As you get known locally, the attending fire and police officers will often smooth the way for you to do your job without being too obtrusive or upsetting the victims more than they already are.

So the majority of your pictures will be of things like school reunions or the launch of a new minibus for the elderly. Local interest is what counts. A group of a dozen schoolchildren receiving an award on the front page will generate a lot of sales for the paper; every parent and many of their friends and other relatives will all want a copy.

Anyone who has experience in wedding photography or shooting family groups would be well suited for the everyday work of a local news photographer. Shots of the WI or school fete will inevitably involve organising people in much the same way as a wedding photographer has to organise family members into groups. Here people skills are probably more important than photographic skill. There is always one who wants to stand at the back with their head turned away and you must make sure everyone is looking straight at the camera.

Sporting opportunities

Although I was earning a little from news photographs it wasn't until the editor passed a shot of a runner in the annual Gwastedyn Hill Race to the sports editor that I started earning a good regular income.

Soon I was being asked to cover local

Local minor league football matches are a staple of most local newspapers. This picture features Mid-Wales League sides Saint Harmon and Brecon

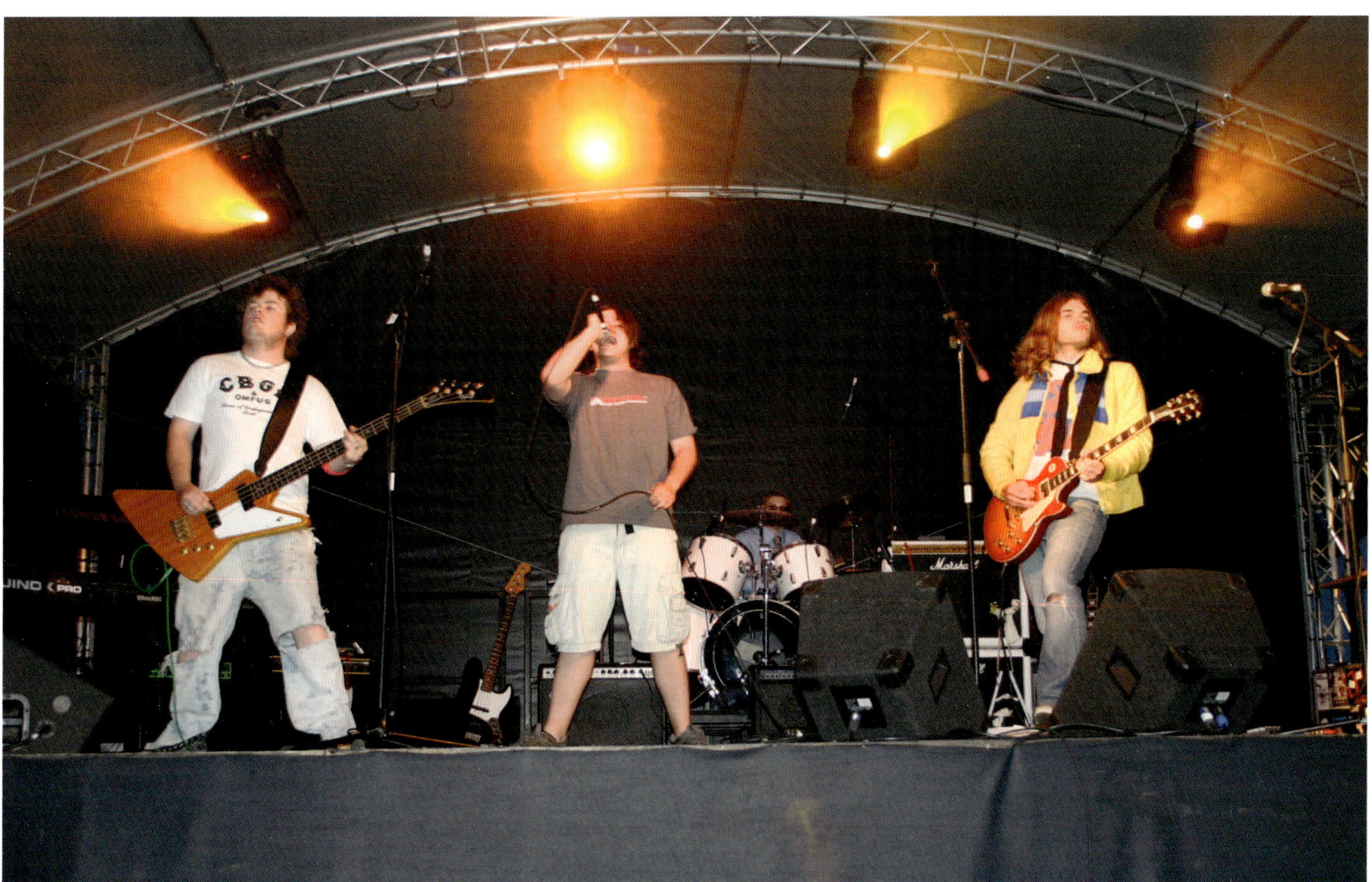

football and rugby and in the summer months cricket, tennis and bowls. Each picture pays more than straight news photos and from a photographer's point of view these events are much more fun to cover.

Whilst many news pictures entail waiting around for ages to get one shot, sports photography is usually continuous action, with countless opportunities for that special photo that makes yours stand out from the crowd.

On a typical Saturday afternoon I photograph up to three or four different football or rugby matches. With luck, kick-off times will vary, allowing me to cover a football match starting at 2pm, then travel ten or fifteen miles to cover one starting at 2.30, and finish up covering both football and rugby in another town. Obviously the ability to work quickly is vital, but staying on at a match for another ten minutes to get the shot you want is better than rushing off with only mediocre pictures.

I occasionally have to send in a report with my sports pictures. It can be difficult trying to concentrate on getting a good shot while remembering who crossed the ball that led to a goal or who cleared the ball off the line, and making notes only when you have a few seconds while play is at the other end. But with practice it becomes easier and an ability and willingness to add words to your pictures will always endear you to editors. The end result will be more sales.

Extra income from print sales

Extra income can also be earned from selling prints to the people in your pictures. I

It doesn't have to be the Rolling Stones. Local bands performing can be very saleable for the entertainment pages of your local newspaper

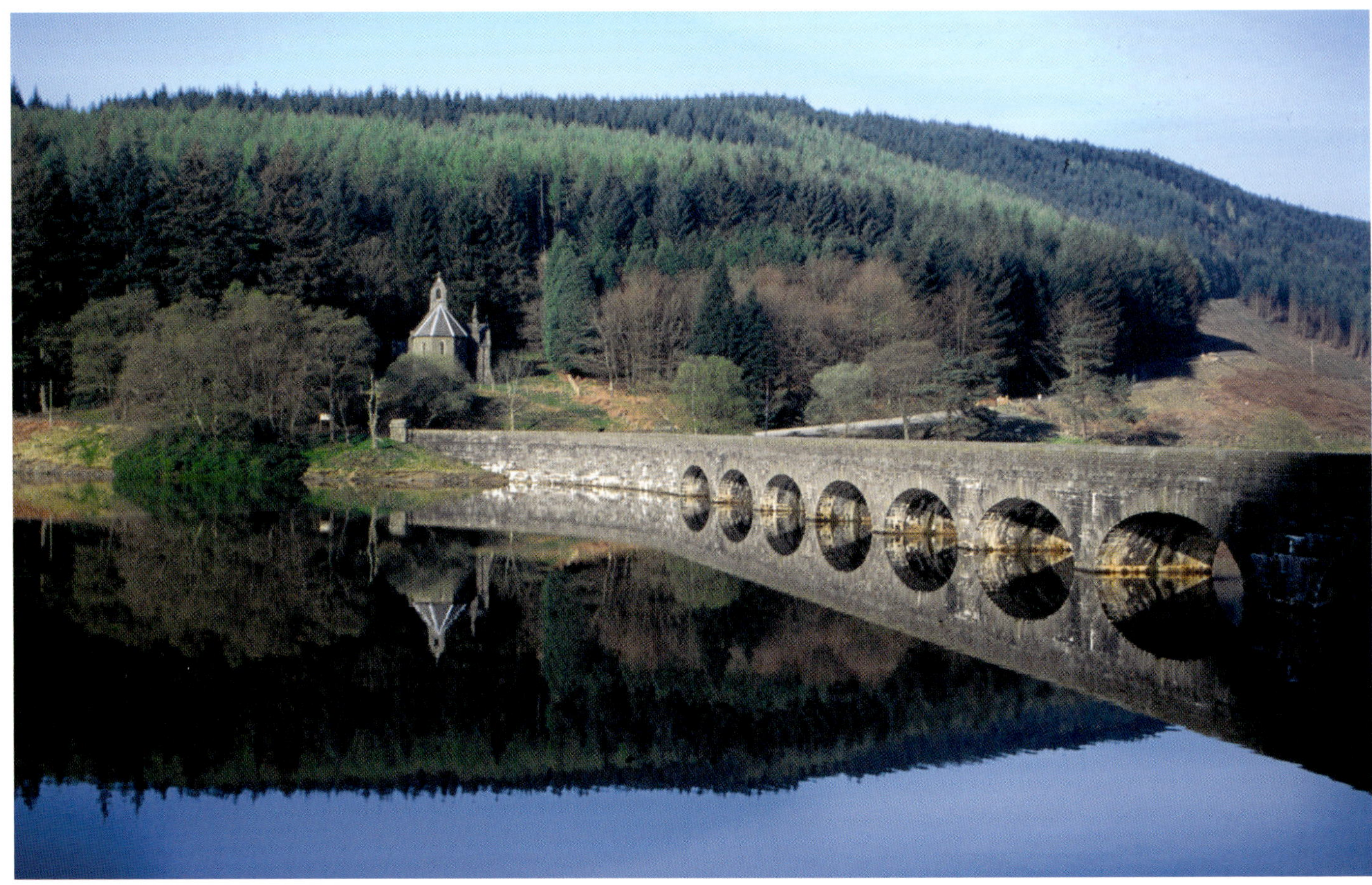

recently covered a charity abseil on the Claerwen Dam. Forty courageous fundraisers descended two hundred feet down the face of one of the largest dams in the country. Knowing the local geography I had the best possible vantage point and managed to photograph every participant

Among those taking part were Kirsty Williams, Welsh Assembly Government Member for Brecon and Radnor. A shot of her descent was used on the front page of the *Mid Wales Journal* while other local papers used a shot of a wheelchair user taking part. But apart from the reproduction fees, over half of the participants ordered at least one print.

I do give away the occasional print, which helps create a good working relationship with the local community. Kirsty Williams received a shot of her abseiling

adventure. Next time she opens a village show or school sports day, I know she will be only too happy to co-operate when it comes to the photo-call.

I recently gave prints to a couple of kids at a Halloween party. Next time I need a shot at the school I know they'll be helpful, and when their parents are looking for a photographer for a family portrait, who will spring to mind?

There is probably a carnival of some kind in your locality each year. Apart from making sure you are there on time for the big moments like the crowning of the carnival queen, photograph all of those in costumes or fancy dress. The paper may give a whole page over to it and you're bound to generate sales of prints.

When covering sporting events I am frequently asked to take a team photo-

Occasionally a good landscape can sell to the local paper, either in its own right or to illustrate an article. This shot of Garreg Ddu Dam made the front page of the Brecon & Radnor Express

graph, especially after a cup win or promotion to a higher league. This can bring high value sales, especially in the case of a rugby team. With fifteen team members plus substitutes and management committee members, sales of thirty or more prints are not uncommon.

Local newspapers will usually have their own facilities for ordering prints by the staffers, but as a freelance I am free to market my own.

The importance of captions

One important aspect of newspaper work, which must not be overlooked, is the need for full and accurate captions. However good your photograph may be, it will be of no use to your editor without a caption. A good photo may even be used in its own right if you can supply just a paragraph or two answering those basic journalistic questions: who, what, why, where and when.

When photographing a group of people get everyone's name *before* you start shooting. Leave it until after and people will be wandering away, leaving you with only half a caption.

You may get away with a caption such as "Chamber of Trade chairman, Joe Bloggs and committee members". But it is far better to be able to name the whole committee, so your caption becomes "Chamber of Trade chairman, Joe Bloggs with committee members John Smith, Mary Brown and Peter White". Add an extra line of context and it becomes: "Chamber of Trade chairman, Joe Bloggs and committee members John Smith,

Mary Brown and Peter White are pictured at their annual general meeting held at Anytown community centre on Thursday."

You now have a usable caption for your picture. Add a short quote from the chairman and you have enough information for the picture to be used in its own right.

Remember it is always better to give too much information than too little; it can always be edited later.

Captioning shots of football or other sporting events can be problematic for a number of reasons. Firstly, at minor league matches there is rarely a programme to refer to so it's worth asking each manager for a team sheet. But with the players wearing their numbers on their backs, identifying individuals in your shots can still be tricky. Again, a word with the guys in the dug-out is usually helpful.

Look for that gap

So if you think you have the necessary skills have a look at the local press in your area. Can you supply the kind of shots they use? Is the sports page full of team photos but short of action shots? Is this a gap in their coverage that you can fill?

The editor's name and contact number will be in the paper, but don't phone a weekly the day before it comes out. The editor will have much more time for your call a day or two after publication.

Freelancing for your local newspapers won't make you rich, but combined with other freelance work it has, for me, proved very worthwhile.

Selling travel photos

by KEITH PLANT

The thought of travelling and selling your pictures to pay for that same trip is very attractive. It's fortunate, then, that holiday brochures and magazines are such a large and lucrative market for freelance photographers.

A glance at any newsagent or travel agent will convince you that the market needs thousands of pictures every month. But which publications or companies are most likely to buy from a freelance and how should you go about contacting them?

Who will buy your pictures?

The big holiday companies will almost certainly have their own team going out to photograph specific properties and they generally buy other shots from picture libraries. It's the smaller, more specialist companies that are most likely to buy from freelances.

Look in an independent travel agent but also check the travel columns of your weekend newspapers. The great thing about travel brochures is that they're free!

Some companies are so focused (for example, they might specialise in educational travel) that they won't advertise in conventional markets. However, a search on the Internet should bring up a list of addresses.

Unless you have an exceptionally friendly newsagent, assessing the magazine market is more expensive. You will need to study the individual magazines in the way described in the Introduction to this book. When you make your initial approaches to a company or magazine you'll need to have a number of suitable pictures available. There is nothing more embarrassing than having a positive response from a potential client and then having only three suitable shots. I usually try to send off between 20 and 60 images. Picture buyers like to have a choice!

And there's little point in sending off ten strong pictures and making the number up with second rate material – that just devalues the impact of the good work.

These days it's a good idea to e-mail a marketing manager or editor first to see if they're interested in receiving work. It's also important to check when they want to receive it – brochures are typically put together only once a year.

Similarly, remember that, as indicat-

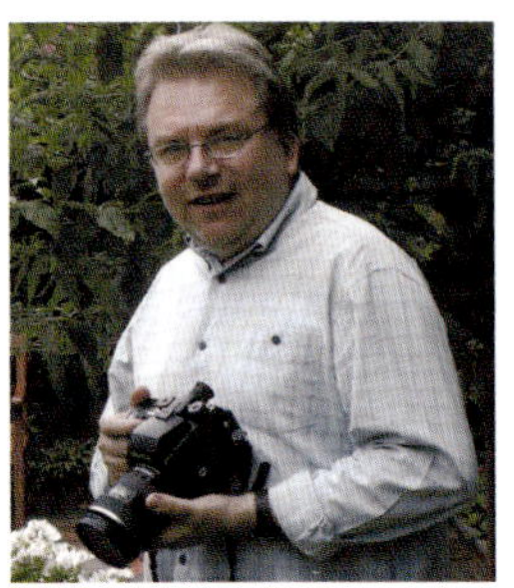

Keith Plant is a teacher who freelances during the holidays. He shoots in medium format and 35mm. His work has been published in a wide range of magazines, brochures, greetings cards, postcards and is held by three picture libraries. Keith is a popular guest speaker at local camera clubs.

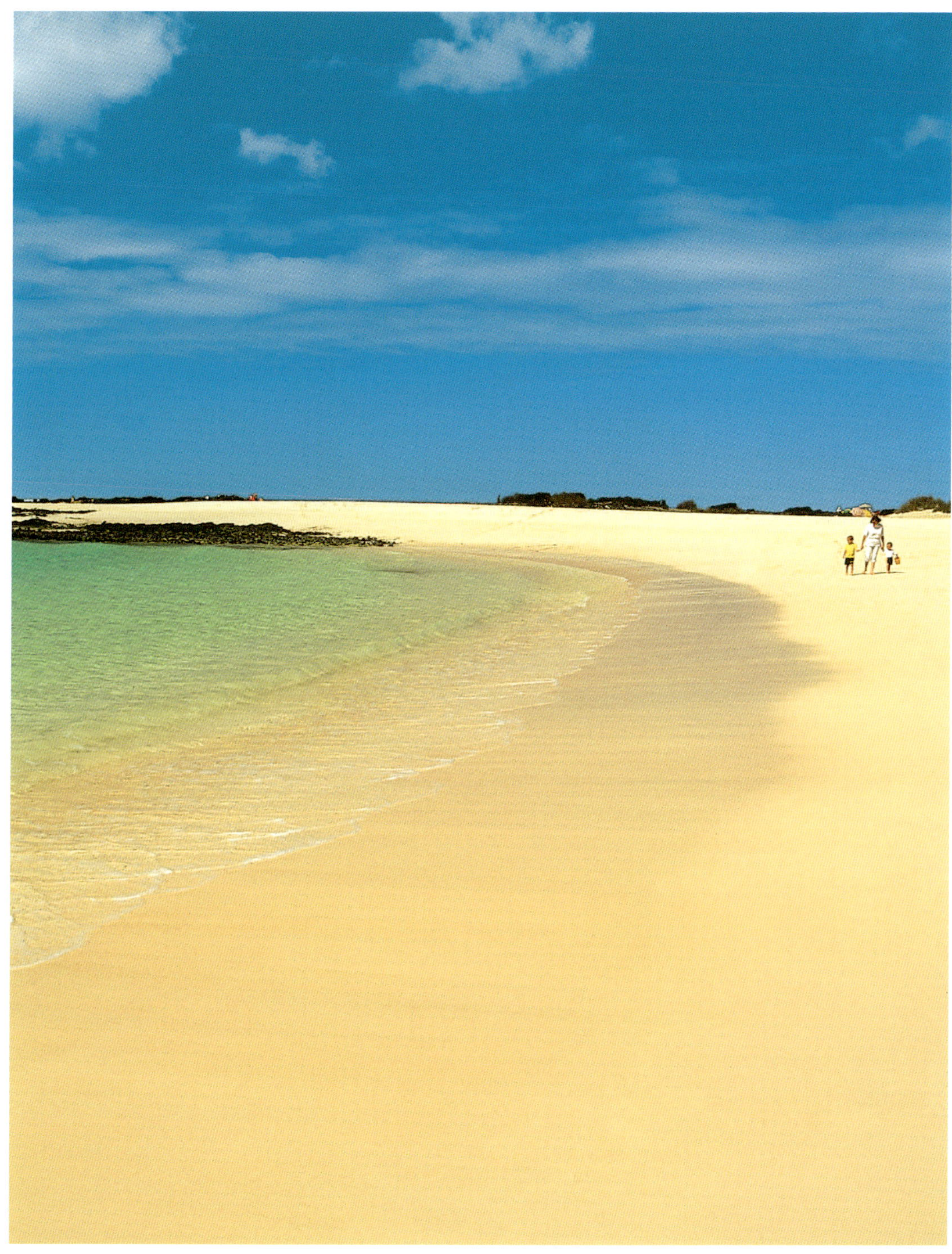

Sun, sea and sand – three words that sum up what many people look for in a holiday; and what those seeking travel brochure images often also require. Here, a wideangle lens emphasises the expanse of sand

edearlier in this book, most magazines want seasonal images and that editors work with lead times where typically they will want pictures of Christmas lights in September or October.

As you become more confident that you can produce the quality of work needed, you can become more audacious. I once booked a holiday with a specialist company and then e-mailed the owner to ask if he would be interested in photos for the following year's brochure. He was enthusiastic, told me the style of image he was looking for, and my photograph duly graced the next cover!

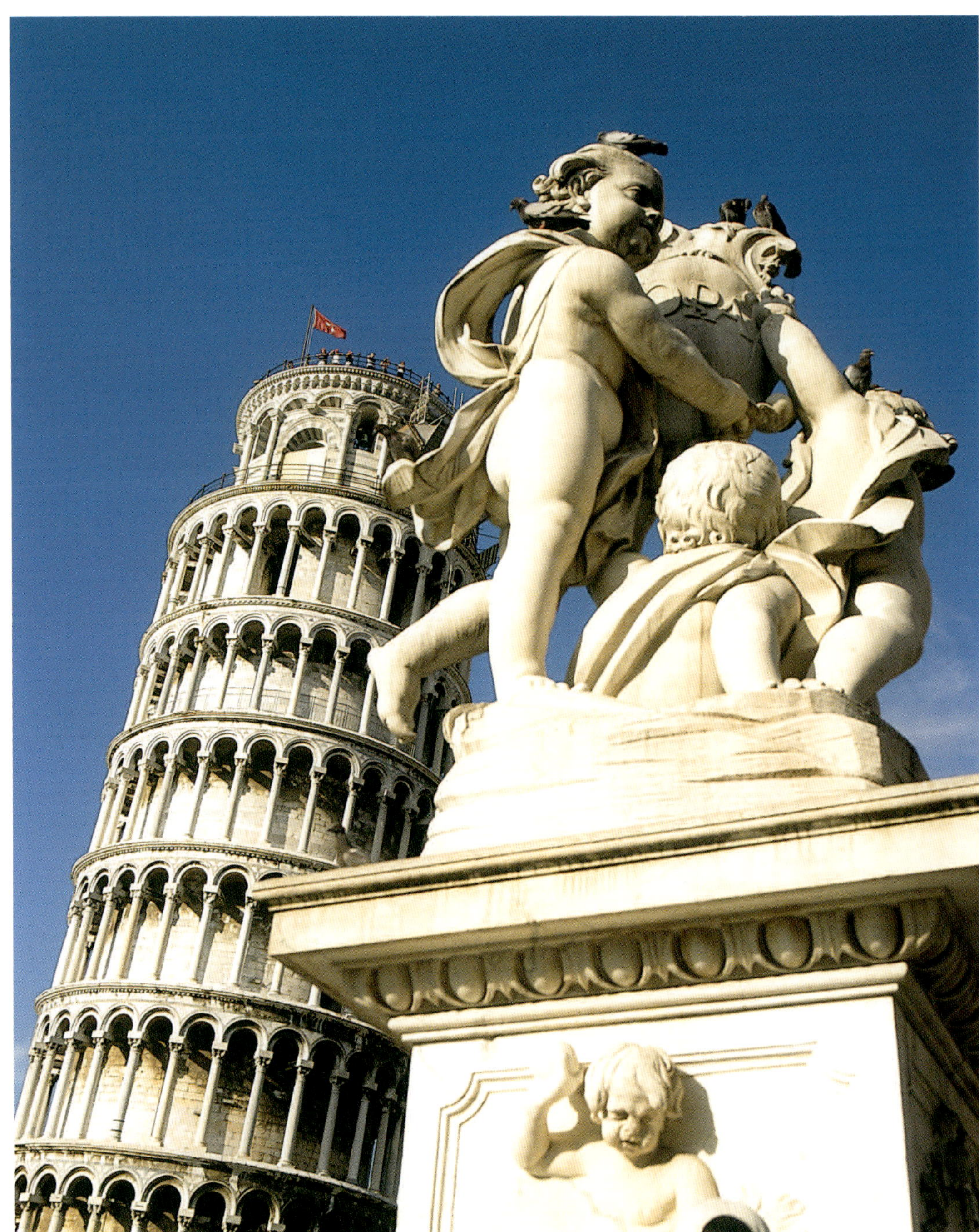

Leaning Tower of Pisa: don't fail to capture iconic images – but try to find a way of being a little different

Composition and content

As you look at your chosen publications, notice how shots are composed. If you hope to get a picture on a cover, it's pointless to shoot in landscape format and you will almost certainly need to leave "dead" space for the editor to drop text into. Note whether this is at the top, bottom or side. A cover composition certainly won't be the same image that you would send to a postcard company.

Naturally holiday brochures want to make destinations seem desirable. That usually means polarising filters, sunshine and blue skies. Avoid overcast conditions or the harsh light in the middle of the day – shoot when the sun is lower in the sky. If it docs rain, one solution can often be to shoot at night when reflections in puddles can enhance a shot.

Look carefully around the image. Yes that piece of litter in the foreground can be digitally removed, but it's better not to have it there in the first place.

Remember that you're more likely to be successful with potential cover or large-scale reproductions if you can submit high resolution images or medium format transparencies.

Check how people are used. Including people helps readers to relate to the location, but notice how most markets want the people to look fit, healthy and attractive.

What people are wearing can be important too. Publications aimed at walkers invariably want people in their pictures, but they also want them properly clad in walking gear. Note too, how often a model is wearing something red!

It's a good idea to seek the permission from any identifiable people in your photographs, or even ask them to sign a model release form as they may not be happy to see their faces turn up on a magazine cover. Be especially wary of including children without their parents' permission.

Does your market use conventional images with blue skies and golden sand, or is it more adventurous using differential focus and unusual compositions? In fact it's surprising how unadventurous most editors are.

There are already hundreds of thousands of pictures of familiar landmarks. But that doesn't mean that you shouldn't take more. The Eiffel Tower, for example must be one of the most photographed buildings in the world, but I wouldn't dream of sending a submission to a company specialising in Paris without including images of it. This is because the Eiffel Tower just says "Paris".

Take the straightforward pictures first, then look around for unusual ways to compose the shot so you have something that little bit different. Looking at postcards can give you ideas about what to photograph and how to photograph it looking at its best, and can suggest alternative treatments.

Homework

It should be clear by now that the successful freelance must do a lot of the work before going out to take the picture. Use of maps and guidebooks will highlight the most photogenic spots and even enable you to work out when the sun will be in the right place. The Internet is also an incredible source of information. Careful planning will enable you to draw up a shooting list before you set off.

Of course you don't have to go abroad to shoot saleable travel images. There are lots of small holiday companies concentrated in the UK and almost every county has at least one regional magazine.

If I were on holiday in Dorset, for example, I would visit a newsagent early in my stay and look for copies of both *Dorset* and *Dorset Life*, noting the style of picture and the editor's contact details.

Sometimes you don't have to leave your own street. I once had a picture printed as a cover of a county magazine that was taken in the lane next to my house!

Local tourist boards can also be worth approaching. And if you visit a stately home or garden that produces publicity material, it costs nothing to e-mail the administrator saying that you have images available for their next promotion.

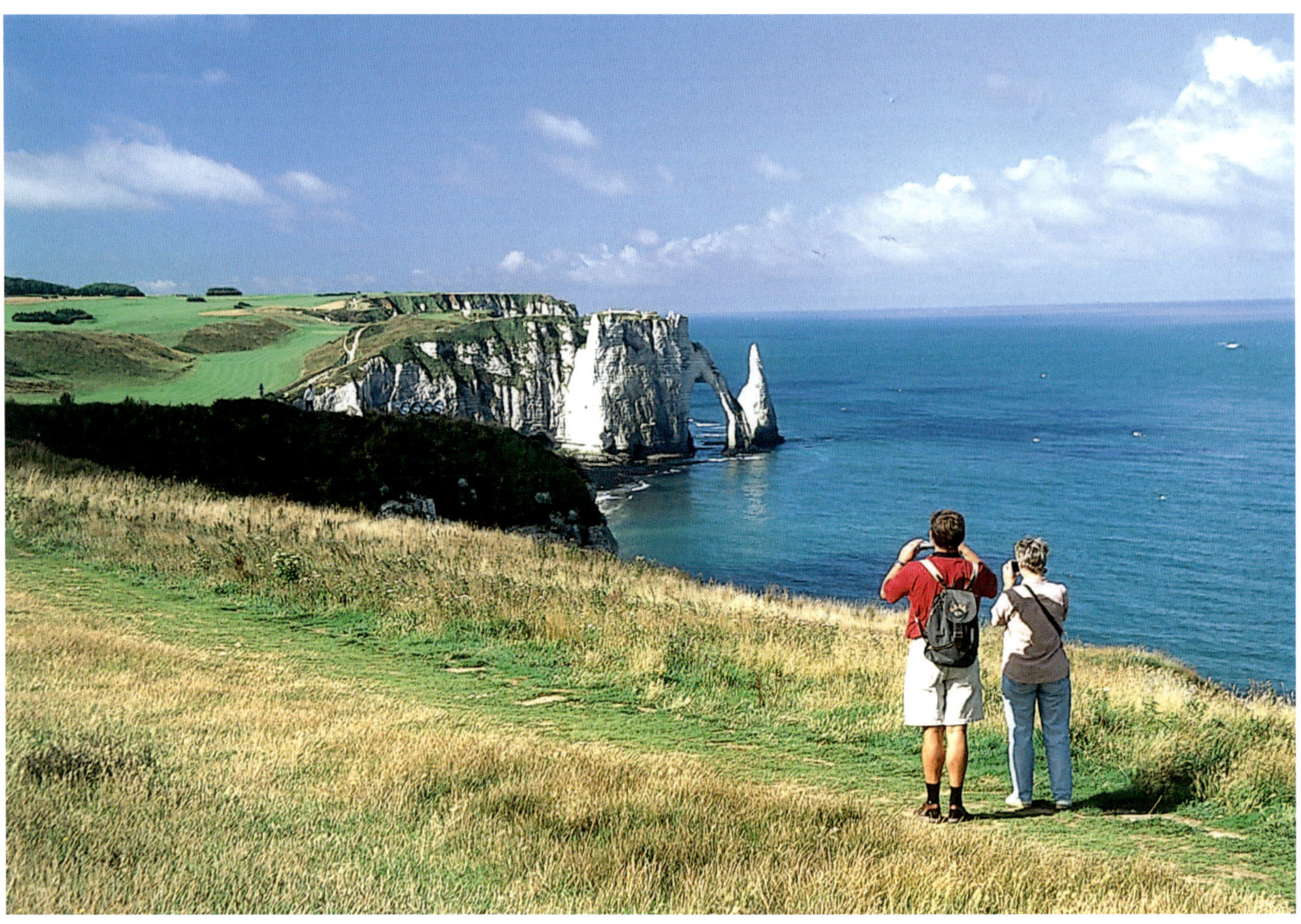

Generic shots and fillers

You'll notice that a number of holiday brochures use generic images – pictures which simply suggest the location. This might be a shot of a horizontally striped sweater in Brittany, a sign saying "Taverna" from Greece, or a jug of Sangria from Spain.

So while you're away, look around for the picture within the picture – it might be a flag or a market stall-holder in a beret – there are countless opportunities like this.

Of course it's perfectly possible to arrange your own still life; indeed convincing shots that suggest a foreign location can be set up in your own garden or kitchen if you're careful about backgrounds. Amstel beer, hummus and black olives are all available in the local supermarket. Add a check tablecloth and an out of focus background – you've brought Greece into your living room!

Generic shots are usually reproduced as small images that brochure publishers refer to as "fillers". This means that a 35mm camera is perfectly adequate. Other types of filler, such as a shot of a pretty girl with sunglasses, someone holding a red ball on a beach, or a couple holding hands in the sunset, can be shot anywhere.

It is perfectly possible to make Blackpool look like Benidorm. I have even had a photograph taken in my local churchyard used as a European holiday brochure cover that was very lucrative!

Include people in your pictures to give scale and context. Red is a particularly good colour to use for clothes

Reaping the rewards

So, you're looking at your excellent images after a successful UK shoot. You've decided to send a selection to the local county magazine and the tourist office. You sit back hopefully awaiting the response.

But you haven't maximised the sales potential of your pictures. Why not target an angling magazine with those pictures of anglers in the sunset? A caravan magazine with the images from your campsite? The company running the longboat holiday business with the shots of their boats you took on the canal? The list goes on and on.

The point is to think creatively. Ideally, of course, you will have worked out some of these options before the shoot, but there are always shots that arise out of the blue that you can find a market for.

Holiday brochures and magazines pay similar rates. A small filler will normally pay about £18 and this rises to around £100 for a cover. Some of the up-market magazines with large circulations will pay up to £250 for a cover, but competition is fierce and I find it more profitable to direct my energies towards more modest publications.

Once your work is accepted, travel markets will very frequently use more than one image. One specialist holiday brochure that I supply uses nearly £500 worth of images per year.

Brochures will often use the same image year after year because this keeps the production costs down. One very straightforward picture of mine with a girl looking at French posters has been used for five consecutive years now. I just keep sending the invoices!

Also, unless you have a sole rights agreement, there's nothing wrong with sending the same image to a number of different markets.

Selling architectural photos

by ANDREW COWIN

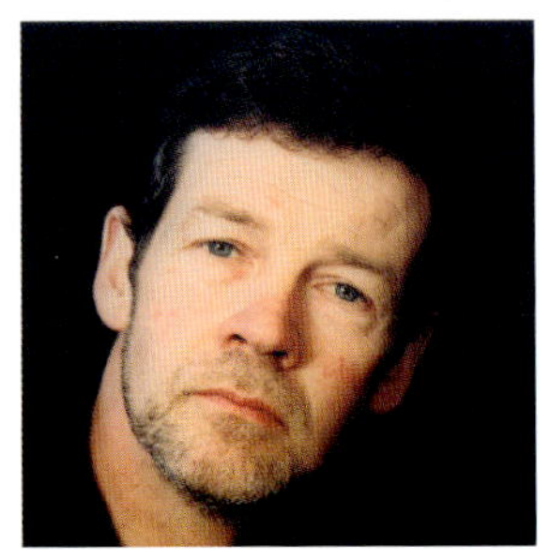

It's a pretty good rule of thumb of free-lancing that you should specialise in photographing things you like and, even better, things you know something about. Having studied history and spent many an afternoon pottering around old churches, I suppose it stood to reason that architecture would become one of my main subjects once I'd learned to handle a camera.

There are other advantages, too. Apart from their intrinsic interest and beauty, buildings keep so delightfully still. Maps help you to work out in advance when the sun will be lighting them perfectly. And, when the weather's bad, many have lovely interiors to work on or are illuminated at night, so that you can, with a little practice, make stunningly colourful twilight shots even in the rain.

If it weren't for the scaffolding, parked trucks and other imponderables that can ruin a planned day's shoot – to say nothing of the dreaded "converging verticals" – it would be fun almost all the way. Especially as there are plenty of opportunities for selling good architectural pictures.

When you think about it, a large pro-portion of the world's most popular desti-nations owe at least some of their attrac-tion to the remarkable buildings they con-tain. So, photographs that adequately cap-ture their beauty and uniqueness serve both as an incentive to potential visitors (travel brochures, magazines) as well as a souvenir of a trip (postcards, guidebooks).

Of course, the style or historic features of buildings may also make them relevant for more specialist architectural works, whereas some particularly charming detail or symbolic quality may again open up other markets where "prettiness" is sought (calendars, greetings cards, gift books).

All this leads to the first rule of archi-tectural photography: when tackling a building, consider carefully its potential appeal for as broad a range of markets as possible.

It may be that its only exceptional fea-ture is a perpendicular doorway. Unfortunately, though, the market for straight shots of late-Gothic features is small and not especially lucrative. In con-trast, the surrounding pseudo-Tudor half-timbering might be architecturally worth-less, but that climbing rose transforms it

After working for several years as a history teacher, Andrew Cowin moved to Germany where, from 1989 onwards, he began working as a photo-journalist initially specialising in travel. As he soon found that he enjoyed taking photos more than hammering away at a keyboard, he moved up to medium format and was soon drawn to architectural subjects, which have since become a particular focus of his work.
In addition to ongoing work in the calendar, postcard and gift-book market, he has produced the photos for books about several German cities including Heidelberg where he now resides. A particular speciality is Gothic architecture, which is not surprising as he has an MA in Medieval Studies.

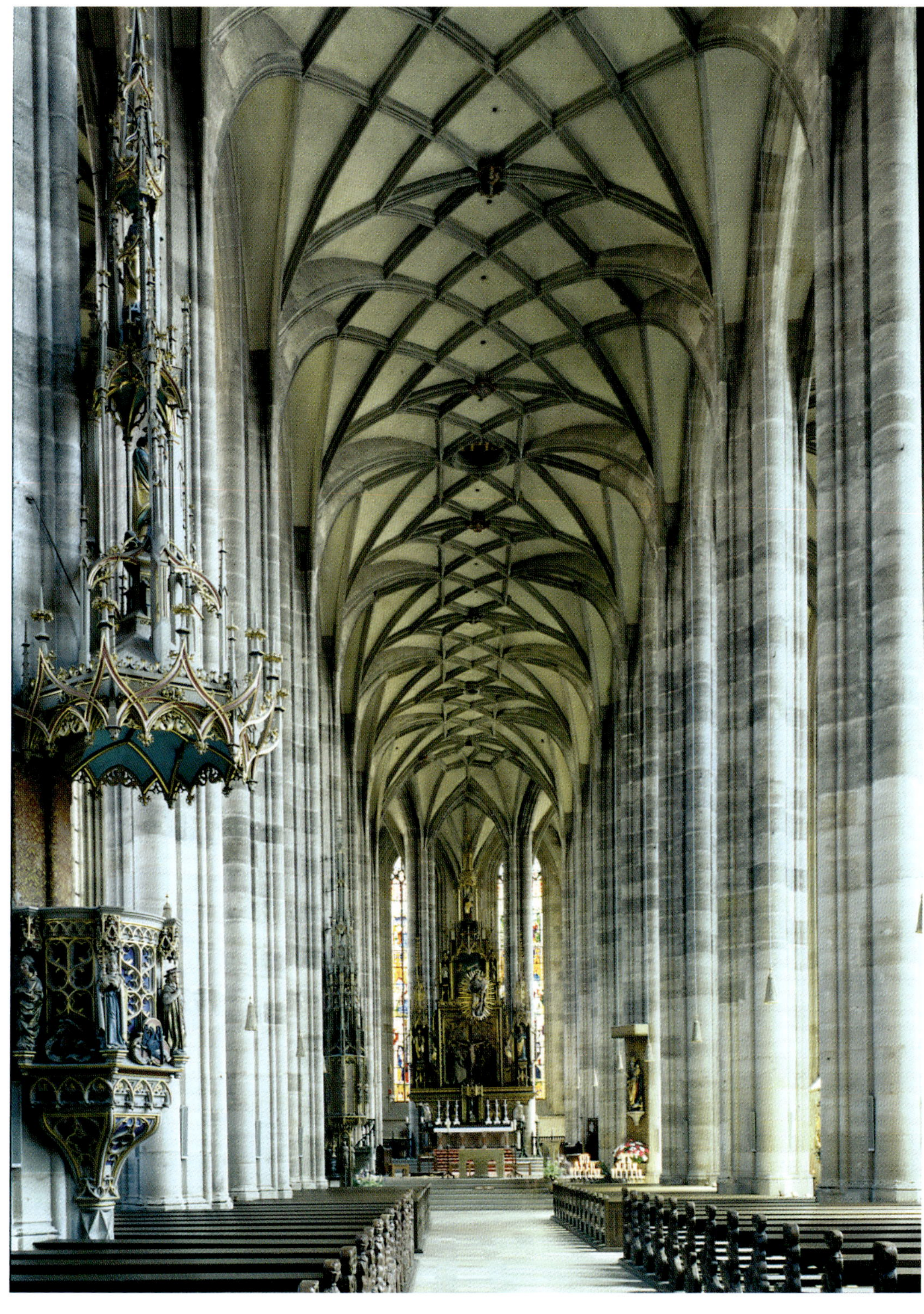

Dinkelbühl – St Georg: this picture was used full page in Paul Frankl's classic, Gothic Architecture, *published by Yale University Press*

into a sure winner as a greetings card.

It cost you time and money to get to the place in question, the weather's playing along, so it makes sense to milk it for all it has to offer.

Exploiting the home advantage

That last sentence implies that being an architectural photographer involves a lot of travelling, which is largely true. But, at least

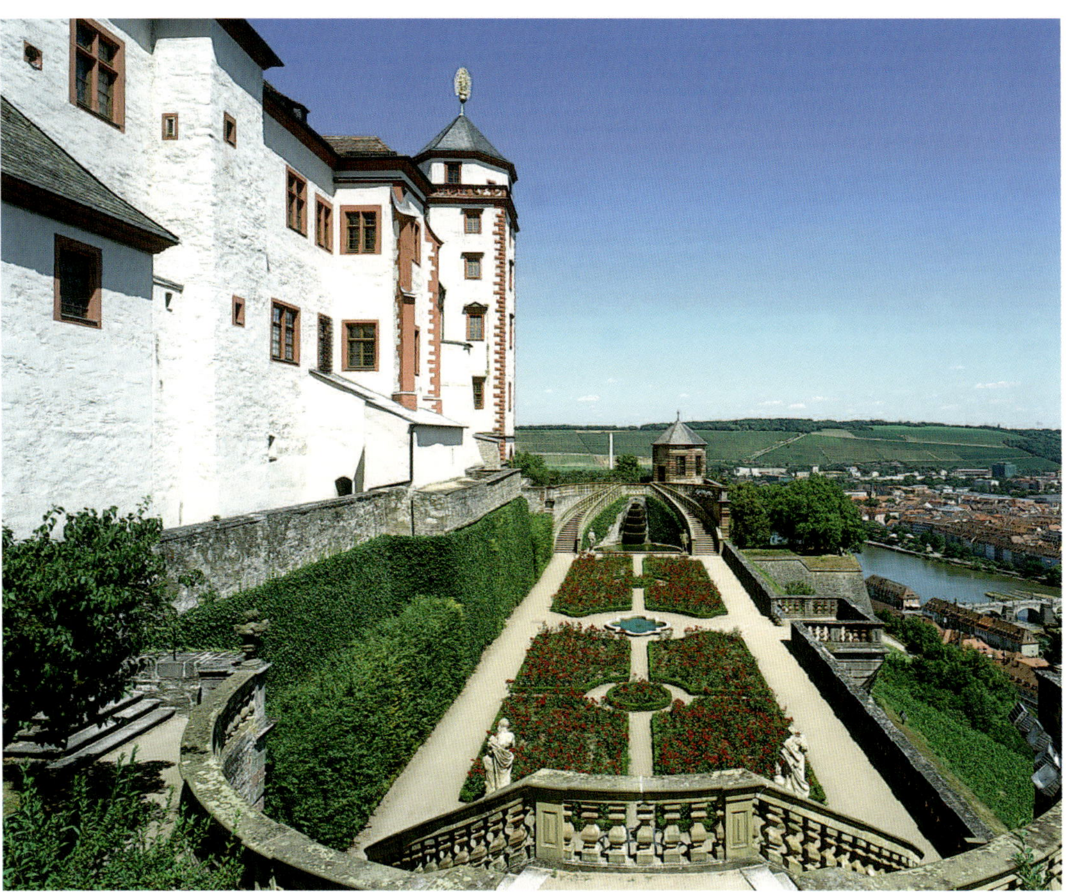

Würzburg – Festung Marienberg. This picture was taken as part of a project for a new guidebook about the city of Würzburg

when you start out, this doesn't have to be the case.

I have the good fortune to live in the beautiful city of Heidelberg in South Germany, whose castle attracts about three million visitors per year, so I've got a rewarding subject plus a number of ready-made markets for it literally on my doorstep.

Even if you don't live directly by a popular destination, there's probably a tourist town or famous building not so far away, and you really should try to exploit this "home advantage" to the full. Start by trying to get a clear overview of the existing markets while taking a close look of the sort of images they favour.

If we take postcards as an obvious area for potential sales, I would suggest a two-pronged line of attack. First, you'll see that there are a few standard images that keep on recurring. Although your chances of selling these same views to this particular market are negligible, take the shots anyway. These images are clearly what people associate with this particular town or building, so there's a good chance of selling them elsewhere.

Second, try to find new or surprising views as well as being on the lookout for unusual moods or seasonal features.

For example, I've established something of a niche for buildings taken in the twilight, these often having a big impact thanks to unusual colour casts. As such pictures are technically demanding and often mean standing around in the freezing cold, there's also not so much competition. A further advantage is that, even if the weather is atrocious, you usually have a brief phase of 10 minutes or so when the sky comes out a marvellous deep blue on film.

Let me also give an example of how seasonal factors can make a difference. Snow is a rarity in Heidelberg, and I had to wait for five years for thick snow with a blue sky. On that one day, I was like the proverbial aphid with a blue rear end, but those pictures are still bringing in money 10 years later and will continue to do so.

Investing in the future

From what I've said so far, you'll see that any budding architectural photographer is going to have to spend a fair amount of time and money to build up a collection of reasonable images before approaching a publisher. You've basically got to show your credentials before you can hope to receive definite sales or commissions.

This means that, like me, you'll probably have to start out on a part-time basis, using safer sources of income to finance the project. But once you've got a good range of images, it's time to polish the doorbells of potential customers.

In addition to postcard publishers, obvious targets are calendar and guidebook publishers. Even if you can't raise any immediate interest, always ask what subjects they might be looking for in the near future. At first, you'll have to follow up such leads without any surety of success, but if you then come up with images the customer likes, you've shown that you can deliver and can press for more specific commissions.

While publishers will be your main targets, remember that local, regional and national tourist boards are often eager to see pictures showing their main sights in the best possible light. Also, many compa-nies are glad to identify with their home town, so they may need images for advertising material or even for promotional gifts for customers.

Again, if visiting such a company, don't omit to say how happy you'd be to take a fantastic series of pictures of their headquarters, while also emphasising that large prints of your images would be just the thing to brighten up the reception area.

Once you establish a reputation of having a good archive of images, you'll find that people start coming to you with specific requests or commissions.

Up to this point, you'll be receiving one-off payments for your pictures, but your final aim should be to expand your collection to a point that a publisher may be interested in making a book consisting entirely of your work, so that you get paid on a royalty basis.

This takes time, of course, but assuming sales are good, it means a sizeable annual cheque for effectively doing nothing thereafter. Bearing in mind that your first phase involved working for nothing, this is only fair and just.

Also, a book can be your visiting card and certification of merit whenever you drop in on potential customers.

Looking farther afield

While your home patch will be an important foundation on which to build, always keep a close eye on other markets where your architectural photography might be appropriate.

I've already mentioned the national and even international greetings card and calendar markets where more "romantic" images of buildings might find a place. In my case, I struck lucky with a market that's more developed in Germany than in the UK: the gift-book. These normally consist of about 20 photos linked with edifying texts or poems. Reasonably priced, it's the perfect small gift when you don't want to spend the earth.

Here, the demand is for doorways, windows, stairs, bridges, pagodas: in other words, anything with a vaguely symbolic quality, preferably with an upbeat, positive feel about it. I'll make no bones about the fact that I'd much rather take shots of a Romanesque interior than a corny old thatched cottage, but then again, 50 books in 12 years with a Munich publisher have taught me not to be so dogmatic!

And, once you have your foot in the door of such a market, you'll be surprised about spin-offs from such motifs that, in my case, have included bookmarks, diaries, tablemats and even Christmas decorations.

Furthermore, don't ignore any market slanted towards religious subjects, as evocative shots of churches, stained glass and so on are always welcome here.

As your collection of images grows, there'll come a point when you really should consider working with a picture agency. After all, these have direct access to markets that most photographers would never stumble on by themselves.

The benefits of a good working relationship with an agency make it worth investing some time in finding the right one. I personally would recommend finding a small specialist agency where you will not just be one among hundreds of faceless contributors. Check its publicity material and website: does it seem professional, is it expanding, who are its customers?

Serious equipment

Up to this point, it would be quite possible to establish yourself in the field of architectural photography using "normal" equipment, by which I mean, in my case, a Mamiya RB67 with three lenses (50mm, 127mm, 250mm).

However, once the serious commissions start coming, you'll increasingly be faced with shots that are "impossible" because of those dreaded converging verticals produced by tilting the camera upwards. As long as you're not using a wide-angle lens, the results may not be too disturbing, but even an expensive shift lens won't help you much for really tall structures.

While this problem may teach you to be creative in your choice of vantage points, there will come a point when you really have to consider investing in a plate camera if you want to become a true specialist in this field. Here we are talking about a large sum of money, so it's not a decision to be taken lightly. Nonetheless, if you do take the plunge, the advantages are enormous.

Thanks to the movements of the camera, you don't just banish converging verticals forever, you can frame your main image with absolute precision, so that all distracting elements are excluded. You can select the viewpoint that you feel is absolutely the right one for a particular building to show it in all of its grandeur. And, because you're one of a select few with this sort of equipment, the images you'll be marketing are obviously different from most of your competitors.

But clearly, with such costs involved, you would need to broaden your marketing operations with a vengeance.

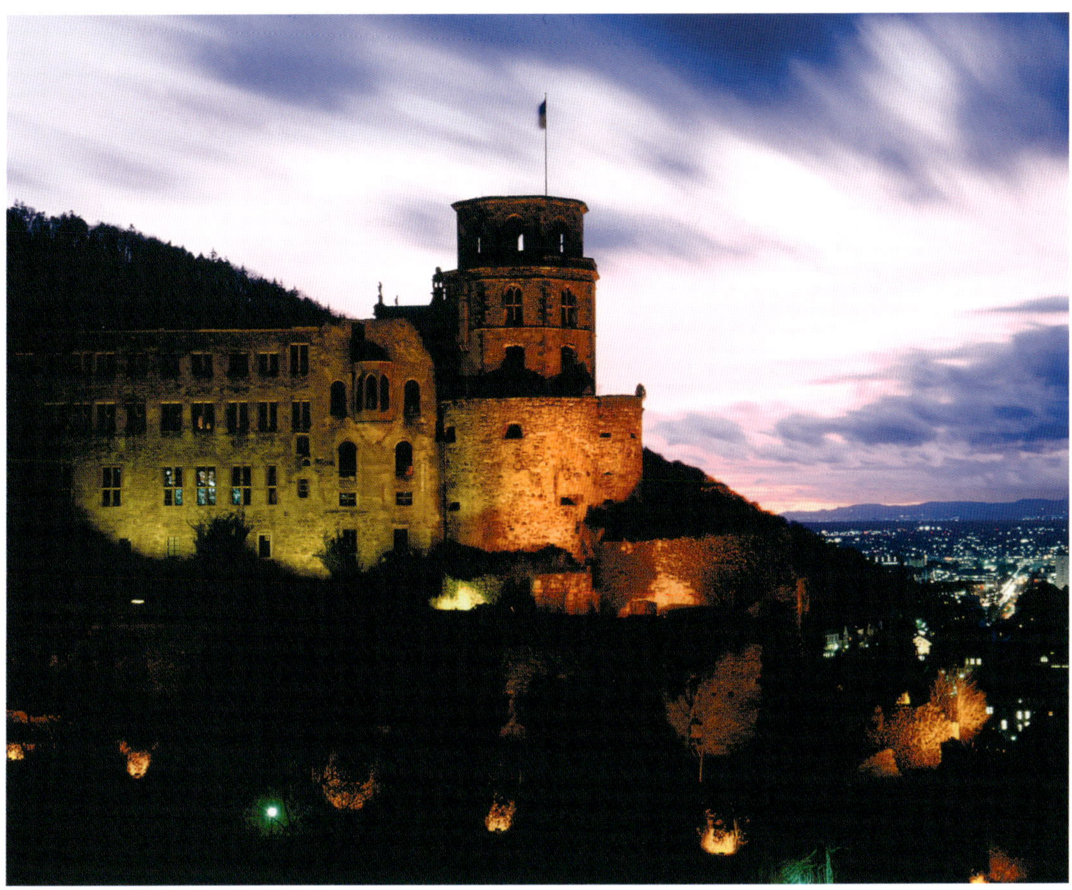

The benefits of knowledge

The technical tricks and tips that you've picked up on the way are almost certainly of interest to amateurs who perhaps aspire to follow in your footsteps. So, don't ignore the large market comprising photography magazines, where architectural shots are frequently used.

For example, after I'd bought a large-format camera, I produced a feature with pictures that served as a "how to" guide for anyone buying such equipment, and thus helped to finance it.

Only when you've got the right equipment and have learned to master it will you be in the position to submit work successfully to more specialised publications. These might be magazines devoted to modern architecture or interiors, or those books dealing with architectural history that demand not only perfect images but an understanding of the features which make a particular building so special.

This highly desirable market is small and not particularly well paid, but there is great satisfaction in producing a definitive image for a classic work on architecture. Here, a lot depends on luck and being in the right place at the right time, but persist long enough, and you'll end up making your own luck.

Heidelberg Castle photographed from the East. This picture has been used as a postcard, in a book about Heidelberg, for the lid of a box of chocolates, and in a technique piece in a photographic magazine

Selling angling photos

by LESLEY CRAWFORD

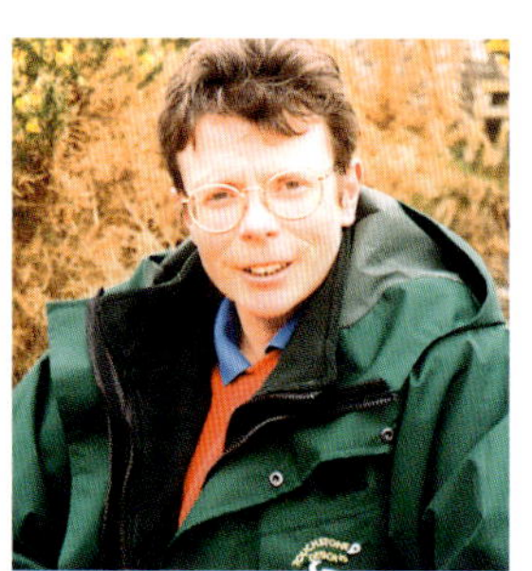

Lesley Crawford is a highly experienced freelance writer, author and photographer working in the angling/fieldsports market. Her work has been published across the angling press since 1990 with illustrated features in national newspapers, fishing magazines and Internet sites. She also undertakes trade brochure work and general environmental photography. At the time of writing Lesley is working on her fifth angling hardback book for Swan Hill Press.

It goes without saying that if you are going to break into any photography market you need to do your homework first. The angling sector is no different. To sell well in what is a potentially lucrative area you must have a real affinity with your subject.

To this end it helps greatly if you are a fisherman of sorts, or at least have easy access to fishing venues and can study all the sport's facets first-hand. You might not think this important; after all anyone can take a snap of an angler on the bank. But to sell consistently you need to grasp all the fishy nuances, and believe me there are many!

Fishing facts: know your market

For a start there are three separate branches of angling: game, sea and coarse. The equipment, method and venues for each sector are very different and you must always keep your photography in context with the market you hope to sell it to. For example, there is no use submitting a picture of an angler clasping a specimen carp proudly to his chest if the publication you are aiming at specialises only in salmon and trout fishing.

After you have made your decision on which angling sector you are going for – and I suggest it's the one you know or can get to know best – take an in-depth look at the already published photography on the subject.

Check out all the magazines, newspapers, books and websites you can find. You will quickly see the different fishing methods have dissimilar styles of photography. In sea fishing publications many pictures involve a close-up of a guy holding up a big cod while perched on a rocking fishing boat; in coarse angling it will often be a beaming fisherman at a lake's edge cradling a specimen fish; in game fishing the pictures nearly always have an angler elegantly casting a fly line in a fine landscape.

It is possible to cover all of these different angling markets, but in practice the photographers who sell best nearly always start their career dedicated to one sector.

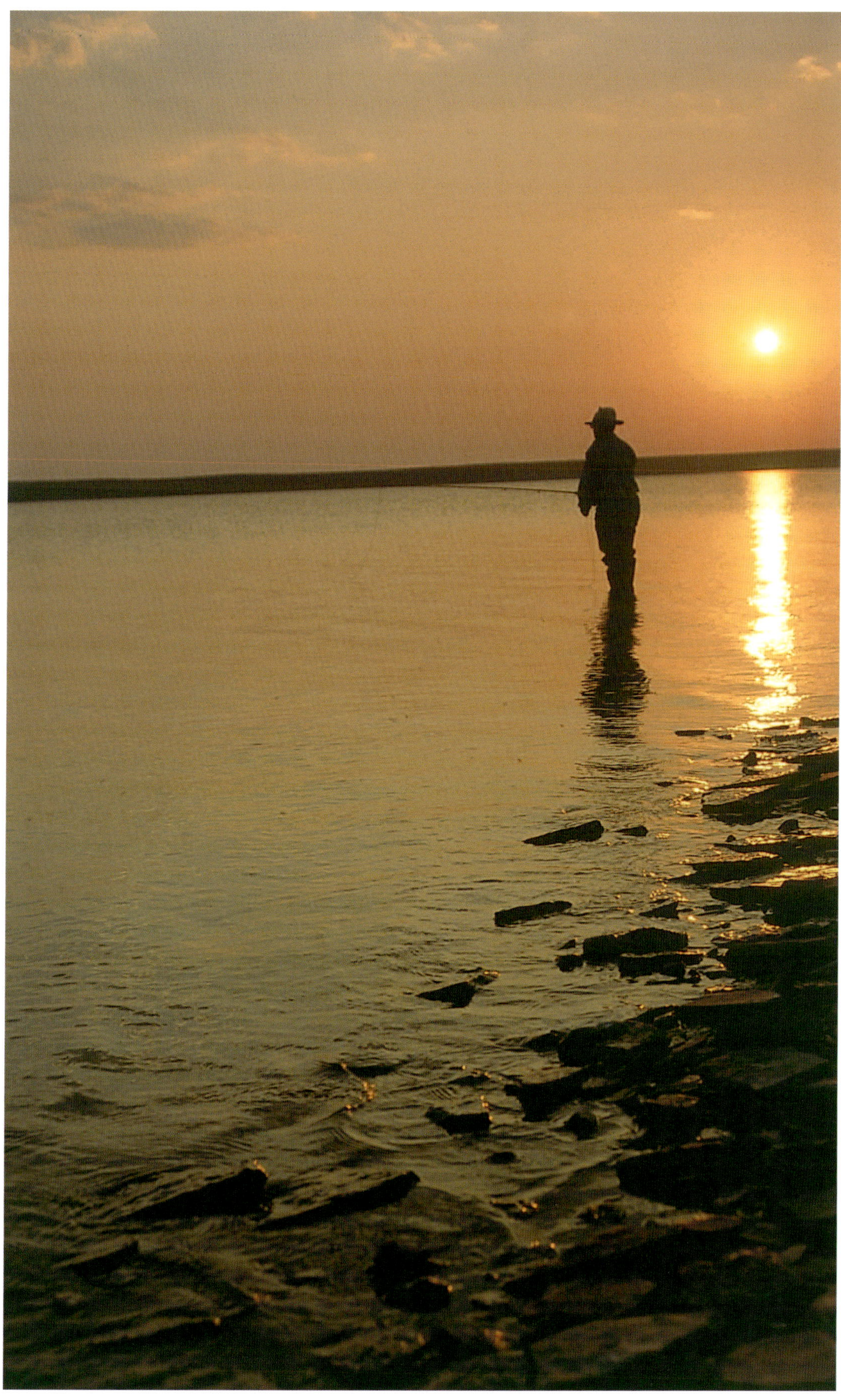

*Atmospheric shots like this
sell well. This has been
used in angling magazines
and in a book on the subject*

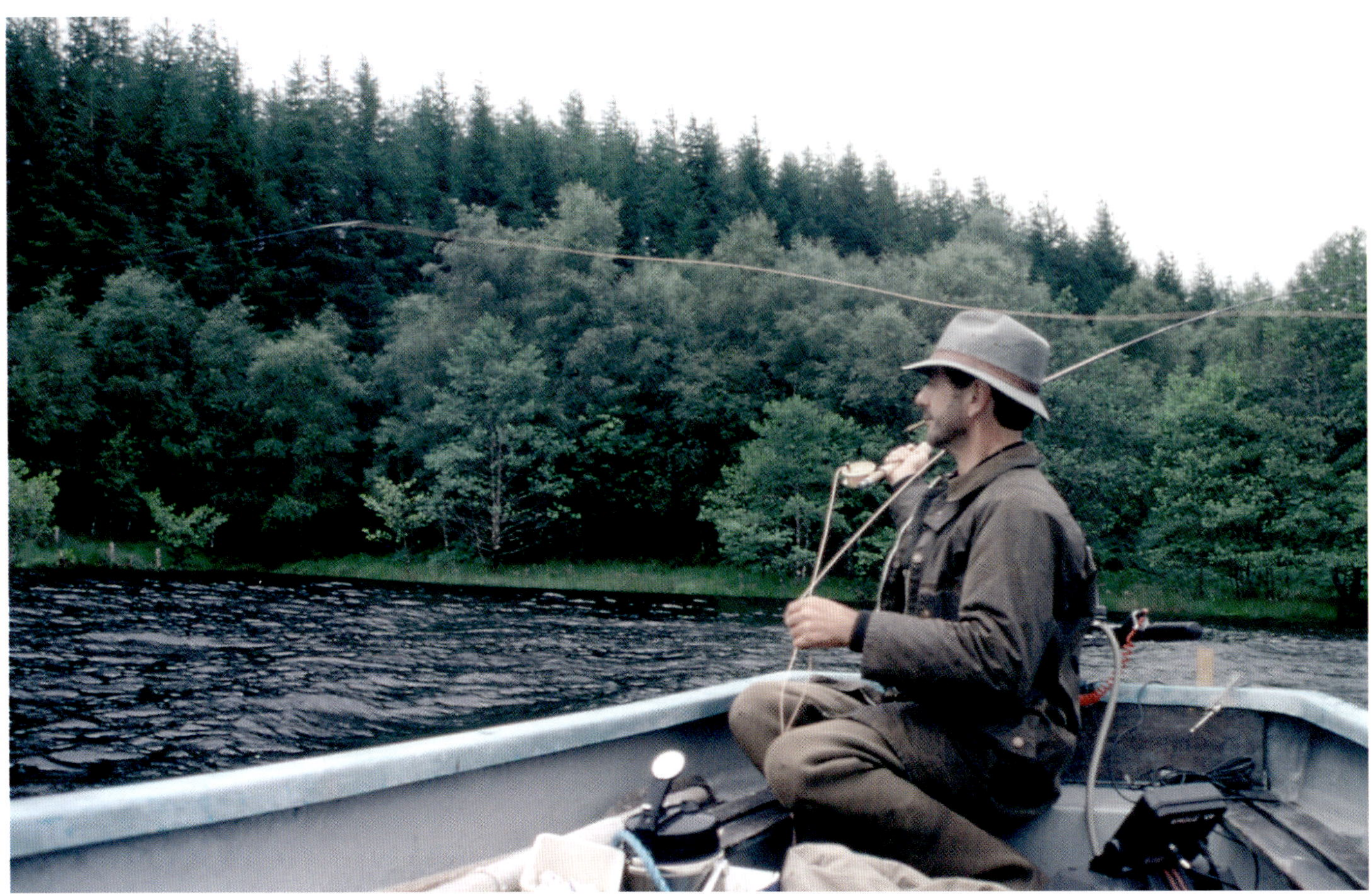

Casting a line: pictures that feature the fly line in the air sell best

Breaking into the market

There are three ways to break into this market. First you can take a variety of different shots of your chosen form of angling and submit them as a portfolio on spec to a specialist magazine that deals with the topic. It must be said that the success rate for this method is often on the low side. Unless your shots feature a catch of a record-breaking fish or an unusual event, busy editors will often ignore your work even if it's technically brilliant, in favour of that produced by their staff or regular photographers.

The second way is to try to break into this market is to try to contact the editor personally (not easy!) and see what his future requirements are likely to be. Go for one of the smaller publications to begin with; the big publishing houses nearly always slant work to their known contributors first. As you will know by now, magazines work months in advance and there is usually a demand for good quality photos way ahead in order to cover the different fishing seasons. For example Scottish salmon fishing starts in January and pictures of game anglers in snow on the banks of freezing rivers are de rigueur for that month.

The third and usually most successful way is to become an "expert" and write words to go with your pictures. As with other markets, illustrated articles as complete packages often sell better than just producing a straight set of images without text.

Initially, writing for your photos need be little more than an extended caption – Joe or Jill Bloggs with their record fish (always name the species), caught in June in bright sunny weather, at such and such a water, on their favourite fly, a Blue Zulu. To this you then add a little bit of background: It was their first visit to the lake and the fish took 20 minutes to land… Or it was their first time using a particular rod, line or fly...

Before you know it you have a short piece ready made for an editor, and providing your images are pin-sharp and relevant there is a reasonable chance it will be accepted.

Shots that sell

There are a few important rules in angling photography which you should follow, whether you are submitting with or without words.

The first one is to get in close, but at the same time have some "action" in the shot. It can be the angler casting into a sunset or playing a trout, contemplating a magnificent or unusual catch, or just opening a fly box. The object is to show them doing something rather than just sitting with their feet up. If you can make your reader feel like they are involved in some way or that they would like to be there in the picture, you are well on the way to selling your work.

It's important to bear in mind that modern angling photography has considerably more conservation issues attached to it than was once the case. The days of showing an angler beaming over a row of 20 dead trout or salmon have gone forever. Nowadays anglers are often photographed returning their live catch to the water, so avoid dead fish shots unless they can be done in an aesthetic way.

You should shoot in the best possible natural light. Sun and cloud is better than hard brilliant sunshine, as oddly enough it is for the actual fishing too!

Always try to get a new angle (no pun intended) on your photo. A simple way of doing this is to stand in the water in waders in front or at the side of your subject and shoot from low down looking up at the angler. This gives a slightly different perspective and is more attractive than the straightforward face-on shot.

As editors love casting shots with a line visible in the air, it's worthwhile looking at the angler's casting action and getting the timing right on when to take the shot (not always easy, as different fishers have different techniques).

While anglers are generally a very laid-back bunch, to obtain your images you will need a fair bit of natural charm. Your subject sometimes freezes and the resulting shot doesn't look natural.

And don't forget all the associated accoutrements that go with fishing. When I take shots of anglers I also photograph equipment like fly boxes, rod and line, and so on. These subjects give background to the story and are just as important as the catch.

Also remember that pretty landscapes with a tiny dot of an angler half a mile away do not sell, neither do pictures of stale fish kept for too long in a plastic bag before you photograph them.

You also need a fair bit of luck. Even though the angler might tell you different, being in the right place at the right time when a big catch is made isn't always skill!

The right equipment

Often the best game angling pictures are taken in wild remote areas, so I carry both a small digital camera and a point-and-shoot film camera with something like Kodak Ultra "all weather" film. These

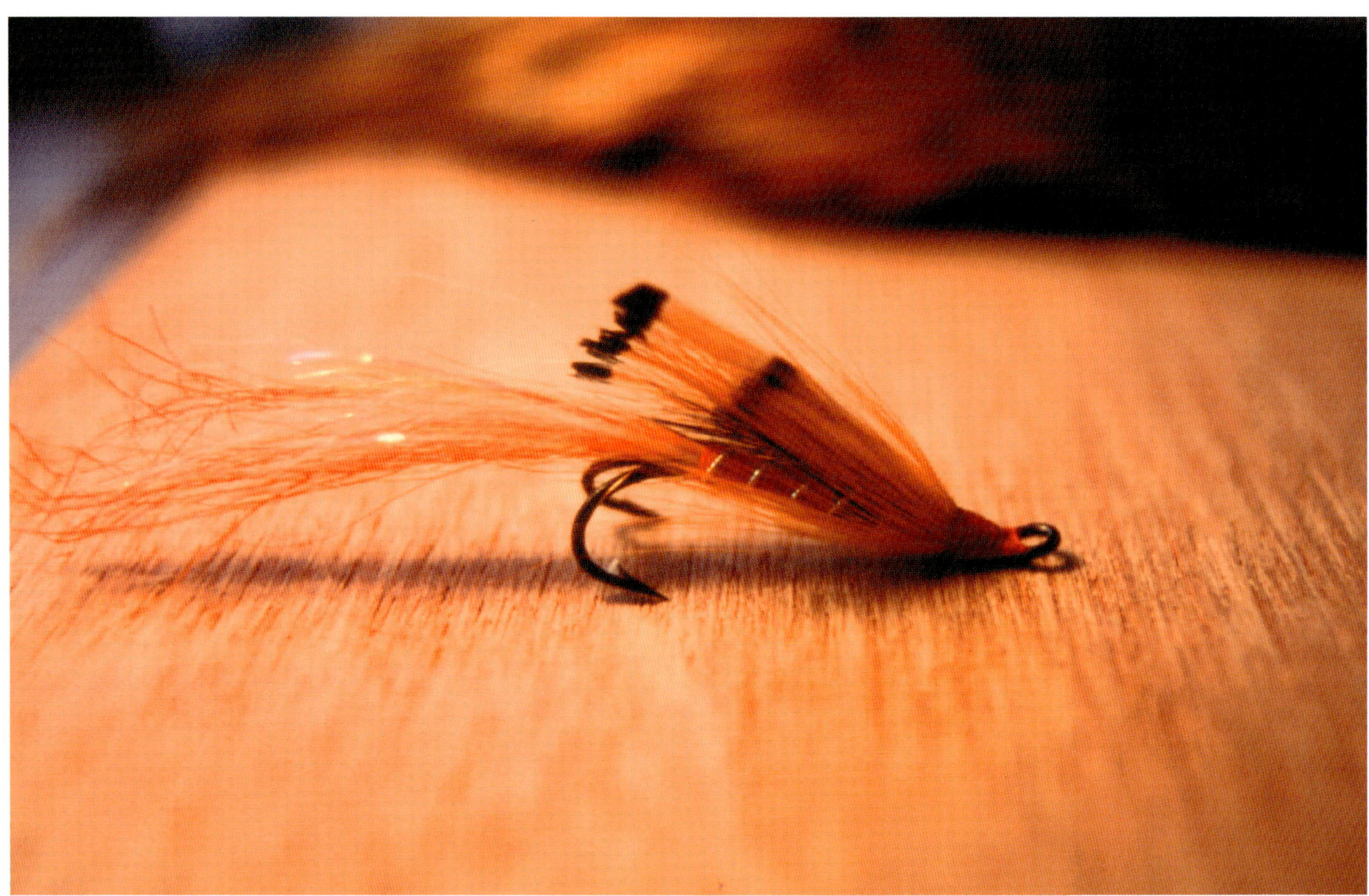

Salmon fly: pictures of the equipment used in angling are always in demand

cameras are light and capture the drama perfectly adequately without being too heavy to carry. The digital camera also gives me immediate e-mail transmission if the image is particularly relevant to, say, a local paper.

When I have specific requests for certain shots, for example showing an item of equipment or anglers fishing on a specific water, I will use my trusted Canon EOS 1000F with Fuji Sensia daylight film, sometimes on a tripod sometimes not depending on the immediacy required in the shot. The lenses are Sigma and if I need to take a tight close-up of, say, an insect hatching (an important subject in fly fishing), I use interchangeable extension tubes on the lens.

Remember that angling, by its very nature, involves water and that your equipment should be well protected in resealable plastic bags. This is especially important if you are going afloat in a boat, and though it might sound a bit basic, do remember to check your lens for water splashes. Even expert angling photographers can be guilty of producing lovely shots with a water blob on them.

Profit from diversification

The great thing about angling photography is that it is extremely versatile and your pictures can be used again and again in a variety of publications. I've had the same pictures published in books, newspapers, trade journals and tourist brochures. I have even sold them direct to the angler concerned, especially if it's his first catch on a specific river.

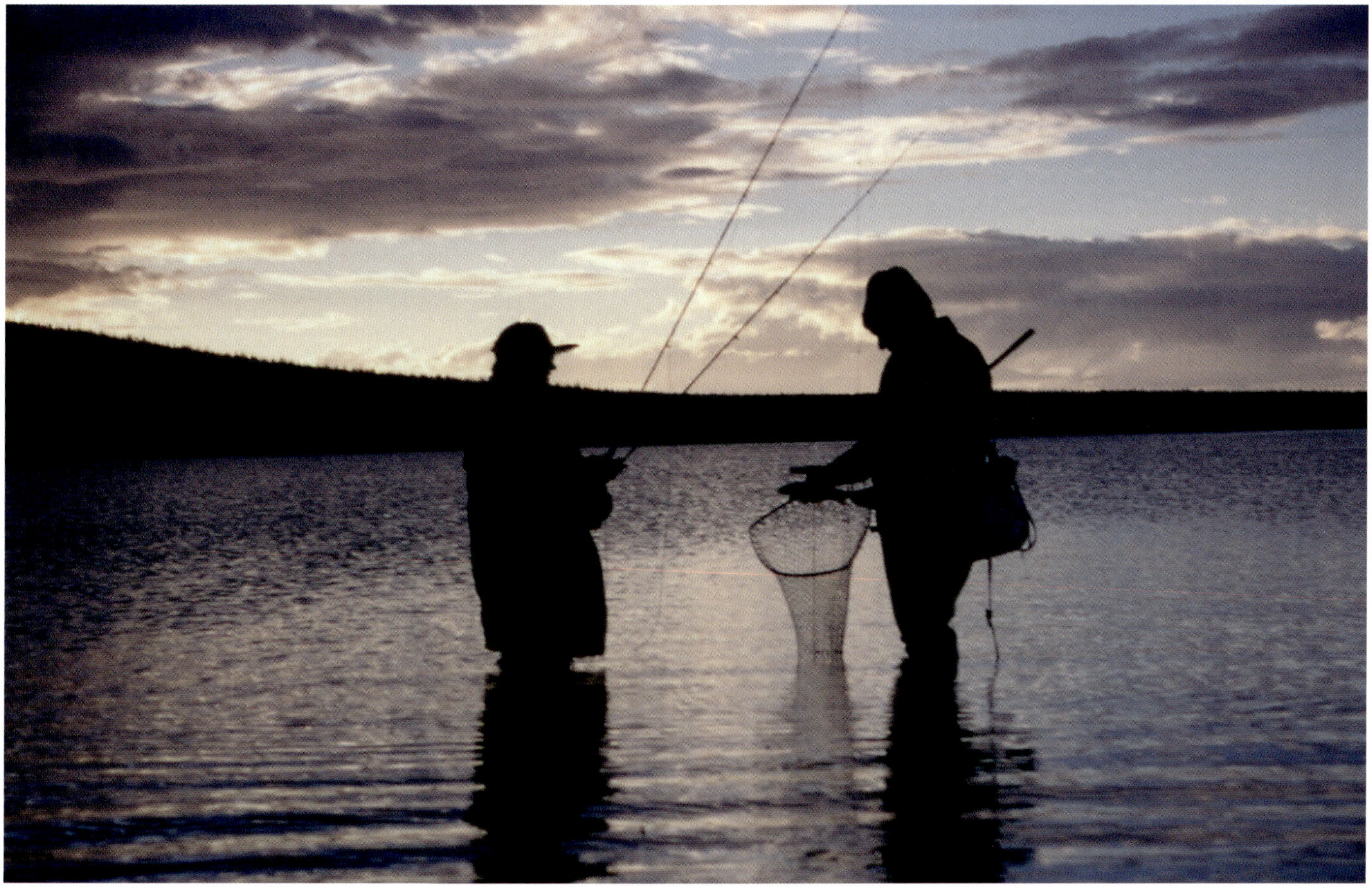

And because you are normally photographing in an aesthetic environment you can take pictures outside of angling as you go along. This means you can build up a library of general country-related images, ranging from wildlife to local history.

If you shoot a huge amount, its worthwhile trying to place some as stock direct with a relevant magazine or newspaper. Stock libraries are another option, but remember they tie up your work and are only useful if you produce a tremendous turnover of shots. From experience I simply run my own library rather than place it elsewhere.

In a nutshell, the best way to stay in the angling photography business is to produce consistently high-quality reliable work, on time, and relevant to the publication concerned. If you can add pertinent words so much the better as it's not rocket science. Just check your facts thoroughly and make your first illustrated articles very short ones.

That's how I started, and over the last 14 years or so I have developed a sufficient enough reputation to be commissioned to do work rather than sending off speculative submissions. Persevere and you can too.

The end of a successful day: this shot has appeared in magazines and on a book cover

Selling generic photos

by DAVID BIGWOOD

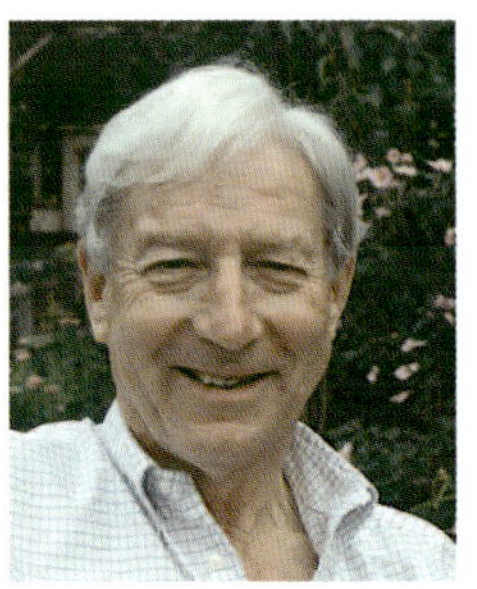

Success as a freelance photographer relies upon maximising our return for every minute that we invest in our business. This is true whether we are full or part-time freelances. We have to keep our cameras working. So, if you are ever at a loss for a subject during a cold and uninviting winter's day, here is something that you can do at home with almost no special equipment.

You will have seen in magazines and newspapers the images that are used in such things as the financial column or on the food or computer pages. Often these images have no direct connection with the words, they are there just to draw our attention to the article and to get us to read it. They are generic images, and it is these that you can shoot simply at home, the only limitation being your imagination.

Imagination is the key. You will be competing with many other photographers who have tapped into this market, so innovation is as vital as technique.

Getting started

The only essential items of equipment other than your camera are a tripod and a cable release and, if you don't have a macro lens, a set of extension tubes. You don't even need special lighting or flash unless you are shooting at night. I usually get by with just window light and an occasional reflector – generally a piece of white card or aluminium foil. Keeping it simple is my philosophy.

While innovation is vital, if you have not previously been involved in shooting very close-up shots, experiment with some simple ideas to begin with. Then, when you do come to shoot your innovative set-ups, you don't have to think about your technique and can concentrate on getting your pre-visualised ideas on to film or file as the case may be.

What you are looking for as generic images are items that can be photographed so as to be recognisable without showing all their detail. With things like books, this can simply mean shooting so that their titles are not visible, but with other items it may be necessary to have just a part of the subject sharply in focus.

For instance if you want to show that it

**David Bigwood began freelancing, both as a photographer and a writer, on a part-time basis many years ago. At that time it was a very stop-start affair as other factors in his life such as a job, a mortgage and a family made their presence felt. Eventually, however, he left full-time paid work, and freelancing became his prime occupation. David's words and/or pictures have appeared in over fifty publications, beginning with black and white pictures of his children. He still gets a thrill from seeing his images in print and from the thought that somebody felt they were worth paying for.
David is a Licentiate of the Royal Photographic Society and writes a column on freelancing in *f2 Freelance + Digital*.**

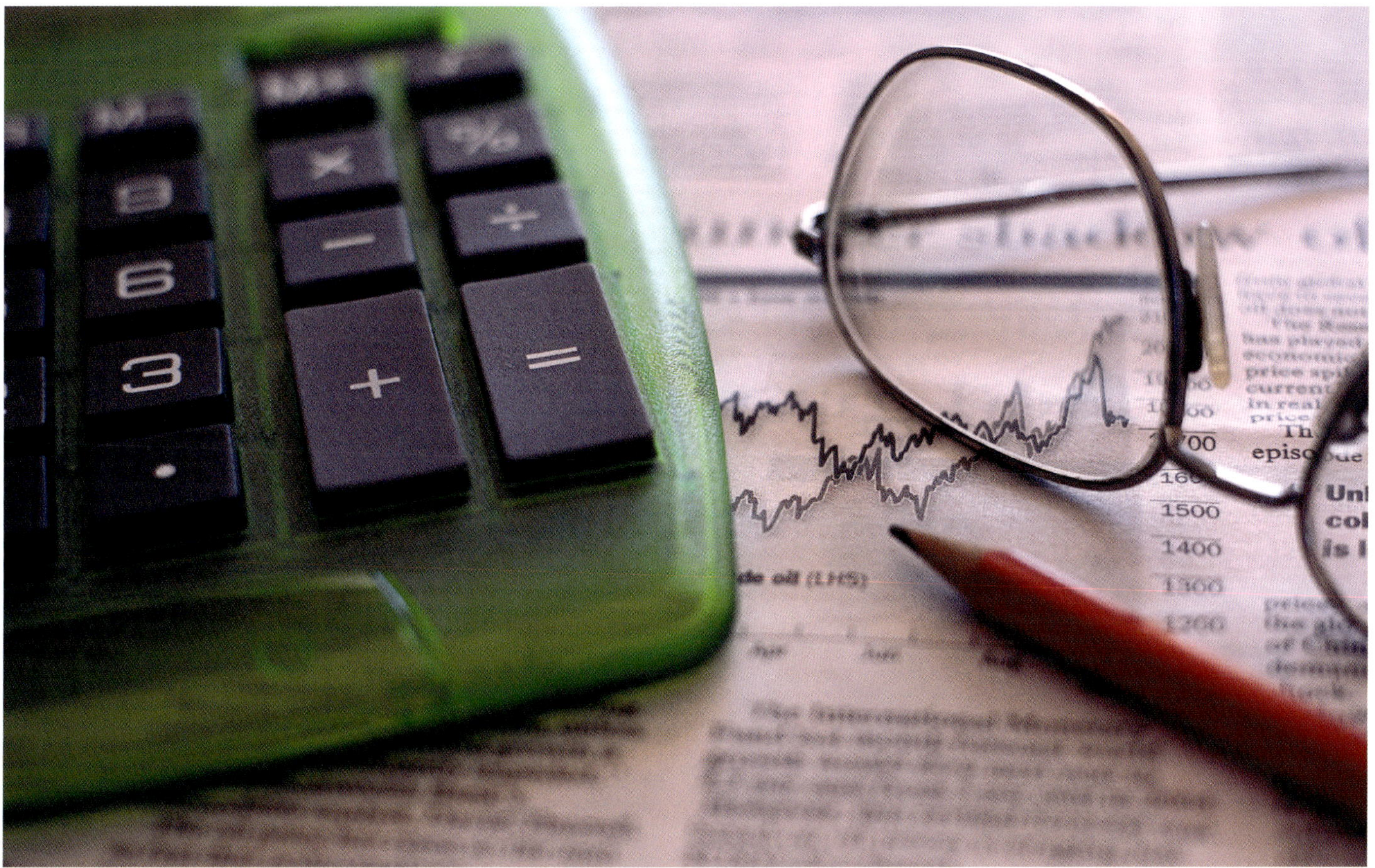

is a camera without showing its make, use a large aperture to reduce depth of field and focus on the shutter button, or the side of the lens, or anywhere where the name of the manufacturer doesn't appear or can be thrown so out of focus that it is illegible. Or you can do the same with a credit card without giving away important details such as its number.

Grab a pen and some paper and start listing your ideas for generic images. In quick time you will probably have up to twenty written down.

In less than 10 minutes I came up with:

Books in a pile not showing titles
Telephone directories
Focusing on the word "freelance" in a dictionary
Credit card
Telephone
Calculator
Spectacles on a paper or book
Computer insides
Coins
Pencils
Pills
Playing cards
Keys
Invoice
Cheque book
Personal organiser
Mobile phone
Watch or clock
Fountain pen and paper
Bottles

Nothing particularly difficult about that lot and all readily available in most homes.

The type of image that is often used to illustrate finance features in newspapers and magazines

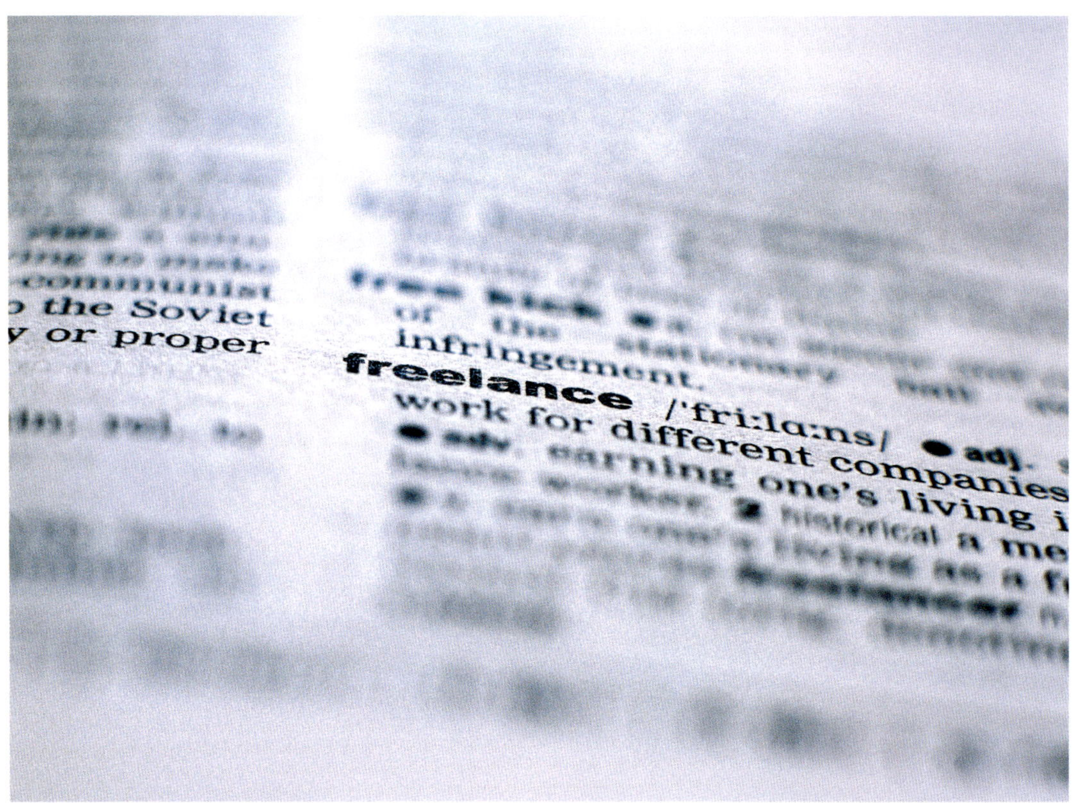

My personal project

To illustrate this project I began by using my Olympus OM1n on a tripod. I used a 50mm lens with, as I do not have a macro lens, a 27.5mm extension tube. The film was Fuji Provia 100F and exposure was calculated using the built-in exposure meter with an extra half stop allowed when shooting black text on white paper to increase the contrast.

Focusing at such close range was the most difficult part. I soon found out that it was sometimes easier to focus roughly with the camera's focusing adjustment and then move the item being photographed backwards or forwards until I had the part I wanted exactly in focus.

To make this easier, I put the item on a large sheet of cardboard on a smooth surfaced table. This enabled me to make very small movements of the cardboard, which is the difference between being in and out of focus at this range, while I looked through the viewfinder.

I was shooting to begin with at maximum aperture, in my case f1.8. Trying to make sure that I had exactly what I wanted sharp, and nothing more, was not as easy as it sounds.

When the film came back from the lab I found that in some cases I didn't have enough in focus and should have been shooting – for example with the dictionary – at about f4 to create the result that I wanted. The aim was to have the word "Freelance" in focus along with some of its definition, with the rest of the words fading away.

I re-shot several of the items and by the time the second film came back I found that I was settling into the groove and the results were looking much more like my pre-visualisation. Still not very innovative, but at least the technique was being established.

Freelance defined: this could be used as an illustration in an article on the subject in a photographic or writing publication ... or in a book like this!

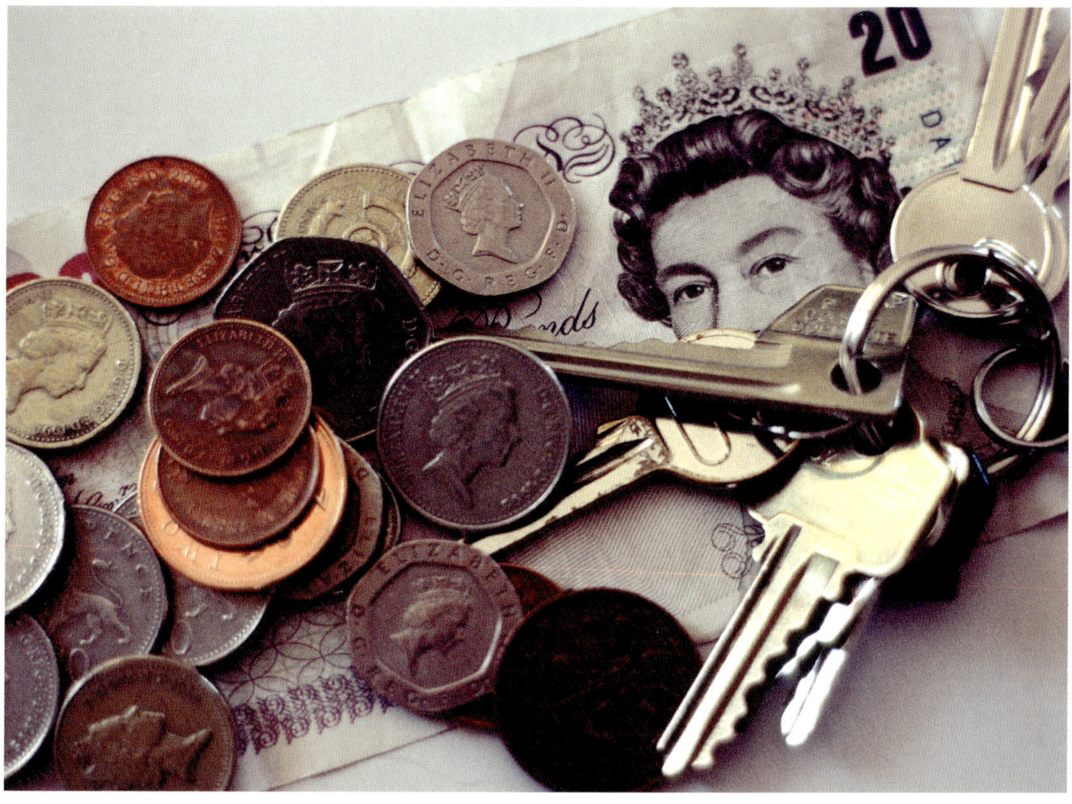

An image that can be used to illustrate a variety of editorial topics

Marketing

But, as any freelance will tell you, that was the easy part of the exercise. How do we get a return from the images? How do we market our generic pictures?

If you already are a contributor to a photo library then that should be your first port of call as it is picture libraries that are able to reach markets that individual photographers often cannot. And this is probably more important with these generic images. But, if you don't use a photo library or your library doesn't accept your pictures because they have other similar ones already on its files, or you are new to freelancing, what do you do?

My immediate reaction is to turn to my faithful and well-thumbed *Freelance Photographer's Market Handbook*. As generic images are not my first specialisation, I have to turn to some, for me, unusual sections.

Almost at once, in the "Business" section, I came across a magazine for accountants that lists among its requirements for illustrations, "creative and innovative images which can be related to the subject and which attract readers' attention." A little thought about accountancy, finance, law and management and you should be able to produce some images that may interest this publisher.

There are many other publications in this and other sections that can be worth an investigation. Their requirements may not be as obvious as the one quoted above, but I guarantee that among the listings are many magazines that use generic images and, if you can come up with a new approach, you may be able to establish a new market for yourself.

Begin by looking at the sections on Business, Electronics and Computing, Food and Drink, Health and Medical, Industry,

Science and Technology, and Trade. But don't ignore the others – generic images crop up in the most unexpected places.

Additionally, see if you can recognise places where generic images might fit but are not currently being used. And, of course, keep your eyes open for where other images that you have on file could find a home.

Naturally your images won't sell if they are in your files and not in the marketplace. If you are convinced that your pictures are of publishable quality then send them out.

I have started by putting some of mine with the on-line photo library to which I contribute. I am also including appropriate images in selections of pictures that I send regularly to a number of publications.

Post production

As contemporary photographers with tools like computers and PhotoShop on hand, we are in the fortunate position of being able to produce a variety of results from what may begin as very ordinary images. No longer do we have to shoot with tungsten-balanced film in daylight to produce a blue cast over the picture, as we can add the blue by using the Levels command in PhotoShop. Nor do we have to resort to cross-processing transparency film in C41 chemicals to produce some often bizarre results. We can do it all in the computer.

While I do not generally fiddle around with my shots, these generic images, to my mind, fall into the category of advertising, and producing eye-catching results is what advertising photography is all about.

If using the curves command can make my images stand out and have a better chance of being used by a publisher, then I shall use it, just as I used dodging and burning and all the other tricks to "improve" my pictures when I used a darkroom.

Generic images may not be the most exciting of pictures to shoot but they can be a good way of keeping your camera active and earning its keep on days that are not conducive to much other photography. They can be one way of maximising the return from a freelance business.

Selling to house mags

by JOHN WADE

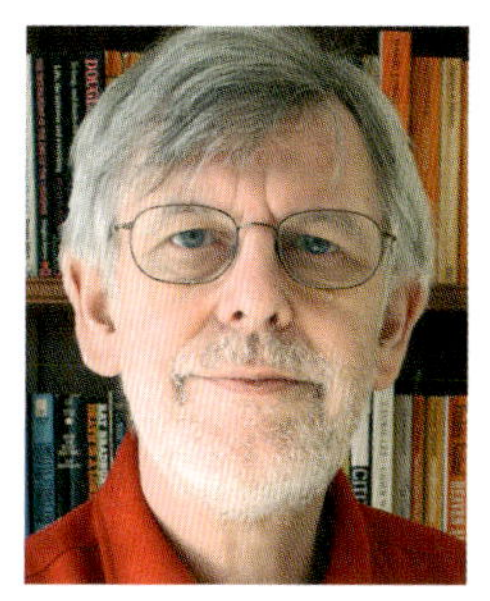

Following a seven-year stint as editor of a national photographic magazine, John Wade turned his back on regular employment in 1984, to work as a freelance writer, photographer and editor. Today, his business is mainly involved in the writing, editorial production and design of house magazines for a number of top-name UK companies, although he still finds time to write and illustrate magazine features and books, most of which concern photographic history.

We should begin by defining the term "house magazine". Contrary to what some believe, we are not talking about a magazine for houses – *House and Garden*, *House Beautiful*, *Ideal Home* and the like. What we're talking about here is a publication that is produced by a commercial company or other large organisation. Its readers are usually employees, sometimes customers, and often anyone who has an interest or a connection with that company or organisation.

You can't buy a house magazine in your local newsagent. In fact, they are usually distributed free. But don't run away with the idea that this makes them any more downmarket or less lucrative to the freelance photographer than those well-known titles with which you might be more familiar.

Take *BT Today* as a case in point. Actually it's not so much a magazine, more a tabloid newspaper which goes out to all BT employees. That's a circulation of just under 200,000. Each month it turns out 24 pages of national news, plus an eight-page section that is changed six times for different lines of business. That's a total of 72 pages every month, most of which have at least one and sometimes a couple of pictures on them. Nearly all of these are commissioned from freelance photographers. What's more, the company commissions even more pictures to go with online stories that appear daily on one worldwide and ten UK regional websites on the company's own intranet.

Add all this together and you find that *BT Today* has an annual photography budget, for both the national newspaper and those localised websites, of around £200,000 – far in excess of what you might expect from some more well-known national magazines.

Big spender

Of course *BT Today* is one of the bigger spenders, as befits a very professional publication produced by one of the UK's largest employers. And it has to be said that the photography for the national paper is commissioned mostly through two or three agencies, while the regional website photography is commissioned by freelance writers under contract to BT. For that reason, this particular publication is not open to a speculative approach as might be the case with some others.

All need pictures

However, at the other end of the scale there are much smaller publications, published by very much smaller companies. Some of these amount to no more than two or four A4 pages, published only once or twice a year, with circulations of as little as 500 per issue. But they still need pictures.

Between these two extremes, are medium-to-large size companies that produce regular publications of around eight A4 pages per issue, perhaps four times a year, with circulations of maybe 5,000 copies. Many of these produce different publications for different divisions of the company as well. One big transport contractor in the UK, for example, regularly publishes up to four magazines a year for each of eight different divisions of the company. And they all need pictures.

Local, district and county councils are another area worth exploring. Some of these produce publications for their own employees, in the same way as any large company. But many also publish magazines or newspapers that are distributed free to all the residents of the area served by the council.

The circulation depends, of course, on the size of the town, city or county. An average local or district council publication might have a circulation of perhaps 20,000-40,000. A county council publication might be distributed to more like 500,000. With figures like these, they are spending a lot of money on design, printing and distribution costs, so allocating a reasonably high budget to commission freelance photographers doesn't really add that much more to the costs in real terms. After all, a council wants to be seen in the best light by its residents, and they won't achieve that aim by using pictures taken by an inexperienced amateur in the photocopying department who happens to have a half-way decent camera.

In fact that goes for any company that is producing a house magazine for its employees or customers. The main reason for the existence of such a magazine is to make the company/organisation/business/council look good in the eyes of its readers.

Easier to break in

Make no mistake, then. The kind of publications we are talking about here might seem obscure, compared to many more familiar, big-name consumer magazines, but they still demand a high level of quality photography. The difference, for the unknown freelance, is that house magazines can be a lot easier to break into than their consumer counterparts – and they often pay better too.

The fact is that the magazine you see for sale in the high street is there to make a profit for its publishers. It relies on its cover price and advertising revenue to bring in money to pay staff, printers, distributors and – at the end of the line – freelances. A house magazine, by comparison, is never meant to make money. It's there as a service. So when it is set up, a budget is allocated for different aspects of its production, and that usually includes good rates for photographers, as well as travel expenses.

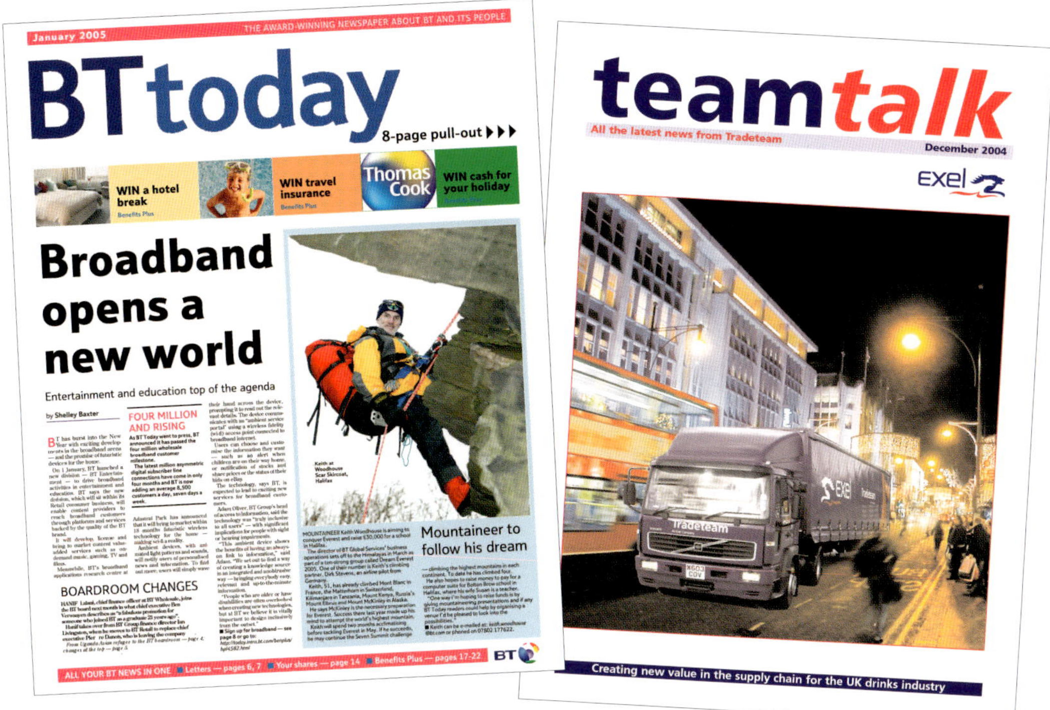

Picture requirements

So what kind of pictures are they looking for?

First of all, in the vast majority of cases, it is just pictures they need. Unlike the more commercial world, where illustrated articles comprising a complete package of words and pictures tend to sell better than pictures alone, this is a market where the words will almost certainly be written by someone in the organisation, who needs a picture to illustrate what they have written.

Many house magazine picture requirements are extremely straightforward. So we're talking about subjects such as cheque presentations, staff training sessions, people with unusual hobbies, employees involved in unusual or important jobs, people who work for their local communities in their spare time, others working on important contracts, those involved in charity work or fund raising, equipment used by the business producing the publication… all fairly ordinary, one might almost say mundane, subjects which are actually very easy to photograph.

Artistry is out…

This isn't a market for overtly artistic pictures. If your subject, for example, is a man working at a computer, don't be tempted to start fiddling with depth of field to throw the computer out of focus, or perhaps photographing the subject through the out-of-focus leaves of a nearby potted plant. In all probability, the whole point of the picture is how that man does his job, using that computer. So the editor is going to want to see both of them, sharp and large in the picture area.

The important thing is to find out from the editor or the person you are photographing, what message they are trying to get across and then to make sure that message is clearly illustrated in your picture.

BT Today is one of the UK's most professionally-produced house magazines – or in this case, newspaper. Teamtalk is one of several house magazines produced regularly by transport company Exel for its different divisions

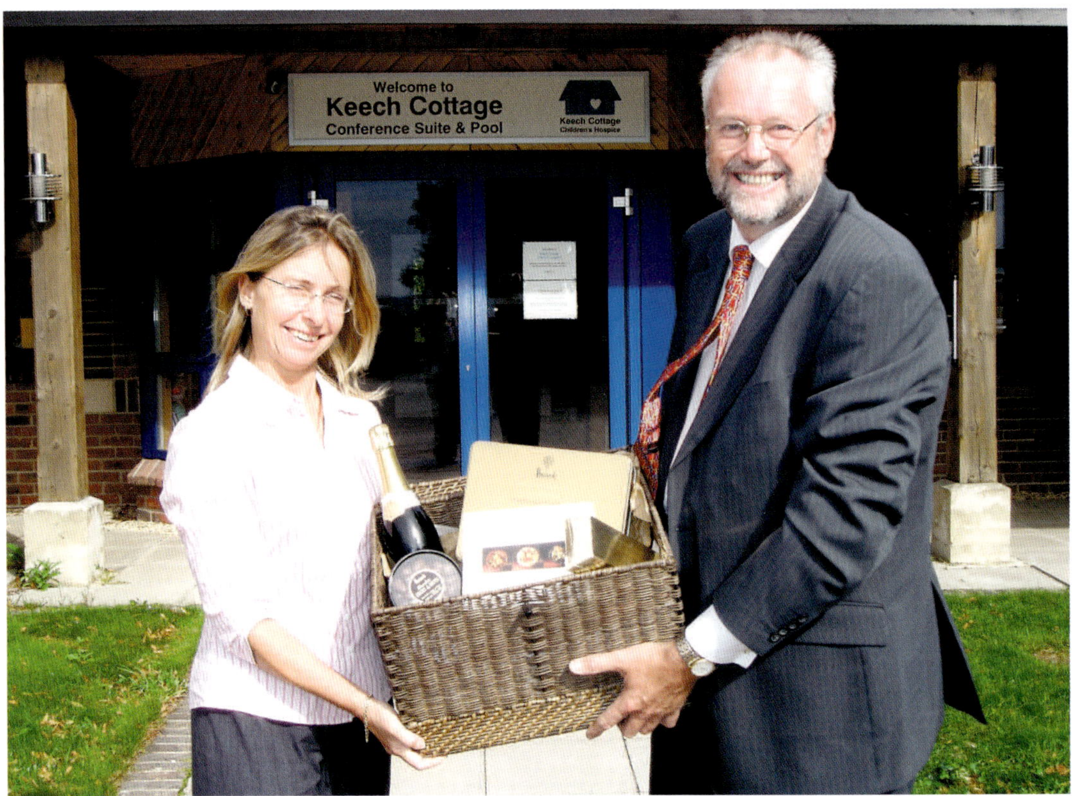

A straightforward charity presentation picture of the kind used by many house magazines (Picture courtesy of RHG)

...But a little imagination helps

Although creativity for its own sake should be avoided in this type of photography, that doesn't mean you shouldn't use a little imagination to get something different from an otherwise boring subject.

Take the traditional cheque presentation from someone who has been raising funds for a charity, for example. The temptation is to simply take a picture of two people, in an office, shaking hands as one hands over the cheque. Boring picture of a boring subject. So ask what the charity is all about. See if you can get an element of the charity into your picture. Say it's a charity for young people learning to sail. That being the case, ask if the picture can be taken at the location where the sailing takes place. Get some boats in the picture. Add some of those young people who are benefiting from the funds raised. Get them in the background, giving a big thumbs up as the cheque is handed over.

Suppose you are asked to photograph a group of people who have been involved in a certain business project. In that case, try to show the project itself as well. Failing that, rather than line the group up like a firing squad, find a different angle. Is there a staircase nearby? Would they look better posed up its steps? Or could you go up the stairs and shoot from above as they look up at you from below? Sometimes no more than a fresh angle or maybe the use of a wide-angle lens to give an unusual perspective can give just that little extra difference to one of these ordinary subjects.

If your subjects have been involved with an unusual job, don't just show them grinning at the camera, show them at work on the job itself. But beware if this involves any kind of manufacturing process or engineering. If that's the case, it

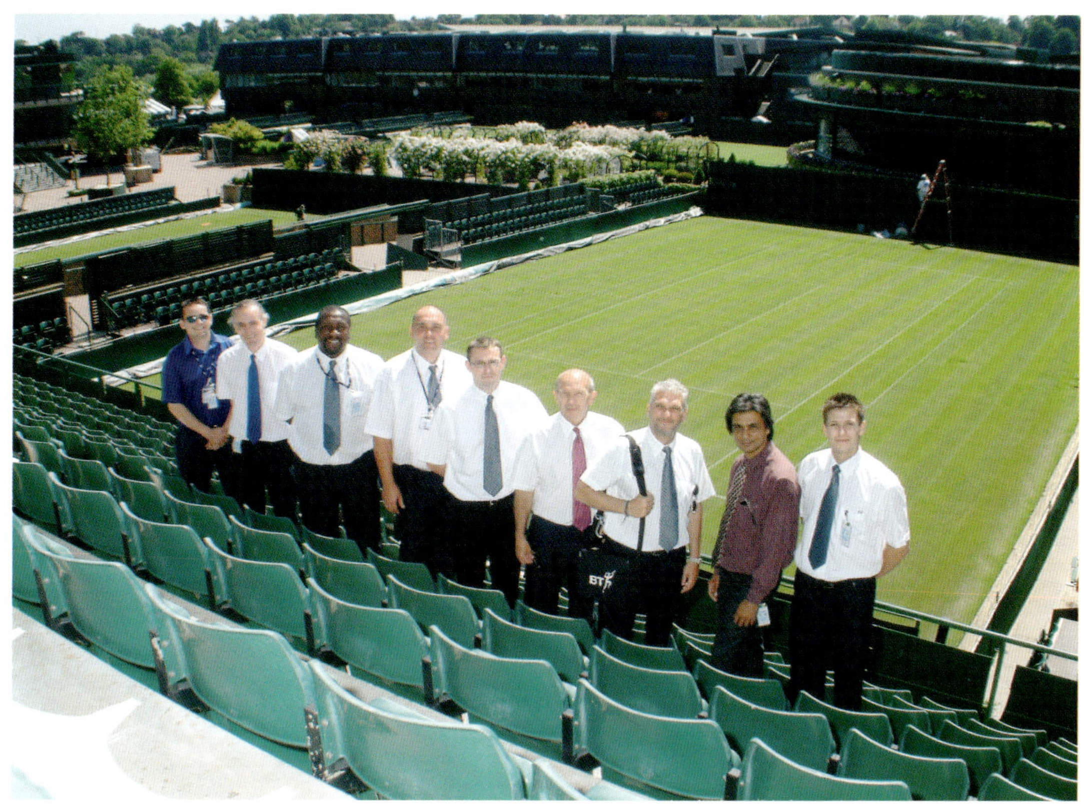

might also mean your subjects should be wearing certain safety gear. You won't know what this is, but they will. So ask them if they are dressed in a way that conforms with their company's health and safety rules. Because if they're not, your picture will be thrown out.

Some of these publications might simply need generic pictures of some kind. Perhaps they run a regular feature on court cases that can't be illustrated other than with something non-specific, like a gavel being wrapped on a block. *Herts Direct*, a magazine published by Herefordshire County Council, for example, regularly buys pictures of Hertfordshire countryside to illustrate the beauty of the county. Many business magazines publish long-winded articles that need to be broken up with an abstract picture that might only be vaguely associated with the subject – clouds, the sea, busy roads, etc.

Making contact

Okay, so now you know the markets and the kind of pictures they need. The next step is to make contact and find out how you can profit. So start by finding a suitable publication. If we're talking about council magazines and newspapers here, watch your letterbox to see what arrives. Ask friends in different towns and counties to do the same. Talk to friends and acquaintances in different jobs. Ask them if their company has a house magazine and if they can let you see a copy. Most feature a request somewhere for story ideas, actually aimed at the company's employees rather than you, but this will give you a name, phone number, email address etc.

Unlike more regular markets, this isn't the place to submit work on spec. Employees of the company might do this, but they won't expect to get paid for their contribution. What you need to do is make

BT engineers at Wimbledon, commissioned by BT to illustrate work their people were carrying out at the world-famous tennis tournament. (Picture by Don Curnick, courtesy of BT Today*)*

direct contact with the person who edits a publication and to offer your services.

If there are no clues to the editor's identity in the publication itself, call the company and ask the name of the person who handles their house magazine. Then, armed with an actual name, ask to be put through to them. If that fails, ask if there is an email address where you can contact them, or a direct phone line that you can call back later. At the very least, get a postal address that includes the name of their department.

Don't make the mistake of asking the switchboard for the editor, because nine times out of ten, the person who edits the publication won't be known as an editor as such, but will be doing the job alongside their more regular employment.

The exception is an extra-large organisation, such as BT, mentioned earlier. *BT Today* has a full-time editor, deputy editor, news editor, production editor and several regular writers, not to mention two freelance sub-editors and ten regional freelance reporters, all under contract. Not many house magazines are so fortunate. Most will be edited by someone in a department with a name like marketing; press office; publicity department; internal, external or corporate communications.

Whether you make contact by phone, email or post, set out your credentials, tell them what area of the country you can cover, show them some of your work if possible and ask if they have something you can shoot for them. If they haven't got anything at the moment, make sure you leave your contact details. Many large companies have a need for pictures from all over the country and there's every chance they'll keep you on their files for when picture possibilities come up in or around your own location.

Working this way is not a guarantee that you'll succeed every time. But there are a lot of companies out there and there are a lot of house magazines. You only need to hit lucky with three or four and you could find yourself with a regular, well-paid income.

Selling transport photos

by PETE TRAFFORD

I am sure many have dreamt about leaving their mundane day jobs to become fabulously wealthy, world-renowned transport photographers. While global recognition will undoubtedly pass most of us by, it does not mean you cannot still be successful.

Of course, "transport" covers a wide range of subjects, and there is a considerable difference between the skills and styles you need for each one, be it cars or motorcycles, rail or aviation. Most photographers tend to specialise in one field and this will probably be your choice too.

Provided you are prepared to be realistic, put in some very hard graft and follow some basic guidelines, there is no reason why your assiduousness will not be rewarded financially and creatively.

Practical considerations

Successfully capturing the diversity of commercially viable transport-related images involves a phenomenal amount of legwork. So to make those long days less arduous, you really need to keep your camera bag as light as possible. While this may seem painfully obvious, it is actually not all that easy, as you do not want to jeopardise your images by not having enough of the correct photographic equipment available when you need it.

In order to get the balance right, you either get some hobbit to carry bags of equipment around for you, or you carefully evaluate your subject, the corresponding surroundings and conditions, possible changes in circumstances, your objectives and market requirements, and of course the ever-changing weather.

Once you have analysed all this information, you will be able to decide what is required while safeguarding against the possible disfigurement caused by humping tons of un-needed equipment around!

Take these examples. If you are planning to photograph planes at an air show, using a very heavy and cumbersome large format camera to take panning shots of an aircraft flying by at 300mph is obvious madness when compared to the advantages of using a much lighter and agile SLR.

The same kind of consideration can be applied to your lenses. Because of the dis-

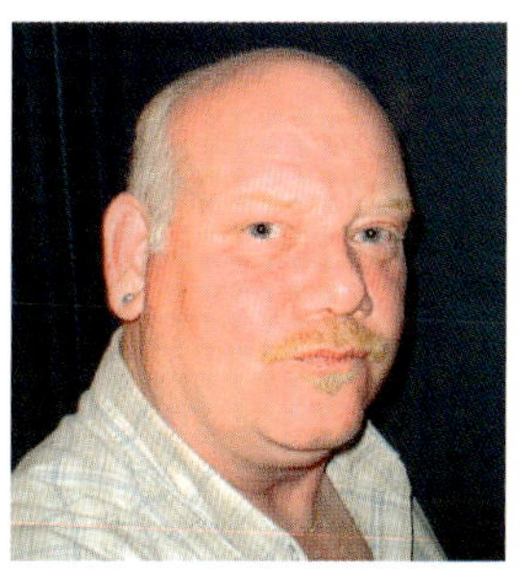

Peter Trafford-Smith spent 10 years as a picture editor on transport magazines for a major UK publishing house and as many years again as library manager of a specialist transport picture agency. During this time he also worked as a freelance photojournalist and is the recipient of *Practical Photography*'s Certificate of Excellence. He has had his work regularly published in various books, newspapers, supplements, advertising campaigns and magazines both in the UK and America.

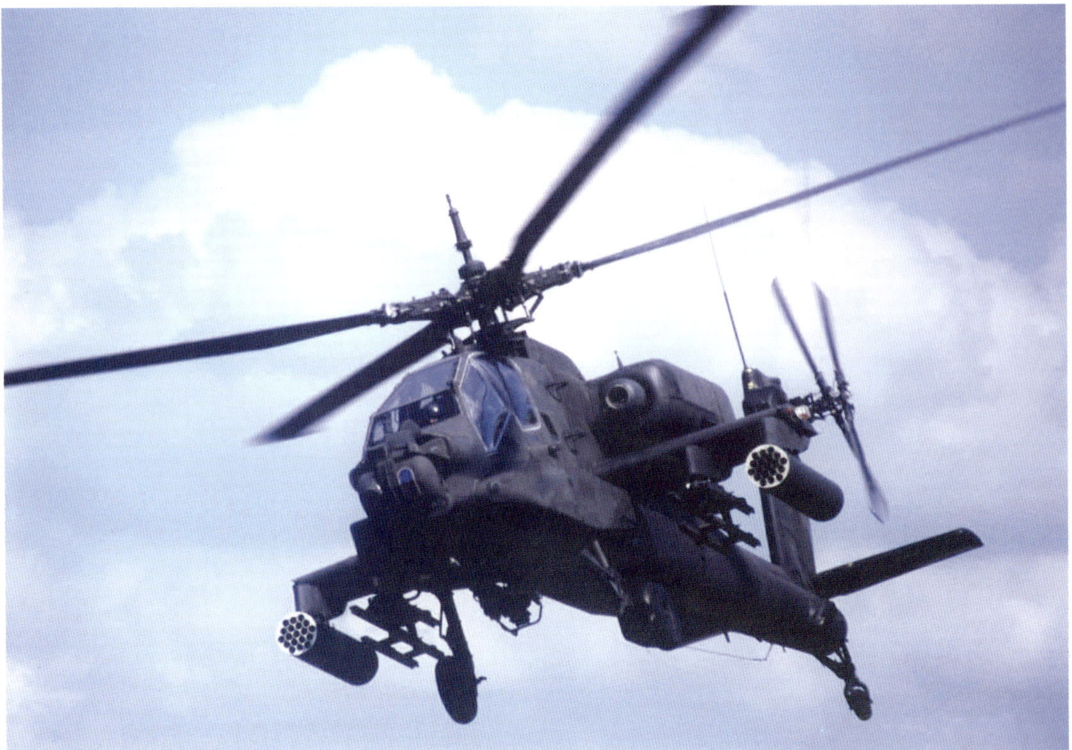

When taking pictures of propellor-driven aviation subjects, set your shutter speed low enough to ensure some blur on the blades

tances you will be from airborne aircraft, you will need a respectable 300mm zoom at least, but you will also need a 35mm for close-in ground-based subjects. I personally use two camera bodies, one with a 35-135mm lens and the other with a 170-500mm lens, and that's about it.

If it's a nice sunny day, the chances are you will not require your tripod or flash-gun, so leave them behind.

In contrast, if you are at an indoor car show, the equipment list is totally different. You will not need your mega-heavyweight zoom lens as you will be very close to your subject matter, but you will definitely need your flashgun. Unless you are using colour-corrected film or filters, you will be using a tremendous amount of flash, so in this case, you need to ensure you have a power-ful and versatile flash unit, complete with plenty of batteries or battery packs.

A sturdy tripod is also a good piece of kit for two reasons. It provides a steady photographic platform, but also deters unthinking individuals from walking in front of your camera and ruining your shot!

So, if you choose your kit wisely, you will have all the equipment you need easily accessible in a camera bag that will be rea-sonably light, and you should still be able to walk upright the following day!

As we suffer from frequent overcast weather in this country, pictures taken on location often include a large amount of bland and colourless sky, no matter how exciting the subject matter might be. In this case some very subtle use of graduated fil-ters can often add some much needed atmosphere. But avoid over-use at all costs! The object is to make the picture look as natural as possible, not like the work of a drug-crazed PhotoShop geek.

I normally pack, just in case, a 50% graduated light blue, grey and tobacco fil-ter, plus a polarisor to cut out unwanted

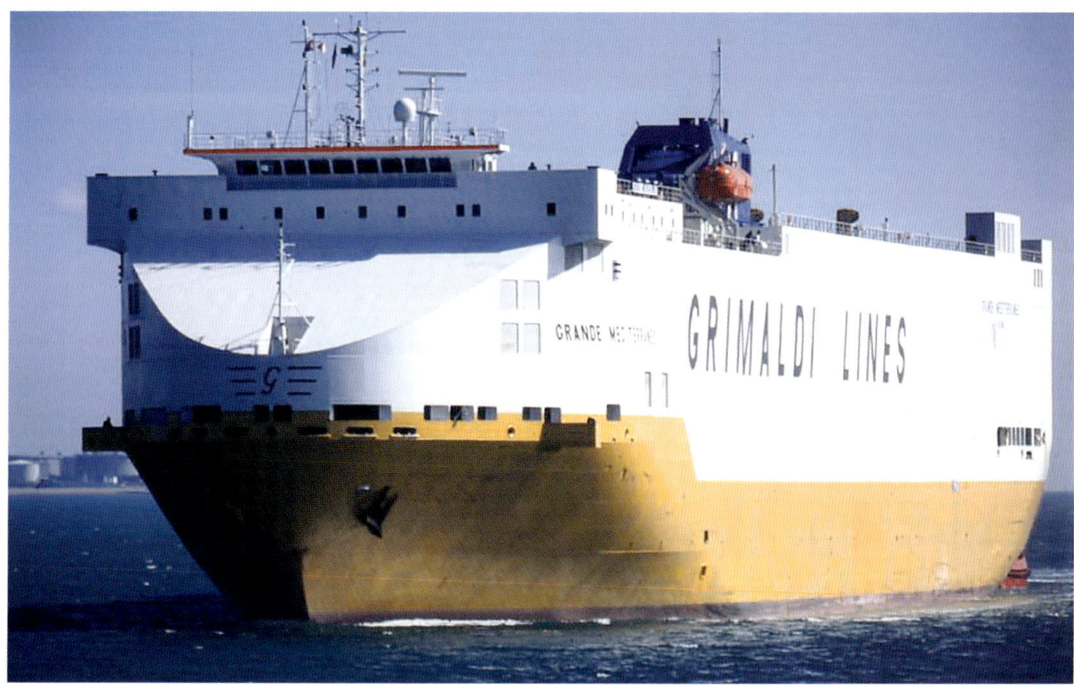

reflections. I am also a firm believer in controlled fill-in flash to liven up close-in shots.

Regardless of what you are using, please remember that transport photography can be dangerous. So be vigilant, and make sure you are not venturing into restricted areas.

Researching your markets

Many photographers shoot first and try to find a market later. As has been emphasised in previous projects, it is important to know the market requirements and subject matter thoroughly.

Before you shoot one frame, do your homework meticulously and see what is currently being published. Take time to look at as many transport-related commercial and trade magazines, e-zines, books, newspapers, supplements, cards and calendars as you can. Record as many details as possible regarding the kind of material being used, by which publisher, and very importantly, the kind of shots actually being used. It should be obvious that there is absolutely no point in submitting pictures of the latest HST train to a steam traction publication – they simply will not be accepted.

You should maintain a database of your transport markets with updated information of contact names, phone numbers and e-mail addresses. The usefulness of *The Freelance Photographer's Market Handbook* in this respect has been emphasised before and you should also not forget internet search engines, which can help with potential foreign markets.

Most specialist publications or agencies have a set picture style format, so try and emulate this, but don't be afraid to try a new spin, provided you have the basic style already covered.

The more you know about your potential markets, the greater your chances are of satisfying their needs and getting published.

Filling the frame with your subject can give your picture added impact. However, sometimes editors need space around the subject to accommodate text – shoot both types of picture to increase sales potential

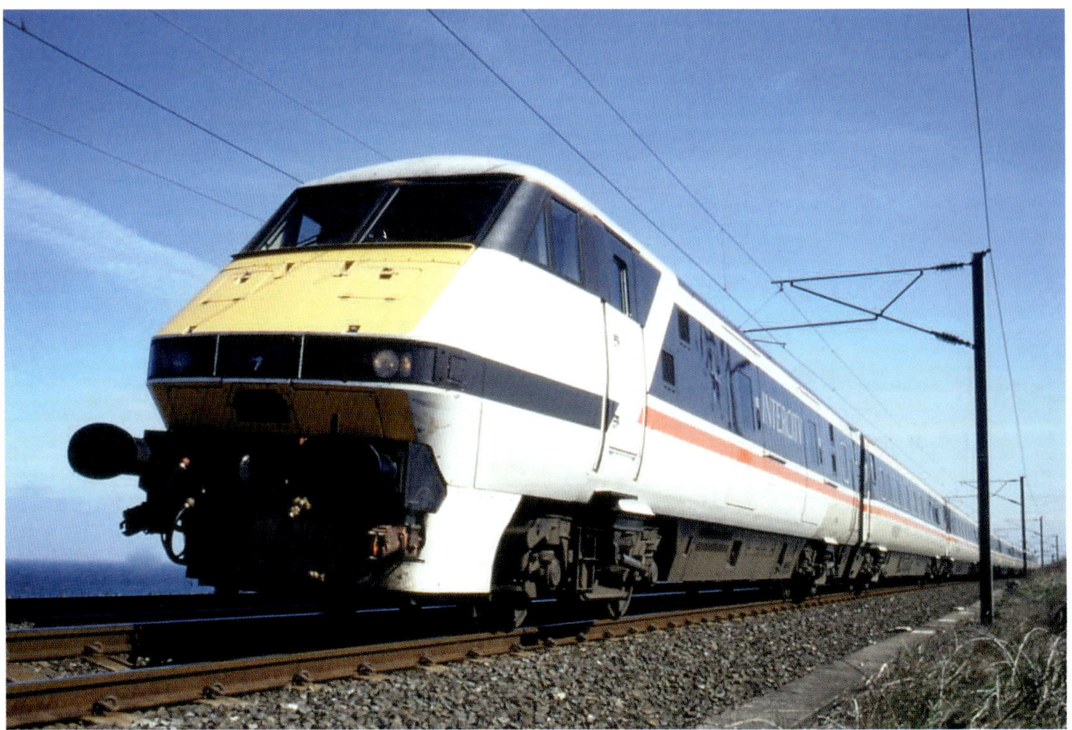

Presentation

Art directors and picture editors are very busy people who rarely have any spare time available to spend pouring over the masses of submissions they are sent every month from aspiring freelances. If you want to get their attention, your submissions have to be professional and to the point, and the first step in this process is your own picture editing.

You have to be brutally honest with yourself here. Your pictures must be perfect in exposure, focus, composition and content. If they are not, don't bother sending them in.

Keep your intended submission to a reasonable number, but make sure that they still demonstrate your expertise and versatility. This is not quite as easy as it sounds, and may take a great deal longer than you think.

Regardless of who you are sending your pictures to, you must adhere to the unwritten "picture etiquette" rules if you want to stand a chance of getting your images noticed and published.

One thing that is absolutely essential in this market is detailed and accurate captions. You should include as much information as you can and be prepared to do some research if you are not sure of your facts. There is no point in just putting "vintage car" on the caption – you need to know the type, year and model. Your intended market will want to know this, so you must supply it.

Cars, trucks and motorcycles are pretty easy to identify as they have their make and model somewhere on the vehicle. Make sure you take a shot of this for your own reference.

Rail and aviation subjects are more difficult though, and you may need to invest in some reference books to help you correctly identify types and variations.

Taking pictures of transport subjects can be dangerous – you need to be aware of your subject and the surroundings. You must ensure that you are safe and also, that you are not violating any laws. This near-track shot of a British HST was taken with official permission

Most of these subjects can be identified by their individual numbers and luckily there are numerous helpful books available.

Maritime reference books are harder to find. Jane's have comprehensive volumes, but these are expensive.

If you have made an appointment to actually go and see an art director, designer or editor, they often like to see portfolios comprised of good quality prints of around 20x16in. The advantage is that these also present a high impact visual of your work. If you are shooting on film, take along a sheet of transparencies in case they want to view on a lightbox, and if you can, leave a low-res CD with them.

Rates and results

At the specialist end of the transport market some low-circulation magazines pay very little, while daily newspapers tend to pay top rates. But if you are lucky enough to supply images for a major car advertising campaign you can book your ticket to the Bahamas!

If you have been commissioned to do a shoot you will normally be told upfront of the job or day rate, but you need to find out who will own the copyright, who is paying for processing, travel expenses etc. Get this in writing before you pack your camera bag, but be prepared to relinquish the copyright if you are shooting for a car magazine as more and more seem to be following this route.

Be aware of long days and fickle art directors who have been known to hire photographers more for their jovial character than their photographic skill! Don't be afraid to suggest ideas or trying something new, but be diplomatic as they are, after all, paying you at the end of the day and are responsible for booking you for other assignments.

If you are still having problems getting published try, as has been suggested elsewhere, submitting words and pictures as a complete package. This has worked for me in the past, but again make sure it is on a suitable subject and written and photographed in the style of the market you are approaching. Most transport publications are aimed at specific sectors of an enthusiast market and the style has to be pitched just right for their particular readership. The initial idea can also be "tweaked" to suit other prospective publishers in due course.

Once you have got your images published, it's time to collect for all your hard work, and who knows, maybe you will be on your way to global recognition!

Selling to home mags

by KEN PRICE

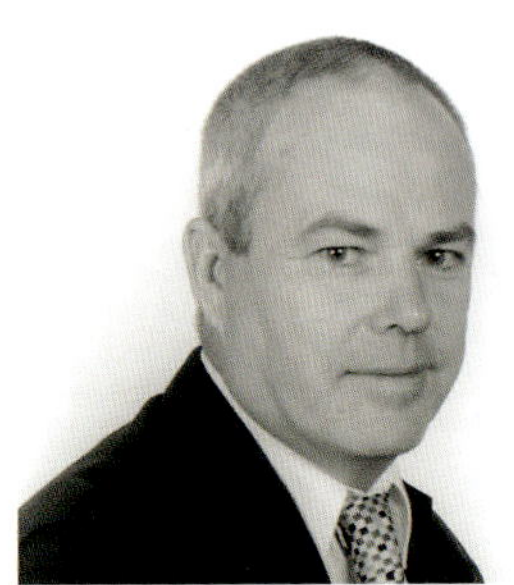

Walk into your local newsagent or supermarket and look at the sheer numbers of magazines devoted to homes – how to build them, design their interiors, furnish and decorate them in a unique style. Published every month are literally dozens of magazines, some featuring as many as 25 different homes.

The featured properties cover a huge range of styles from traditional to modern. They are from all corners of the UK, even the other side of the world. It's absolutely mind-boggling how much effort is needed to produce all this month after month, year after year. And remember that many of these properties are being published for the first time!

Ask yourself how they got there without an army of photographers, writers and editorial staff to produce this huge volume of material in what is, after all, a small proportion of the magazine market. It's exhausting just thinking about it.

Well, the good news is that freelances supply much of this incredible range of material. And the even better news is that editors will pay well to have a regular supply of top quality material to fill their magazines.

The only qualification needed to join this "army" is the ability to provide photos to a certain style, by a given date and to a predetermined standard. This is not a market for purely speculative submissions, but it is easier than you think to get a commission as long as you can deliver the goods.

This project shows you how you can supply this market – and maybe turn a hobby into a living.

Meeting market needs

Begin by forgetting about selling photos.

But hang on, isn't the idea to get paid for the photography? Well, yes of course. But first and foremost it's about meeting the needs of a magazine – or more accurately its readers. If the magazine does not supply what readers want, it does not sell –it's as simple as that. It's like any other market where people buy products. Only in this market the products are the images. Supply the needs of a magazine and you're on your way to successful freelancing, so let's start by looking at this market and how it works.

Ken Price had his first photo published in *The Observer*. After this, sales were made to sports and general hobby magazines on a weekend and part-time basis. He decided to become a full-time freelance in 1999, after 26 years as a Quantity Surveyor. Specialising in architecture and construction photography for the property and construction market, his clients include developers, architects and property consultants. Ken also supplies photos to several home interest magazines, including *25 Beautiful Homes, Real Homes, Home Building & Renovating, SelfBuild & Design, Your Home, Period House, BBC Good Homes* and *The English Home*. Stock images are sold through three specialist photo libraries. More of his work can be seen on his website: www.agimages.demon. co.uk

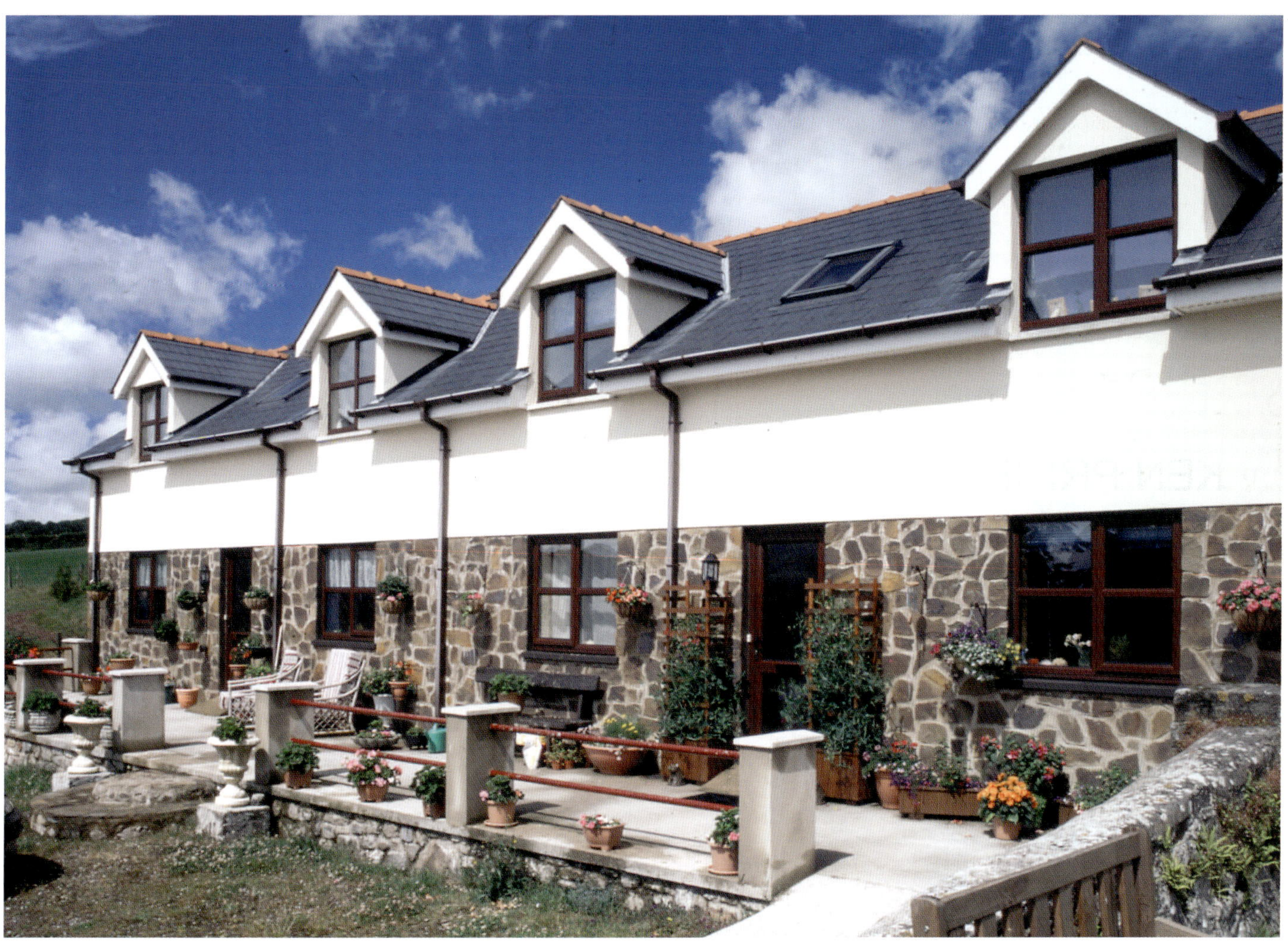

Local markets have stalls offering a variety of goods. Some are quite individual; others have some overlap in the goods on offer. The home interest market is the same, only here the traders are publishers and their products are magazines.

The Freelance Photographer's Market Handbook includes numerous magazines in the "Home Interest" section, but this is only a selection of the magazines that use this type of material. Why are there so many? Are they all providing the same information to a vast readership?

Quite simply, they each target a specific sector of the market, though admittedly with some overlap. Interior design magazines focus on creating visual impact – like a photographer – through composition, colour and style. Self-build magazines concentrate on practical aspects – how to overcome planning restrictions and budget accurately. They are quite different in their needs.

Therein lies the advantage to the freelance; they all need different information, thus providing an even bigger need for freelances to supply!

Self assessment

No, not income tax, but the quality of your photos – your products in the market. Do they already meet the magazines' needs?

This shot of a barn conversion featured in a home interest publication. It was taken in the morning to catch the sun on the front elevation, between cloudy spells and after a shower when the light was really clear

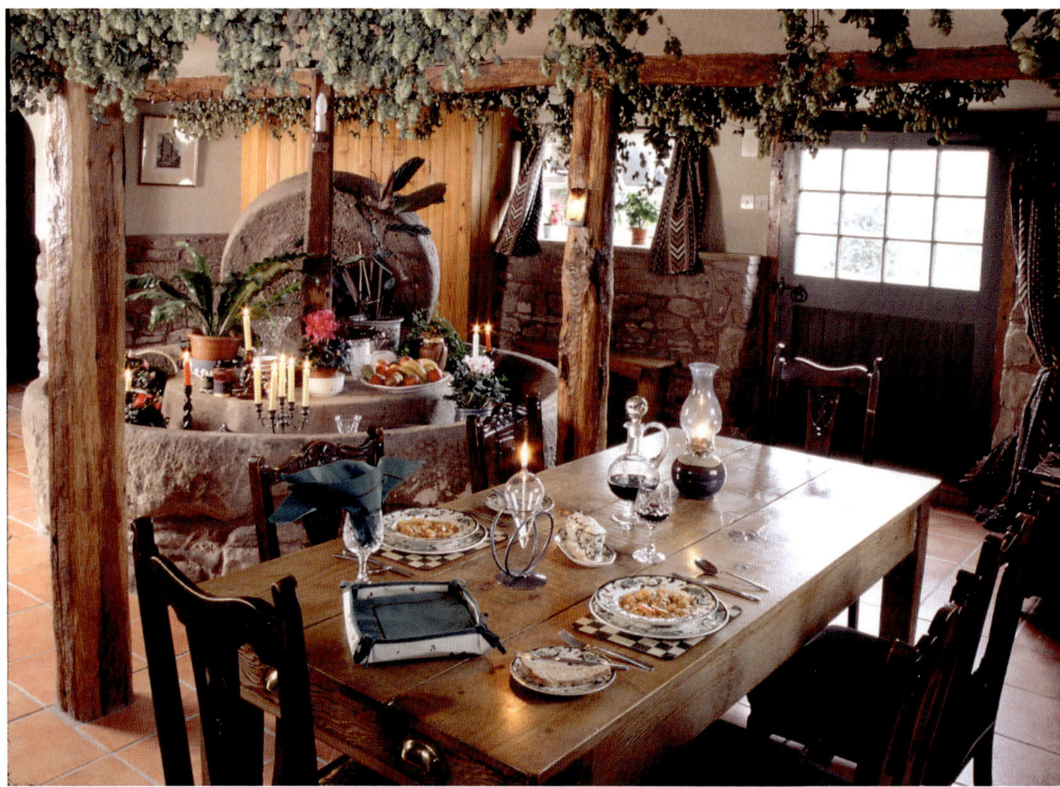

*Shot for another home interest magazine, this shows a dining room interior with an old cider mill in the background. Hops draped along the exposed beams add character to this old country farmhouse.
The table is laid to add interest*

Or do you need to develop your talents, acquire new skills or equipment?

There are certain equipment basics that apply in this field. To supply the full range of magazines available, medium format equipment is a must – most top-level magazines expect it and the competition supplies it.

For sharp photos in low light interiors use a sturdy tripod to keep the camera steady. A studio light helps with fill-in and, using the modelling light, can be used for general lighting. Use a brolly or soft box to provide even lighting and remember to use a filter with daylight-balanced film (80A or B for tungsten) or the photos will have a colour cast.

By all means aspire to be the best you can, but don't expect to be snapped up by top magazines until you've gained experience. Having said that, you have only to produce photos of equal quality to those already in use in the magazines. So let's look at them.

Selecting target magazines

There is no substitute for research, but be selective. To begin, browse the magazine shelves in the newsagent, supermarket, library or even the doctor's surgery. Get a feel for the images they use. Look at them carefully.

Look at the homes featured – are they modern, traditional, period? Exterior shots will usually have blue skies with sunlit elevations. Interiors vary – some go for a moody, dark look – others bright, sunny and well-lit. Detail photos will illustrate relevant points in the text.

Select a few magazines to study with a view to supplying them. Most magazines are open to approaches from freelances, but some only from those with experience. The BFP *Handbook* identifies both and also gives indications of the fees they pay. And if you are a BFP member, *Market Newsletter* also provides updates on their needs and

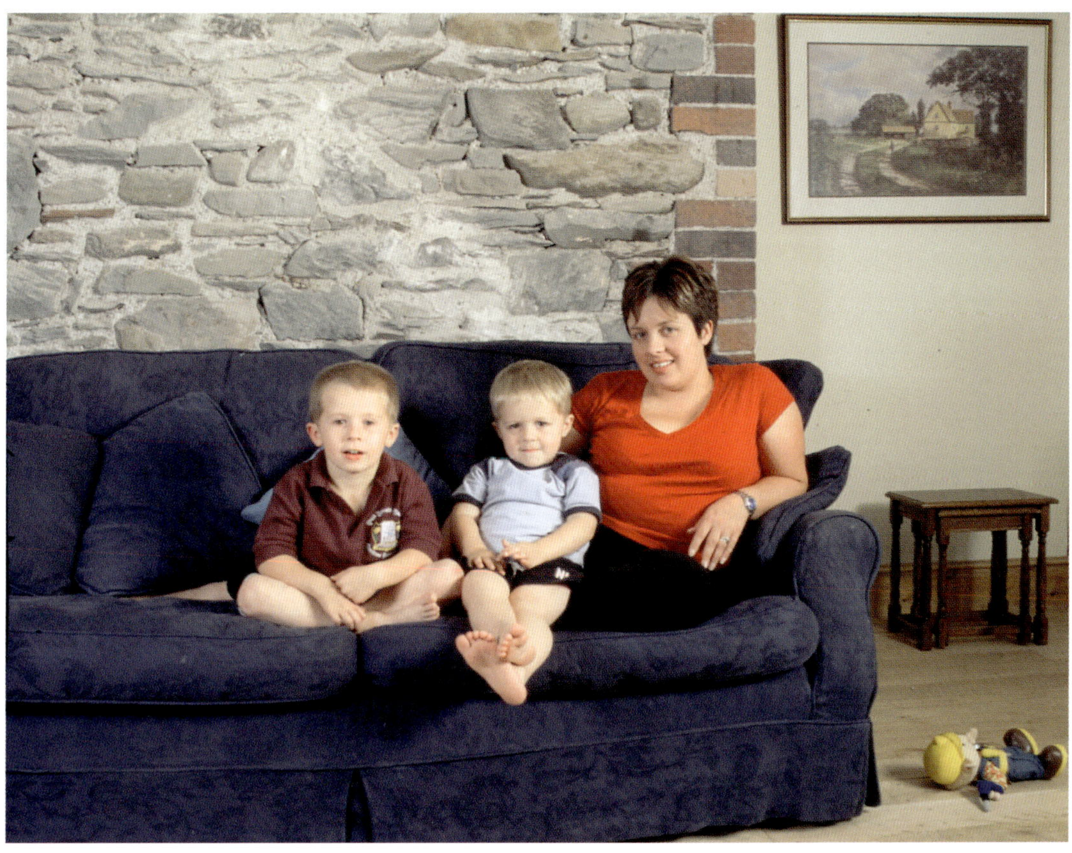

Typical family shot for a Your Home feature about a couple who built their own home. The magazine likes to include photos of mothers with their children

wider market leads and information. Both are invaluable sources of information for newcomers and experienced alike.

Read the articles to understand what information they need; the images and text should work together to inform the reader. Many of the articles are light and chatty, written to fill a tea break or to appeal to the readers' nosy nature. See how long it takes to read the article. As a guide articles are generally between 900-1400 words.

So now you know what types of homes they feature, go out and get them.

Finding your homes

First you need homes to offer for commission. Why? Because that's the quickest way to get a commission!

This is where research is invaluable. It should be obvious, but knowing what properties to look for makes them easier to find. There's no point in offering a traditional thatched cottage to a magazine that only features chapel conversions.

But how to find them? Well, featured homes are owned by people like you, your family, friends and work colleagues. They are the ones to ask first as they already know you and will be willing to help. Tell them what you're doing, what you're looking for.

Take a drive or a walk around the area you live and look for suitable homes. If you know the owners – ask them. If not, a hand-delivered letter of introduction often works. Keep it brief, courteously outlining what you do, on headed notepaper with your contact details. Be aware that unsolicited mail can be unwelcome, so do not follow up unless invited. If interested, the owners will contact you when they are ready.

Be prepared for an encouraging, but sometimes cautious, response. Explain what's involved and answer questions politely and openly. Visit the owners to show them a portfolio of your best – and most relevant – photos in a presentation case. 10x8in prints with cream card mounts look good, show a professional attitude and lend credibility. So does a well-presented photographer in smart, casual clothes that give a relaxed yet professional image.

If you have samples of published work so much the better. This can take time to build up, as publication will probably be a minimum of three months after completing a commission.

When people enjoy the experience they recommend it to others, which is good for future business.

Approaching the markets

No single method of approach suits all magazines, but start with the editor unless directed elsewhere. Some are difficult to contact by phone, relying on a deputy. In other cases it may be the art director who deals with freelances. Be flexible and adopt whatever method provides results; a combination of methods if necessary.

A brief preliminary telephone call to the magazine is all it takes. Ask to speak to the editor, having confirmed their name, with a brief explanation for the call: "To introduce my services and ask if the editor is interested in receiving images of homes for consideration for publication".

This usually results in either the transfer of the call to the editor, a deputy or – more often – an invitation to send in a submission for consideration. Expect them to want to see what's on offer before spending time with "cold callers". Check exactly to whom and where to send the submission.

This initial submission to the magazine is an opportunity to get the editor's attention. Keep it brief – a letter of introduction, some sample images and brief notes about the home is all that's needed.

The covering letter should give background about who you are, what you can offer, what experience you have (if any) and your contact details. Keep it concise; one sheet of A4 is enough. Explain that the submission is for consideration for commission by the magazine and enclose a post-paid reply envelope.

Between six and nine photographs should be enough for the editor to make a decision. These would probably include an external photo and one of each of the principal interior rooms (living, kitchen, dining, bathroom and master bedroom). In addition there should be a brief description of the property, the owners, and any other relevant information to suit the magazine and to attract the editor's attention to a potentially interesting feature.

If possible find out if the magazine has any preference for the submission format. Here again there is wide variation. But always make it easy for them to look at your work, the easier the better.

Delivery of sample images by e-mail is a great advantage if the magazine is responsive and considers the submission promptly. But it's important to check if this is acceptable in advance, as there is no point in antagonising the editor by clogging up their inbox. Keep files as small as possible while still big enough to view on screen. A 72 dpi scan is usually enough; a file size of 30-40K gives a reasonable image on screen.

JPEG files are the preferred format for

digital photos for assessment. Send them separately or in small groups to keep the email size down to about 100K.

For magazines that prefer to have the submission by post, 7x5in prints are clear enough with sufficient detail. Alternatively scan the images onto CD, again keeping the image files small but large enough to view comfortably on screen.

The commission

Having sent in a submission for consideration, just get on with life. The editor may only consider submitted material once a month, so forget about it for at least a month, maybe even five to six weeks in holiday season. Replies will usually come back within this timescale with acceptance or rejection.

Rejections occasionally offer some explanation; usually not. Fortunately there is usually more than one magazine suitable for the home concerned, provided the submission is tailored to reflect that magazine's interests.

For example, by simply altering the emphasis an interior design magazine could still accept a self-build property rejected by a self-build magazine. Keep flexible, with an open mind about possibilities. Be persistent and ensure that every submission is relevant to the target magazine.

Offers of a commission may come via a phone call, letter or e-mail, depending on the submission method. The accompanying brief varies from "I'll send you a copy of last month's issue to use as a guide", to a couple of pages of text describing the exact number, type and styles of photos to be provided.

Be confident in asking what fees are paid. It's generally a standard sum for packages – photos and copy – but may be negotiable if there's something special on offer. Larger publishers may offer contracts for signature, with standard terms and a delivery date; others a commissioning letter with details of fees offered and what's expected.

However it comes, you now have your first commission for a home interest project. That's where this chapter ends and your freelance career really begins.

Selling through libraries

by DAVID ASKHAM

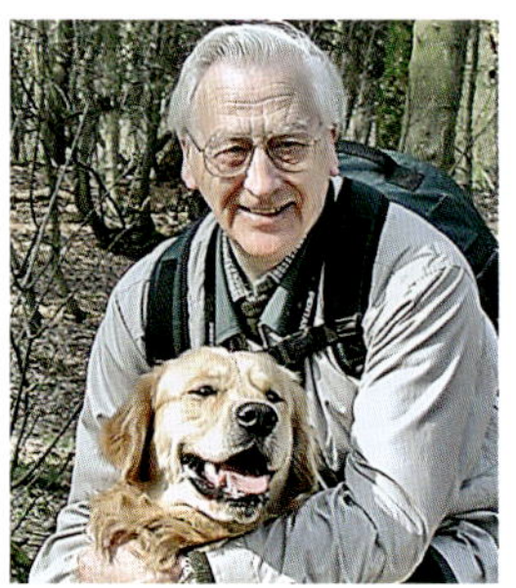

David Askham has been a freelance photographer and writer for nearly forty years. During that time he has operated his own photo library, as well as being a contributor to several general and specialist libraries. In 2000 he wrote the second edition of *Photo Libraries & Agencies* for BFP Books, which has proved extremely popular. In that book he predicted quite accurately how digital imaging would transform the photo library business. David continues to undertake commissions for editors using film, both medium format and 35mm. However, in recent years, he has adapted to digital demands, spending many hours learning the deep arts of Photoshop.

Few freelance photographers can resist the temptation to market their work through a photo library. Why? Well there is a mistaken belief that once the photographs have been taken and submitted, fees from sales will roll in at regular intervals with very little further effort from the photographer.

But nothing could be further from the truth. Without the requisite knowledge it is very easy to tackle this vital market sector and become extremely frustrated and disappointed. Fees do not roll in; indeed they may not arrive at all!

Unrealistic expectations are the root cause of this disappointment. So those photographers who plunge in woefully ill prepared end up giving photo libraries a wide berth. But I believe that you are different. You have taken the trouble to buy this book with the aim of becoming a successful freelance photographer. So it is a pleasure to help you understand the stock library business so that yours becomes a success story.

This project will be devoted to helping the freelance photographer understand how photo libraries work and how you can succeed. It also includes a structured proj-ect to help you on the road to success.

So let us begin by looking at a typical photo library.

Understanding photo libraries

Imagine you are travelling abroad on holiday and you want to borrow a book which illustrates and describes your destination. You visit your local public library, find what you need, and as a registered member take a book out on loan. A books library lends books to readers.

Now imagine that you are a publisher who produces new travel books. You have commissioned a writer for a new title and now need some relevant photographs to illustrate it. You can either employ a photographer or approach a relevant photo library in order to hire suitable stock. If you find what you want, you can buy appropriate rights to reproduce those photographs in your new book. When you have finished, the photographs are returned to the photo library and a fee is paid to that library.

Now just suppose that you had contributed some of those pictures selected by

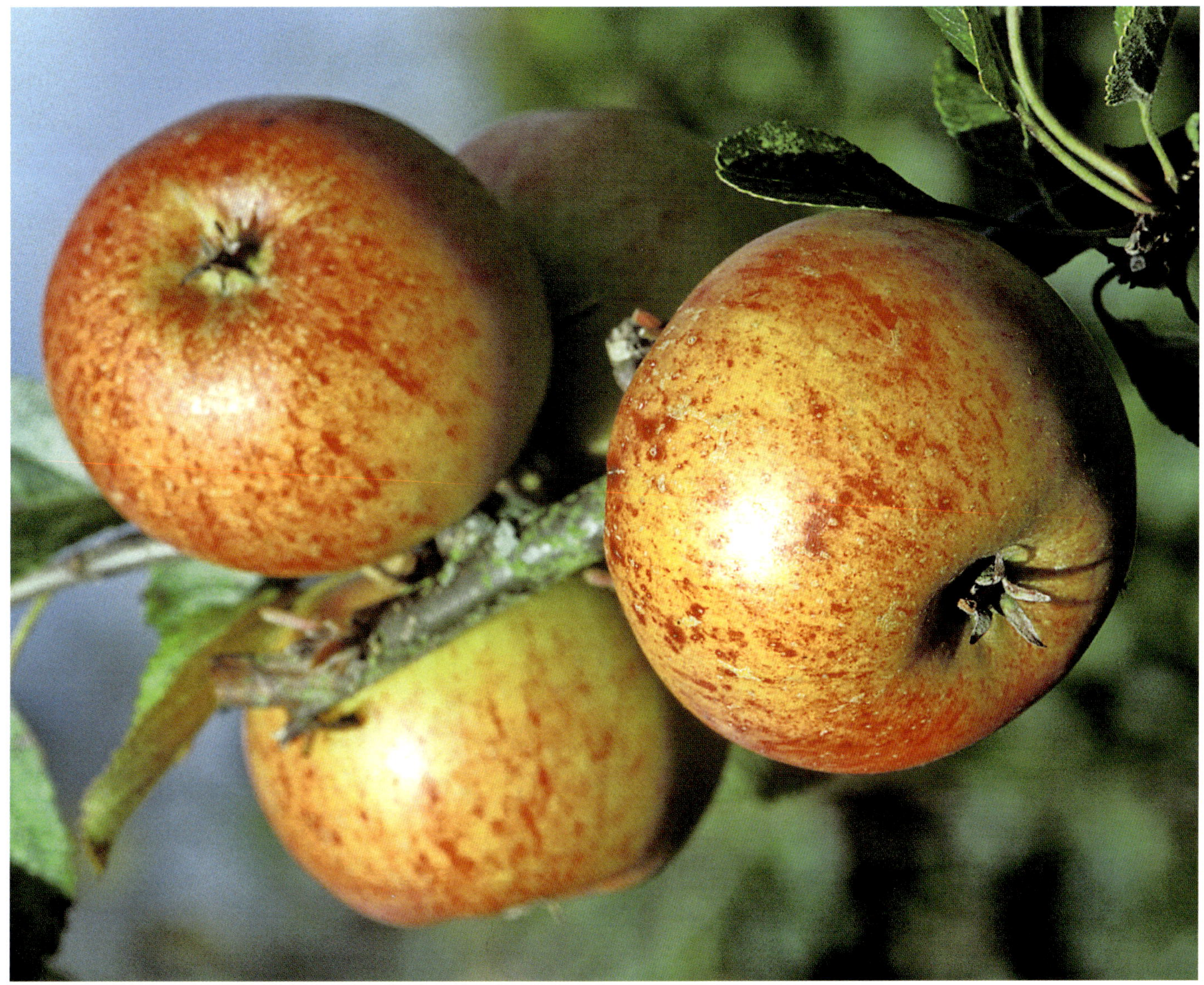

the book publisher. After an accounting interval you would receive your share of those fees and your photographs would then be available for further sales in the future. It is not uncommon for successful pictures to sell many times to markets generally inaccessible to a part-time freelance photographer.

Commercial photo libraries are in business to make a profit from the sales of stock photography.

The more successful libraries run as highly efficient businesses where there is no place for disorganisation and sloppy procedures.

Picture requirements constantly evolve and change. Successful libraries have carefully honed their skills in picture selection, marketing and sales. They know what their markets want and strive to source relevant new material from contributing photographers. Some libraries issue "wants lists" to help their photographers provide relevant new photography.

Traditionally, photo libraries accommodated many thousands – sometimes millions – of colour transparencies, all categorised, labelled and filed ready for picture researchers to view, select and hire.

A good seasonal subject, such as this, could appeal to editors of health and horticultural publications

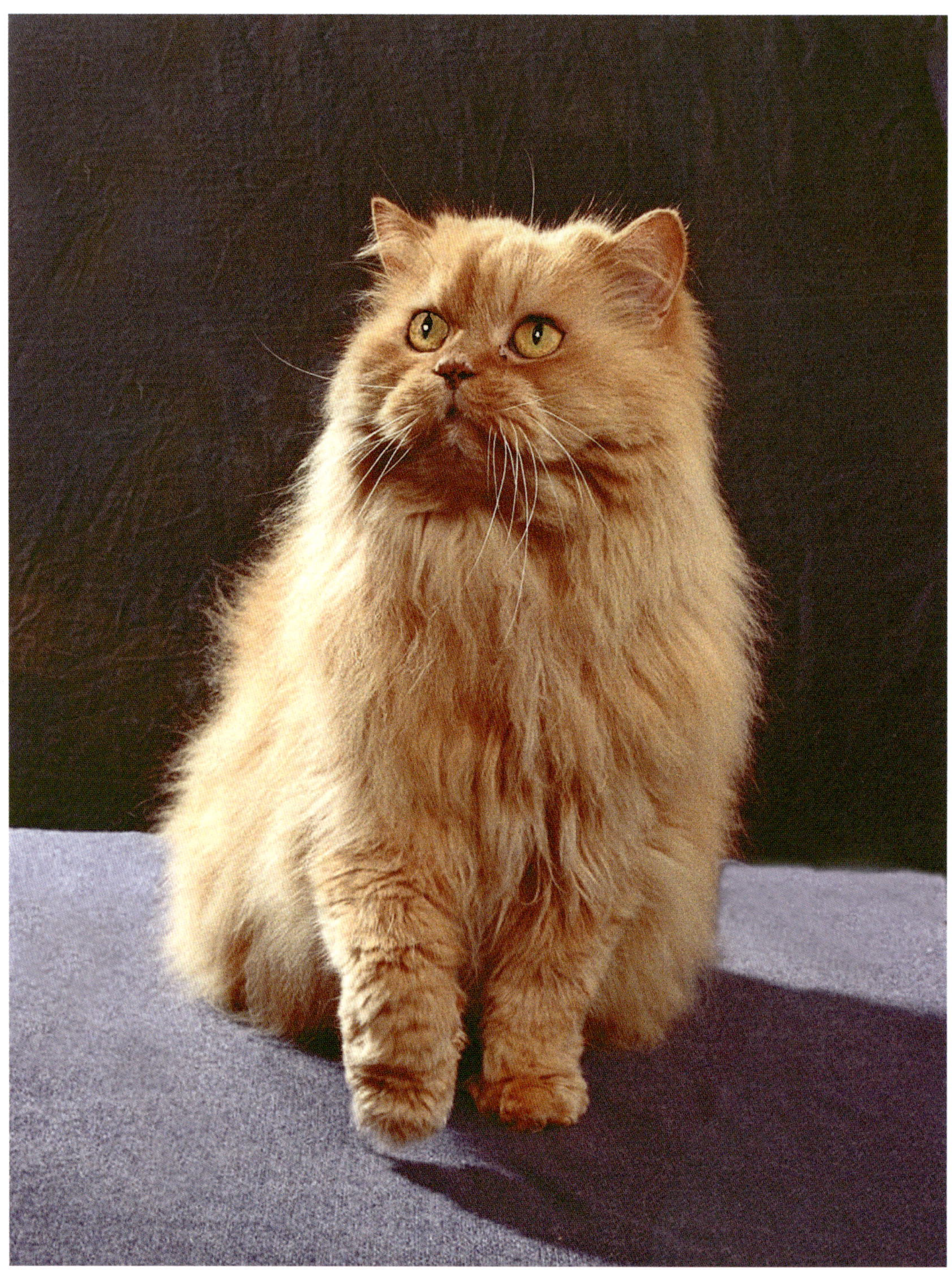

Animal pictures are much in demand and this one has sold several times

Modern technology now makes it possible for images to be digitised and made available for search by computers through the World Wide Web, thus opening up the market in an unprecedented way and leading to global sales.

Whatever the method of storage and delivery, images find their origin in photographers like you. Talented photographers around the world are focusing their lenses on subjects which they judge to have good sales potential. Carefully selected new pictures are then sent to a contracted library where they are edited and the successful ones added to the library stock for marketing to clients.

Fees payable to contributing photographers, traditionally 50% commission on sales, are usually sent out quarterly after clients have paid the library.

A factor often overlooked or misunderstood by new contributors is the long timescale at work in a library. Depending on the staffing and efficiency within the operation, several weeks or months can elapse between the receipt of new material and it being available to new clients. Photographs have to be mounted or digitised, identified and labelled, added to the picture and photographer. Unless they are actively marketed, or are extremely lucky in meeting a current need, pictures spend a lot of time resting in filing cabinets or computer storage. Sales may never be made.

However, lots will sell. But there is a lengthy lead-time between a picture being selected and actual publication. Contributors would be exceptionally lucky to receive fees for new pictures within less than a year of delivery to the library.

So selling photographs through a library has to be seen as a long-term investment. If your contributions are likely to be derived from part-time freelancing, think of any income as an additional small pension fund. Of course, if you become highly professional and devote most of your time to being a successful stock photographer, the rewards can be very good indeed.

Is it for you?

Photo libraries welcome contributors who can maintain a regular flow of new photographs. (Spasmodic contributors, unless of exceptional merit, can be a drain on a library's administrative resources.)

So the real question is, could you sustain such a commitment as a freelance photographer?

Lifestyles vary: some photographers only produce new material on their annual holidays, while others schedule time regularly throughout the year. Guess who is likely to be the more successful.

Equally vital is the ability consistently to produce new photographs of impeccable quality. Only the very best quality photographs will sell. Precise exposure, perfect composition, immaculate sharpness and inspired subject treatment all characterise pictures that will bring joy to the hearts of picture researchers. If you are unsure of your abilities in any of these areas, seek help.

Allied to the foregoing is the requirement to take photographs that are relevant to market needs. Market relevance is constantly changing and is more difficult to gauge. You can judge what types of subjects and treatments are likely to be needed by looking critically at what is currently being used in editorial and advertising.

However, try to avoid slavish copying of distinctive styles. It is far better to establish your own style. Once you have been accepted by a library and have established a good working relationship, you can learn much by consulting the manager about emerging picture requirements. Libraries are at the sharp end of sensing market requirements.

In summary, we have looked briefly at how libraries work and recognd their reliance on good contributing photographers for a constant inwards flow of new material. We have also noted that only the highest quality of relevant photography is likely to be accepted. Assuming you are still keen to succeed in selling some of your photographs through a photo library, it is now time for you to do some work.

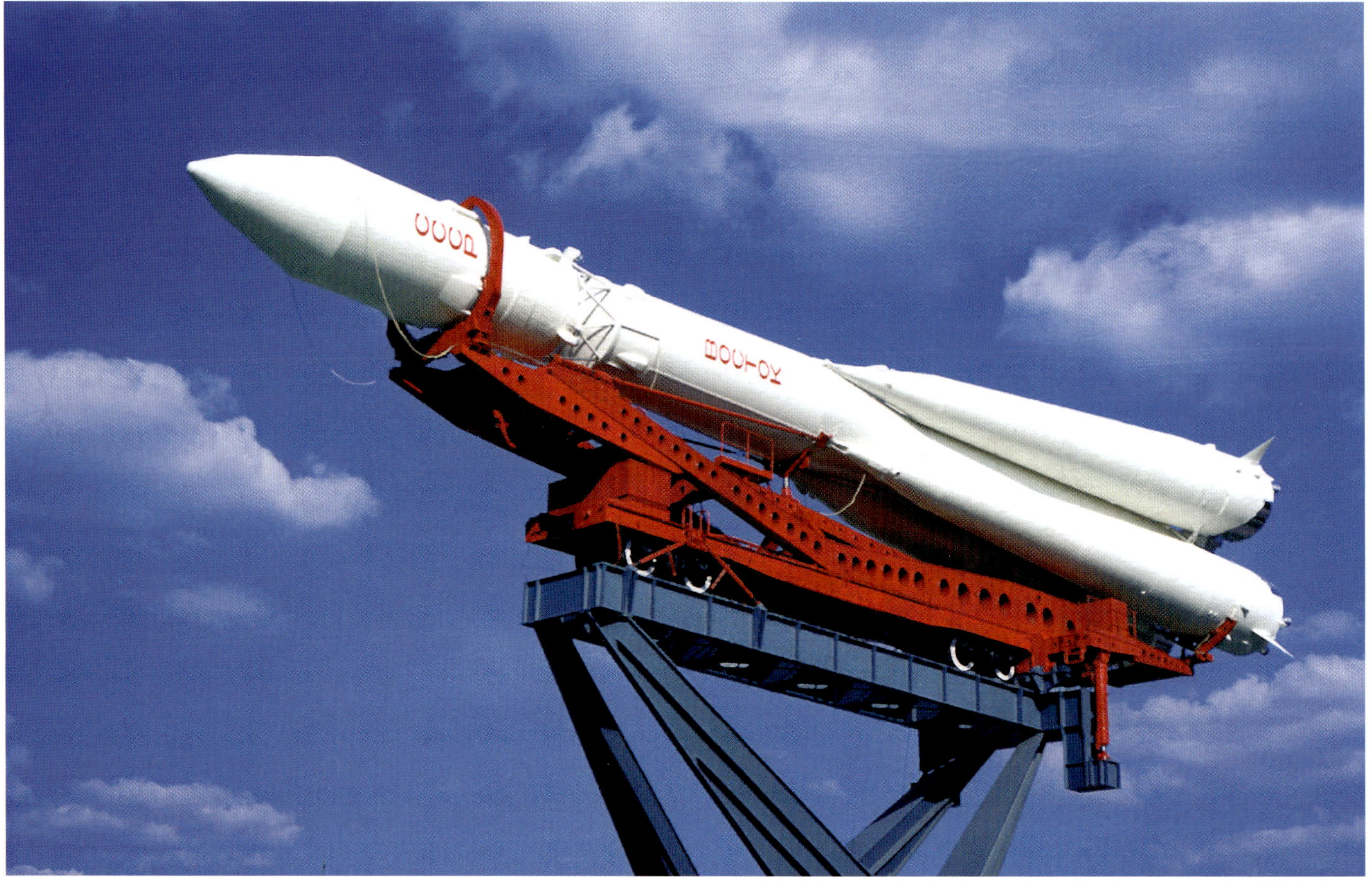

Stock success

Before you embark on the project, it is essential that you understand the scale of the task ahead. Read the first part of this chapter once more so that you fully understand how photo libraries work and the risk of long timescales with no guarantee of success. Now work through the following sixteen steps:

Analyse your photographic strengths and weaknesses
Analyse your lifestyle
Research potential photo libraries
Draft a short list of target photo libraries
Request copies of their Notes for Contributing Photographers.
Study those Notes extremely carefully
Prioritise photo libraries of potential interest
Select and edit suitable material to offer a library
Make an appointment to visit your first choice library
Failing that, make contact by telephone to discuss your initial submission
Send the minimum number of pictures requested
If accepted, study your contract carefully before you sign it
Submit new material regularly
Be patient. Sales take time: payment even longer!
Keep meticulous records of your submissions, acceptances and sales. The taxman will be interested
Assess resulting sales annually and take appropriate action

Vostok 2, on display in Moscow, has become part of space history. A good one for the library

Well it is unfair to leave you at this point, so I will add some words of encouragement and explanation. We will work through the list from the beginning.

A little explanation

We often fail to see our own strengths. The subjects we most like to take are not necessarily the ones which will sell. Produce samples and ask the views of a trusted competent photographic friend who is, preferably, already an established contributing photographer. There may be scope for improving techniques which could be learned on part-time college courses or at photographic clubs. A very successful animal photographer realised that there were times when she needed to use specialised flash, but she had little idea how to do so. So she enrolled in an evening course and learned the techniques. But back to you: in the end it is important to identify those subjects which stand out in your collection. After all, you cannot become a contributing photographer without selecting from your own core collection of supreme images. If your stock is barely adequate, or the subjects are scattered across too many sectors, shoot more pictures to redress the balance.

Does your lifestyle permit the kind of commitment to serious stock photography? It is a valid question which needs to be addressed carefully. If you have a young family, for example, their demands may leave little time for serious freelancing until they are more independent. Do satisfy yourself that you will have adequate time and space to become a dedicated contributor.

Finding the right one for you

Of the thousands of photo libraries operating worldwide, it is impracticable to short-list more than a few. The secret is to identify a selection of libraries that match your main subject interests. Unless you are already a widely recognised photographer, my advice is to avoid the biggest and most famous libraries. Competition within them is fierce. It is far better to join a younger, smaller, more specialised library, where it is easier to develop profitable relationships with the owner/manager. Where do you find a list of libraries? If you have read earlier projects in this book, you will probably have guessed the answer to that question: yes, consult the latest edition of *The Freelance Photographer's Market Handbook* for the latest listings of relevant libraries.

Write to your short listed libraries and request a copy of their Contributor's Notes. Study them carefully and prioritise them. You may need to work down your list as some libraries may not be accepting new contributors. In parallel, study your own picture collection and select at least twice the minimum number of pictures needed for your first submission. Over a period of a few days, look critically at each picture and short list only those pictures that meet the library's brief and are of absolute top quality. Reject any showing signs of unsharpness, lack of colour fidelity, less than perfect exposure, or poor composition. Be ruthless! Squeeze the number down to that needed, but ensure that there is balanced representation of the subjects you shoot.

Now is the time to arrange a visit with the library on top of your list. A face-to-face meeting has so many benefits. If this is impracticable, try to telephone the library to confirm that they would be receptive to

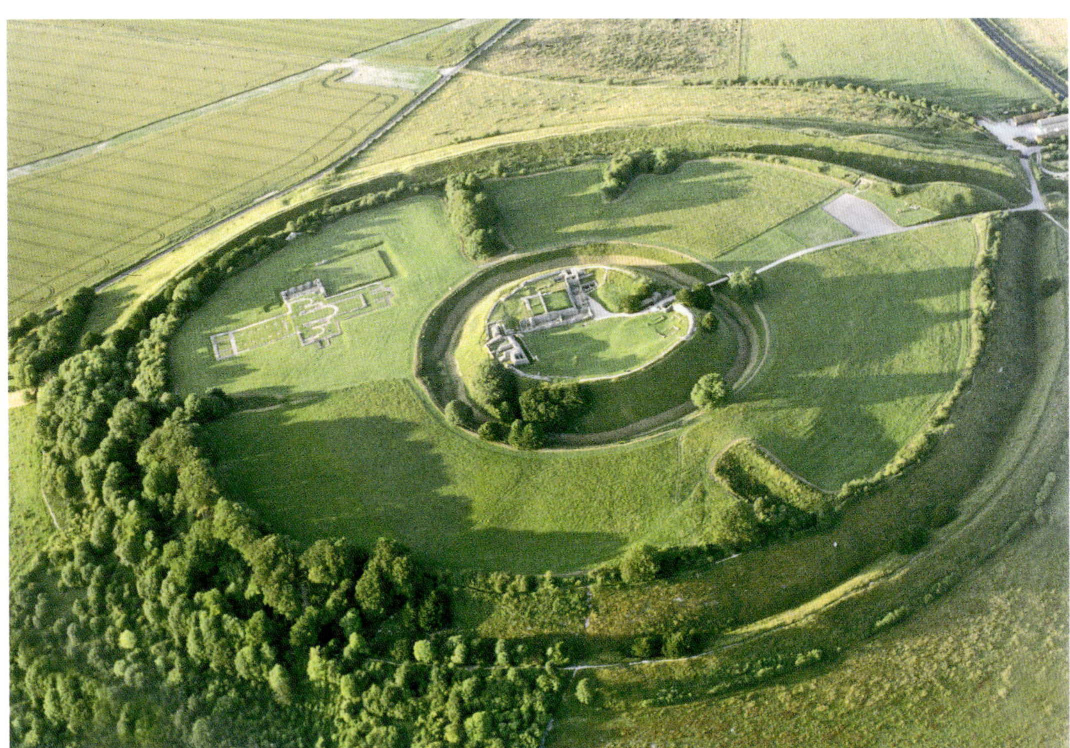

your sending new material. If the library shows interest in your work, they should send you a contract which you must study carefully before signing. Resolve any queries with the library.

Once you have been accepted, set yourself a rolling target to submit an acceptable number of new pictures on a monthly or quarterly basis. Be guided by your library's requirements. Keep records of your submissions, acceptances and sales.

Review your results at least annually, but remember the long lead times. Your first sales receipts may take time.

My final words of encouragement are to persevere and don't become discouraged. Prepare to make changes in your choice of both photographic subjects and library. Perhaps even go it alone. There are possibly many more solo photographer librarians than established businesses.

Good Luck!

Some historical archaeological sites only become apparent when viewed from the air. This shot, of Old Sarum near Salisbury, is a regular library seller

Selling cards & calendars

by DAWN SUMNER

Photographic imagery has become increasingly popular with greetings card and calendar publishers, many of whom are now looking to develop collections of fine art photo-based products. From still life black and white shots to landscapes and colourful floral images, publishers are always looking for creative and innovative imagery to appeal to consumers.

In the UK alone the greetings card industry is worth an estimated £1 billion and the average person buys around 40 cards per year, making it a lucrative market to tap in to.

As a photographer there are two ways to enter the greetings card and calendar market – you can either become a publisher yourself, which requires a lot of investment in both time and money, or you can supply existing publishers with your photography. The latter is the route that most photographers initially take as this helps them to understand the demands of the market without making a heavy investment.

Market research

Whether you choose to become a publisher or simply supply pictures you should, as always, first research the market. Visit newsagents, card shops and gift shops and browse through the stock available to get an insight into the types of imagery publishers are reproducing on current cards and calendars.

Trends in image buying do come and go, with square format designs fashionable one year and more traditional the next, so it is always worth shooting a subject from several angles to give publishers the option to crop an image.

The major trade fairs such as the Autumn and Spring Fairs at the NEC in Birmingham offer another good way to research the market. Many of the UK's leading card and calendar publishers launch their new ranges at these fairs and it is an excellent opportunity to talk to them about the types of imagery they are looking for. While most of the exhibitors will not have time to look at a portfolio most will happily take a business card from you. It is also worth taking along samples of your

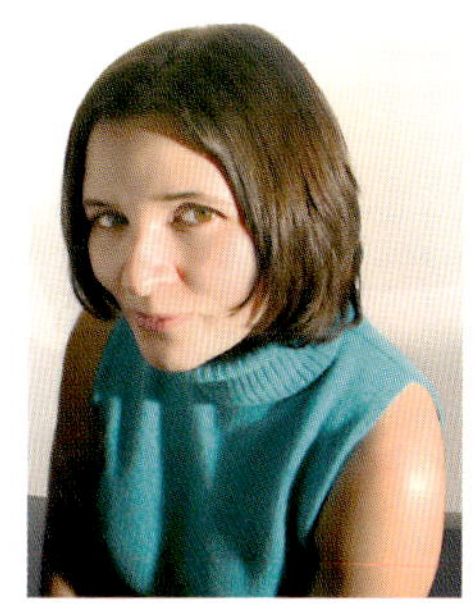

Dawn Sumner is a former features editor of the *British Journal of Photography* who currently works as a freelance writer for a number of photographic publications. She has over 14 years experience as a photographer and currently supplies stock images to two picture libraries, Alamy and RedCover. Examples of her work can be found at www.dawnsumner.co.uk

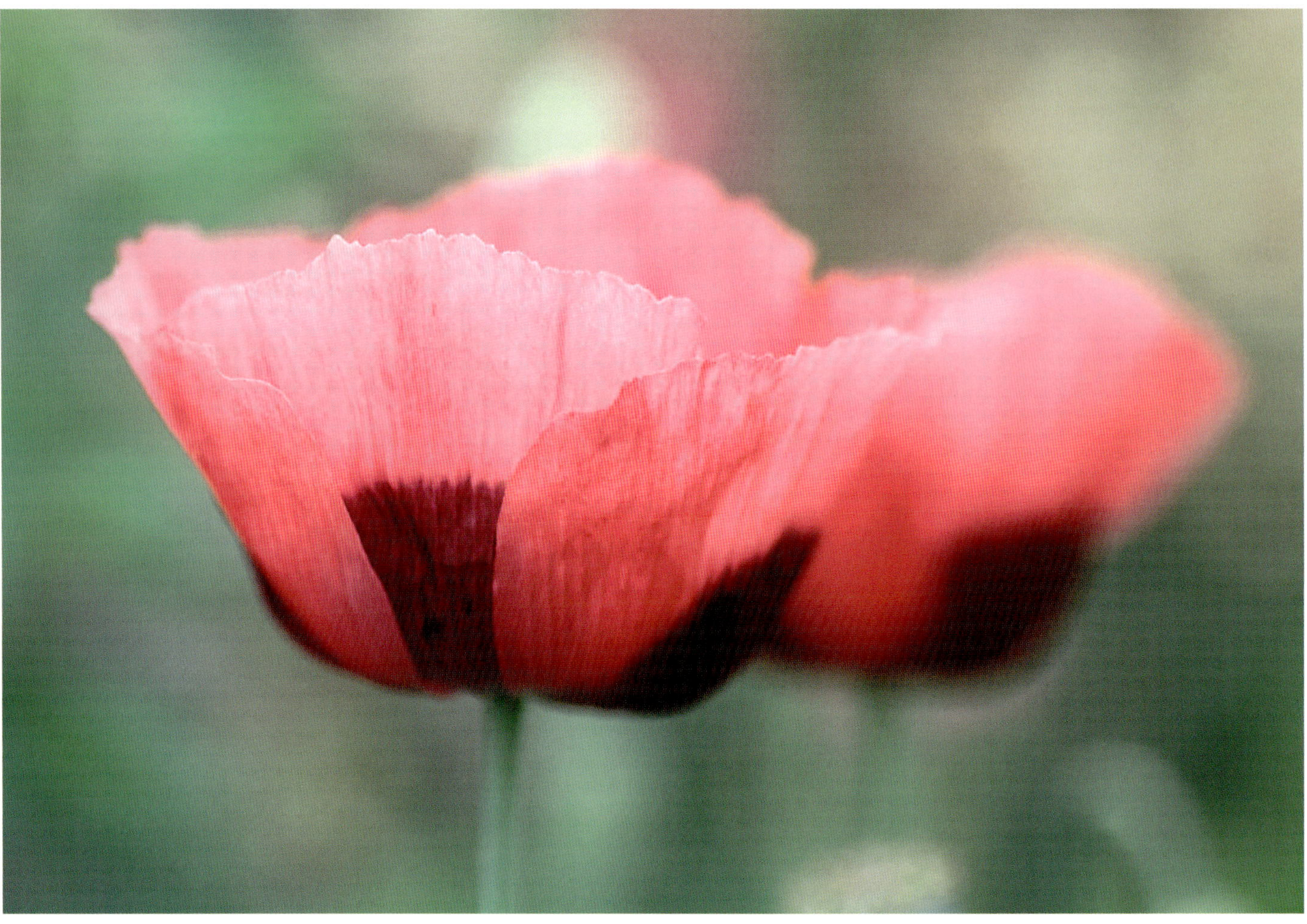

work in the form of a brochure or a CD.

Most publishers accept both 35mm and medium format transparencies and an increasing number will also consider digital images. In particular, the 6x6cm dimensions of medium format transparencies remains a popular choice for calendar publishers, as it allows them to maximise on the image without the need to crop, when producing a square format calendar.

Demand for subjects varies considerably, with some publishers specialising in particular themes such as landscapes, flowers or classic cars. As a photographer, if you become renowned for a particular subject matter, then publishers will come back to you year after year for new images. Therefore it is important to be consistent in the work that you produce.

Approaching a publisher

Publishers work up to six months in advance on card designs and up to 12 months ahead for calendars, so it is important to submit work at the right time of the year when image buyers will be actively sourcing new artwork.

Calendars are made available to retailers from around Easter; therefore artwork (ie images) will be sourced some six months prior to this.

Greetings card publishers tend to launch spring collections during June and July, so it is a good idea to contact them during the winter months when they will be looking for images for the following year's collection.

Pink Oriental Poppy: floral subjects are always popular with greetings card publishers

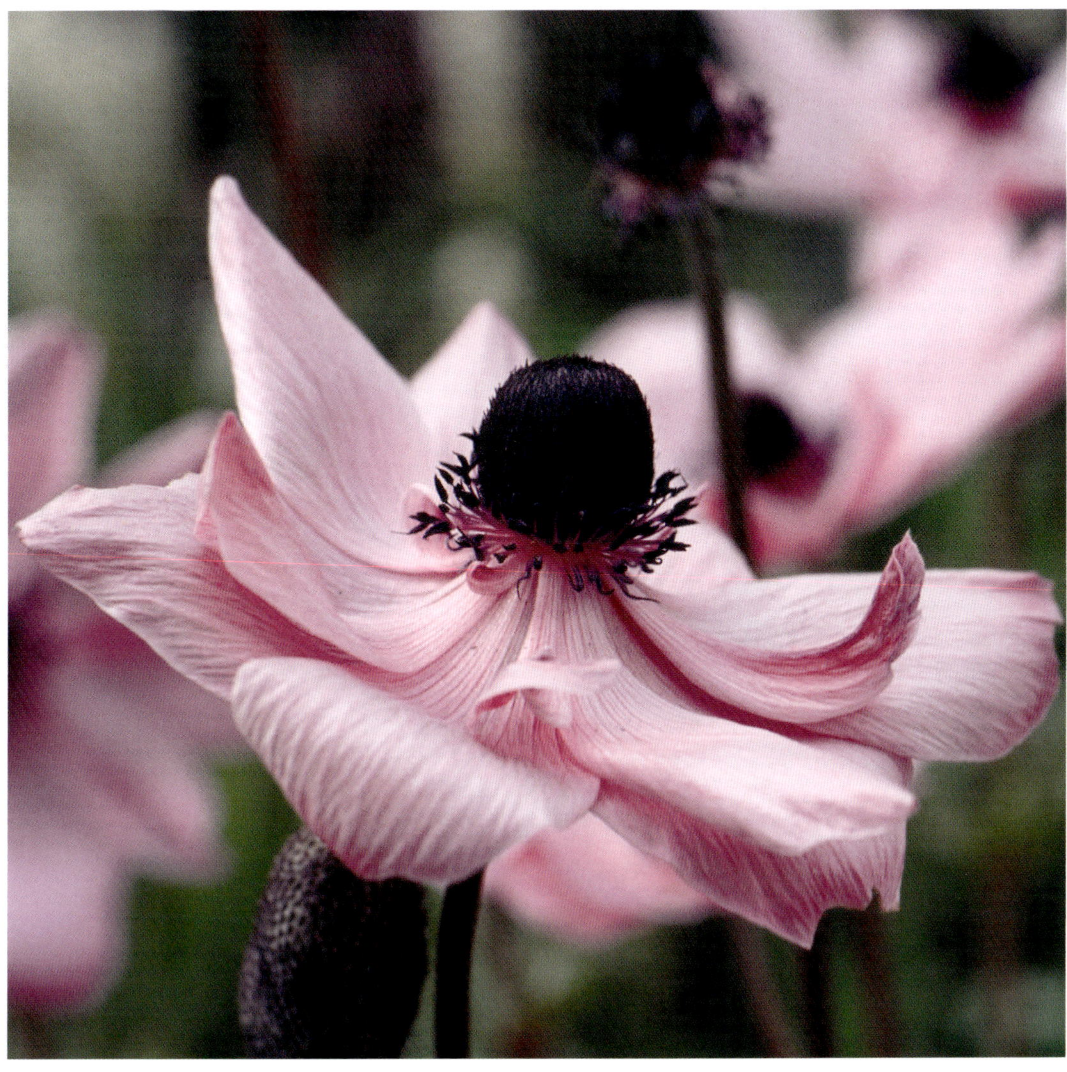

Anemone: this image has sold to a greetings card publisher

While there are hundreds of card and calendar publishers in the UK not all of them buy in photography. Some of the smaller companies are run by photographers and illustrators selling their own work, while a lot of other companies just don't use photography at all. So first you need to know if your chosen publisher is open to freelance work or not.

Initially it is a good idea to make contact by telephone or e-mail to enquire as to whether or not they would be interested in seeing a sample of your work. Most publishers will ask for examples to be submitted on a CD, and only if the work is chosen for publication will they ask to see a high-resolution digital file or an original transparency.

While some publishers will respond to your submission quite quickly, others can take up to two months to respond depending on how frequently they review submissions.

If a publisher decides that they want to use your photography they will either ask to buy the publishing rights for a flat fee or they will offer you a contract. Avoid handing over all rights to your work at all cost, as this will mean that you will no longer be able to exploit the image in the future. By entering into a contract instead you can licence the publisher to reproduce the

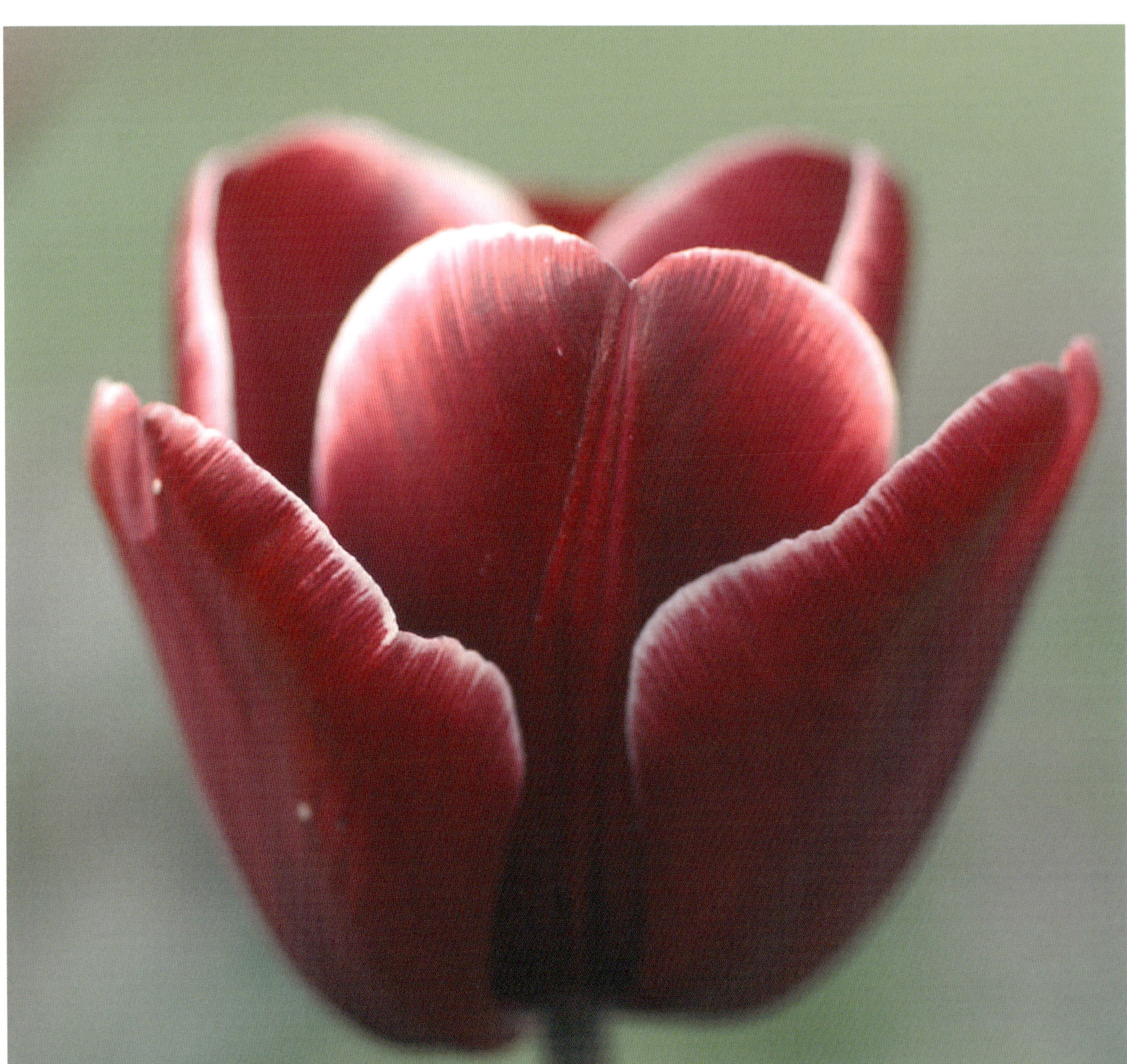

image under terms that you agree to.

The licence will set out rights of usage (eg calendars, greetings cards and gift wrap), territory of usage, terms of payment, and the number of years the licence has been granted for. Most calendar publishers only want a licence for the life of the calendar, so that after that time the photographer is free to try and sell the image to another publisher.

Usually a licence is sold for a specified fee, but under some contracts you may receive royalties every time a card or calendar is sold.

Tulip: another image that has been used for a greetings card

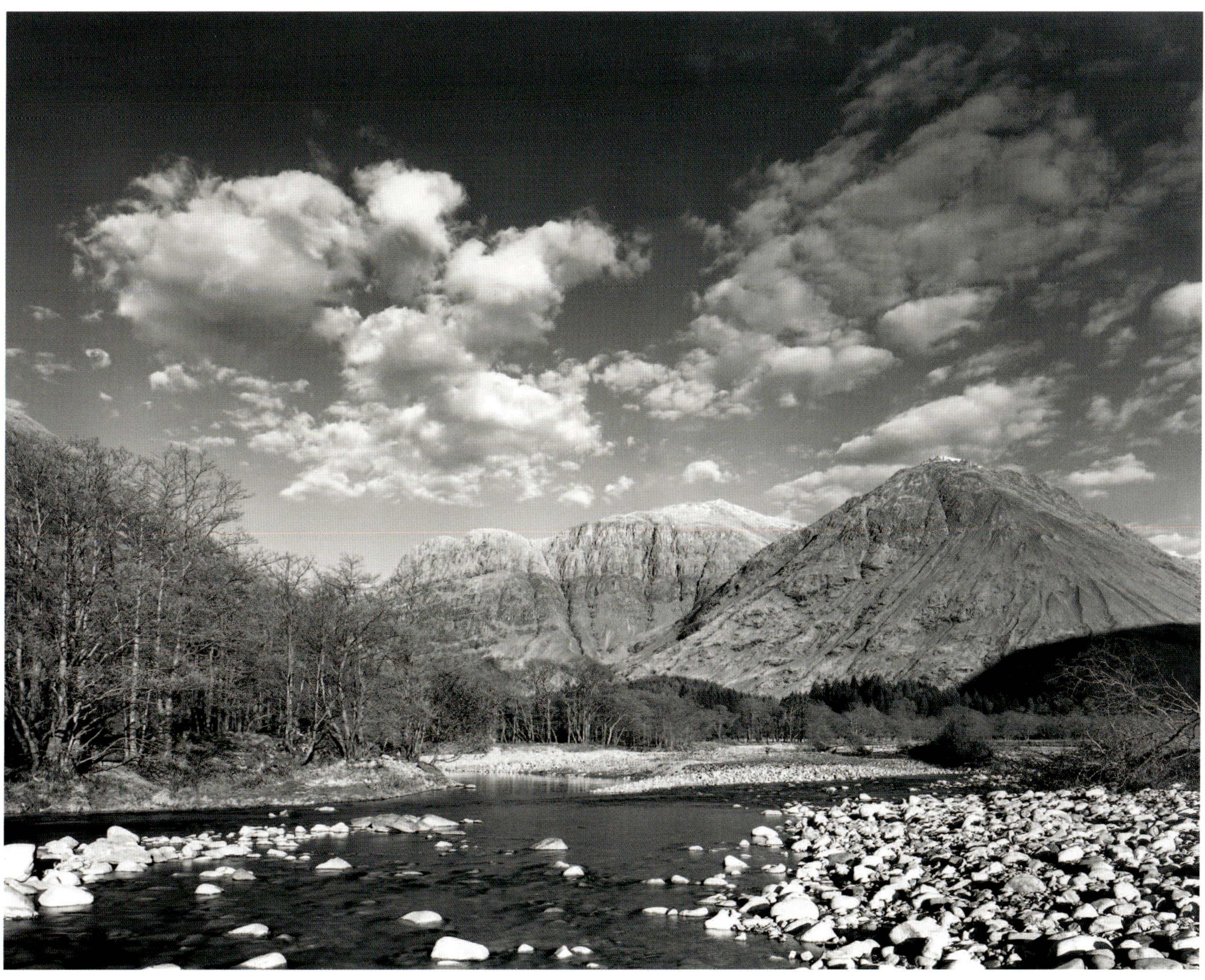

Self-publishing

A large number of established photographers have started to self-publish their work as greetings cards, postcards and calendars. Advances in digital printing techniques and the development of easy to use publishing software mean that photographers can have greater control over the design and printing processes.

If following this path it is advisable to mock-up the designs in a collection and show them to several retailers to get some feedback on which styles they think will be the most popular. Out of a collection of 12 designs, a retailer might only be prepared to buy a small quantity of around five in each design until they are comfortable that the collection will sell well.

Some retailers prefer to buy direct from publishers while others buy stock via an agent, so you may need to consider the benefits of using an agent to promote your own range of cards and calendars to shops.

They often deal with more than one publisher at a time and tend to work with publishers who can guarantee them a frequent supply of new ranges so that they

Craig McMaster, who took this shot and those on the following pages, specialises in photographing the landscape of his native Scotland. He self-publishes calendars and posters of his work

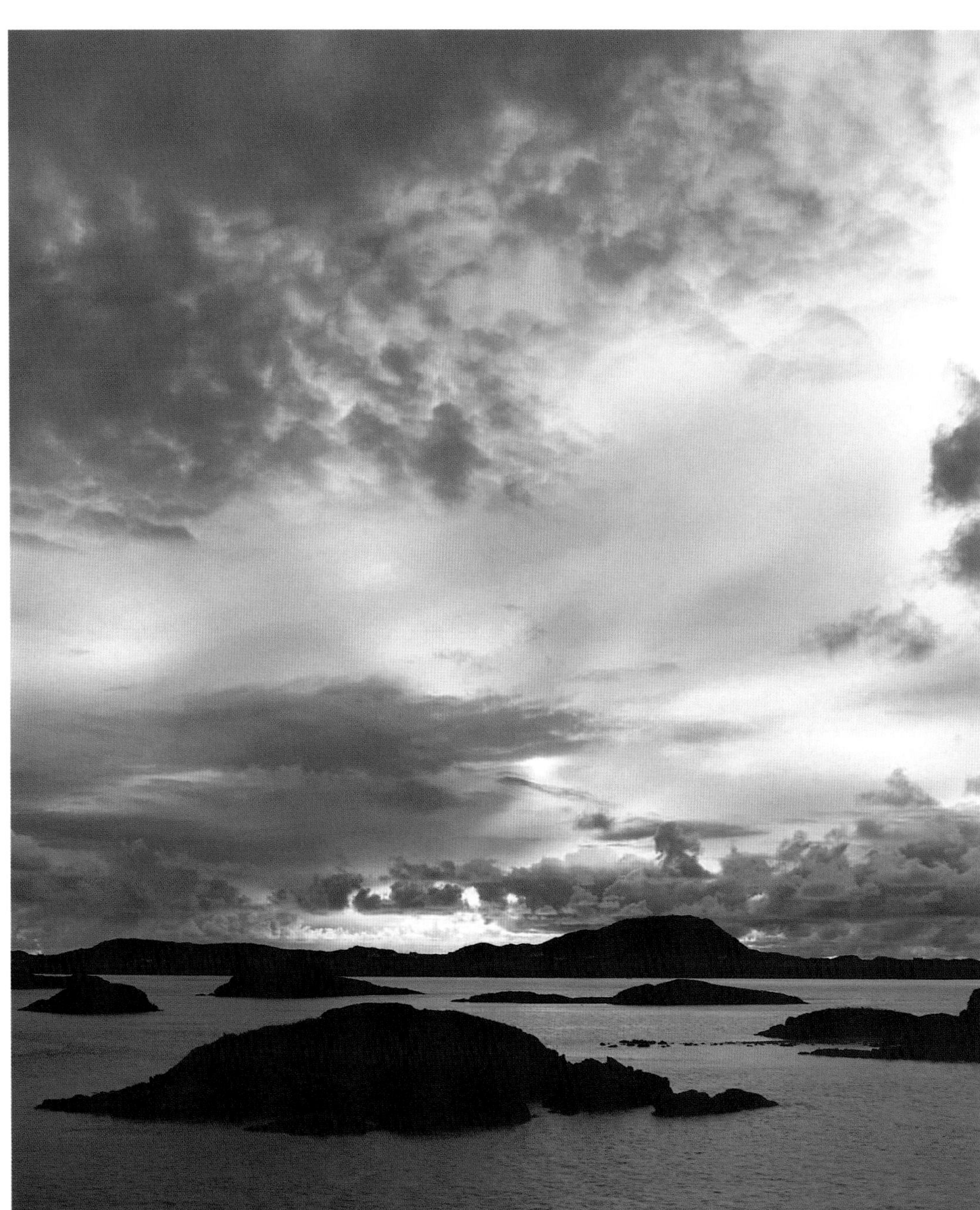

Another of Craig McMaster's superb black and white images

can continually offer retailers new stock.

Although employing an agent has its advantages they will expect to receive a commission of around 15%. Do not enter in to a lengthy agreement from the outset; any reliable agent will be prepared to draw up a contract for a six-month probationary period. After this time if you are satisfied that the agent has met their sales targets you can negotiate a mutually agreeable long-term contract.

The printing process

Once you have decided on your designs you should then get several quotes from printers for your chosen formats.

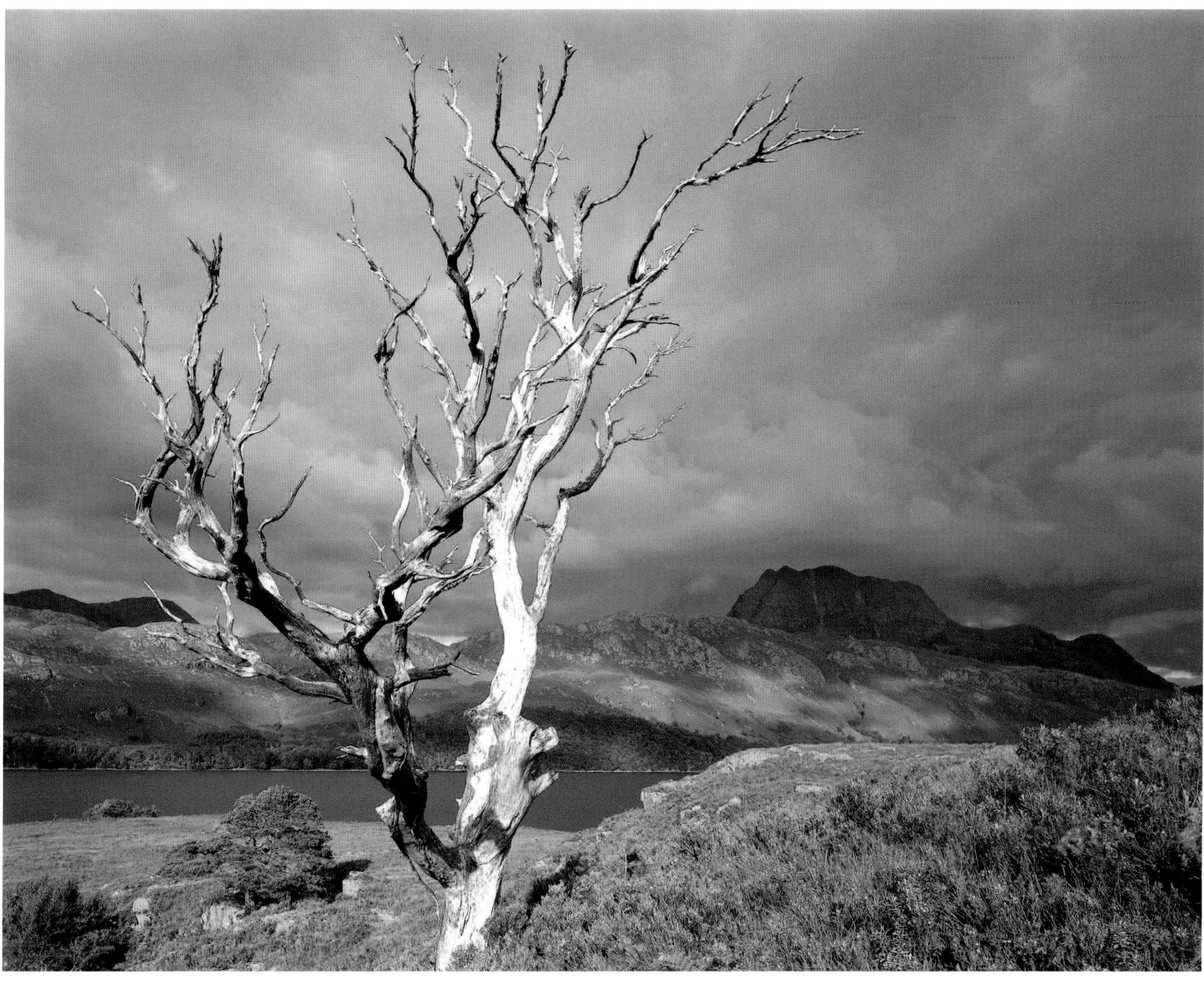

Some of the larger printing companies will offer around 10 greetings card sizes to choose from with 6x4in and 7x5in proving to be the most popular. While a small trial print run of greetings cards will allow you to test the market for each card in the range, unit costs will naturally be much higher for a print run of around 500 compared to that of 4000.

With calendars the type of design you choose will depend on your market. Desk calendars are popular with the corporate market while wall calendars, with room to write appointments and birthdays, appeal to the domestic market.

For a calendar publisher the minimum print run is typically 10,000 to make a reasonable return on investment. But the quantity you decide to print will depend on how many outlets are prepared to take the calendar. If the subject is regional images of familiar sites on the tourist trail for example, these are likely to sell well in tourist information centres, book and gift shops.

The type of print process you choose will largely depend on your budget and the quality you want to achieve. Lithography, which relies on a four-colour process, uses cyan, magenta, yellow and black (CMYK) to reproduce the colour in the image. This tends to be the most popular printing choice for large print runs.

Digital printing is ideal for short print runs of between 500 and 1000, but it does work out to be more expensive per unit in comparison to lithography.

Whichever approach to printing you take you should research the process carefully, because photographs can often reproduce differently in print. Always ask to see a proof before going ahead with a print run.

The financial investment

One of the main reasons why new publishers fail in the greetings card industry is their lack of experience at costing production correctly. It is all too easy to be lulled into a false sense of security when you see how low the unit cost is with the lithographic process. But dividing the number of cards by the printing cost will not give you an accurate cost price. The reality is that you might only sell a third of the batch at full price, so your true unit cost will be based on how many you can realistically sell. You should also factor in the cost of marketing and maintaining stock.

Remember that the retailer will probably be looking to make a 100% mark-up, so you need to produce cards at a cost price that ensures both you and the retailer make a decent profit.

Although the card and calendar market is a competitive industry that initially requires a large financial investment, if you get the formula right there is a healthy profit to be made.

The Greeting Card Association in the UK is the ideal starting point for any photographer looking to either publish or supply images. The association's website holds details of publishers, printers and agents and its industry magazine *Progressive Greetings Worldwide* details the latest news on publishers and showcases new artistic talent.

No freelance photographer can make a living solely from selling images to the card and calendar market but the sales and royalties can be a useful additional stream of revenue.

The opportunity to publish work in this way should also be seen as an opportunity to draw attention to your wider skills as a photographer. By simply adding your website details to the finished product you will be able to direct the buyer to further work and they will then be able to make additional purchases or perhaps even enquire about commissions.

Selling stock with articles

by SIMON WHALEY

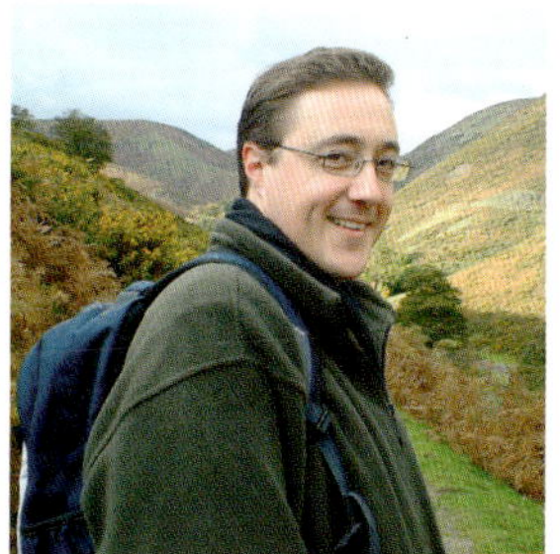

Simon Whaley is a full-time writer/photographer whose words and pictures have appeared in a variety of national magazines including *The Lady, Country Quest, Dogs Monthly, Trail, Walking Wales, In Britain, Garden Ideas, Water Gardener* and *Holiday Cottages.* He is also a regular contributor to *Country Walking* and *Country & Border Life* magazines, as well as being the author of the best-selling books *100 Ways For A Dog To Train Its Human* and *100 Muddy Paws For Thought.*

Someone who can give me a complete words and picture package is my dream supplier," an editor recently told me. "Trying to find the right pictures to illustrate a writer's words takes time, and if I have to arrange for a writer and a photographer to meet up to do a feature, the opportunity for errors is unbelievable. The person who can supply both the words and the pictures saves me a lot of time and hassle."

Ideally every picture you take should be for a specific market, but in reality few photographers sell every picture they take. Rejection often has nothing to do with the quality of the picture, so over time you can amass your very own photographic library. This may also include pictures you've sold for single-use reproduction, which are now available again. And we've all got plenty of those perfectly good shots that just don't seem to meet the requirements of a picture library.

But there is a way of getting some of these more ordinary stock shots into print. It's time to start writing articles.

When an editor is faced with a gap to fill and has two articles that could plug that gap, nine times out of ten it is the person who supplied the complete words and picture package that will be used. And it's possible to produce a highly illustrative package with relatively few words, giving you the opportunity to sell some of those shots that you thought may never see the light of day.

Finding the ideas

The way to sell these photographs to magazines is to use them to illustrate specific points in an article that you write. For example, I've written for several walking magazines and always supply photographs to accompany those articles. Over time, I've collected numerous shots of different waymarks and signposts. As a collection of pictures they are not particularly exciting, but the signs all differ slightly. Some are interesting logos, some blue arrows, others yellow, or wooden. A little research helped to identify that there is actually a system for these waymarks.

So I approached the editor of a walk-

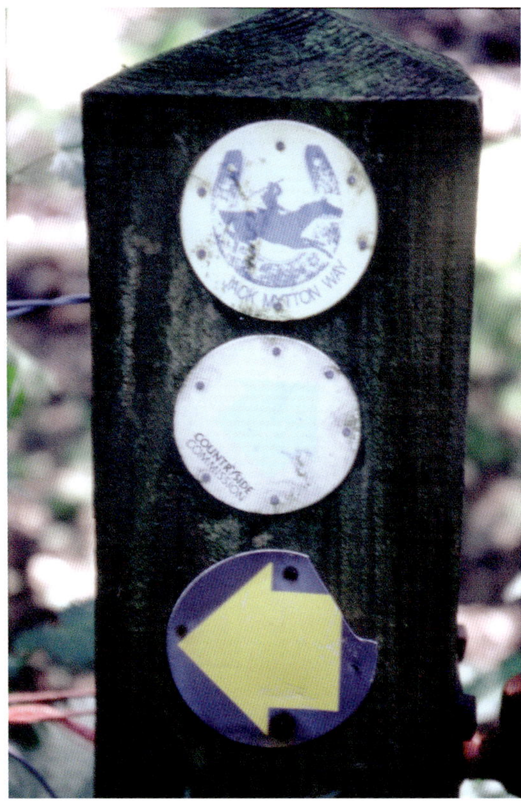

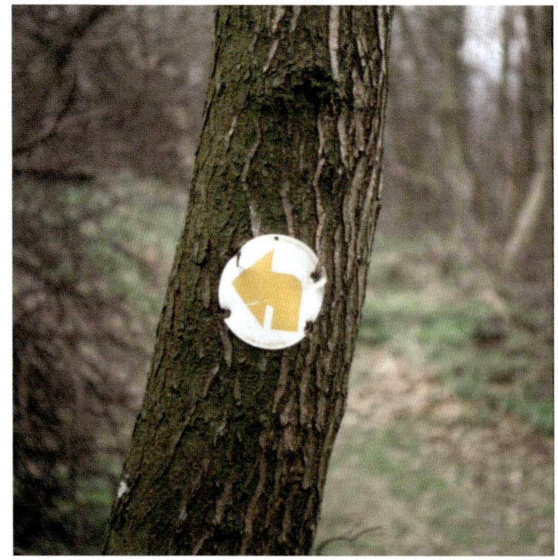

The author has photographed many waymarks like these over the years. On their own they were not good sellers, so he wrote an article on the waymarking system and submitted it with the pictures to a walking magazine. It was published

ing magazine to see if he was interested in an article about the waymarking system. He asked to see the complete package, so I wrote the words and submitted them with the photographs. A few days later he replied accepting the article and subsequently used all the images. Had I not written the article, the editor would not have found a need for those pictures. Those particular words helped to sell those particular photographs.

Like many dog owners, I have several pictures of my dog in typical family dog situations. I selected about 20 of these images, including one of my dog tucked up in my bed, and another of her toys pegged out on the washing line to dry.

With each image in mind, I wrote a short, tongue-in-cheek 700-word article entitled "Twenty Ways To Be The Perfect Dog Owner". Each image illustrated one point. Thus the photographs were helping me to produce the words

that I needed to write.

So take time to sit down and go through your own library. What have you got pictures of? Can you link or theme any of them?

I had several shots of large gardens that are open to the public. I saw that I could write an article about using the ideas found in the gardens of stately homes and transferring them into a home garden on a smaller scale. Picking a specific feature from each photograph, I wrote a brief paragraph explaining how the same idea could be utilised on a smaller scale. It was up to the editor to decide how many of the pictures to use if he liked the article, but the more you tie your article to the pictures, the more likely it is that the editor will use them.

You may see the exercise as writing to sell your pictures; the editor, however, will see the pictures as specific shots for the article.

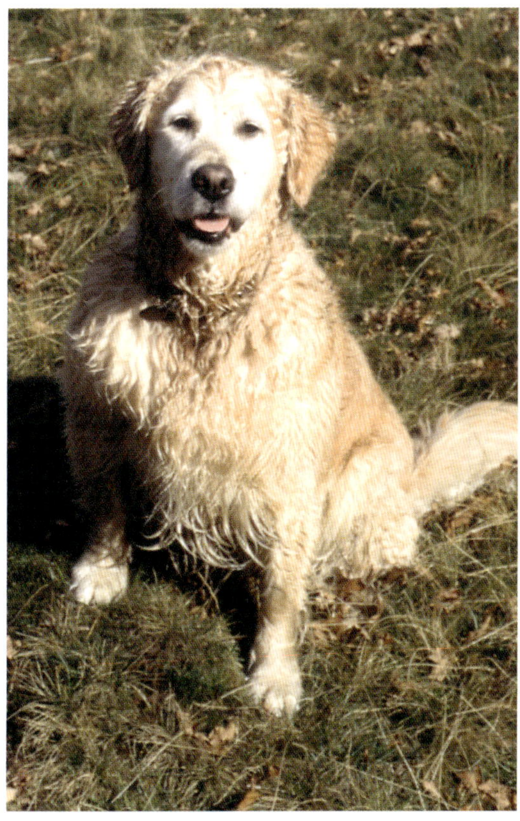

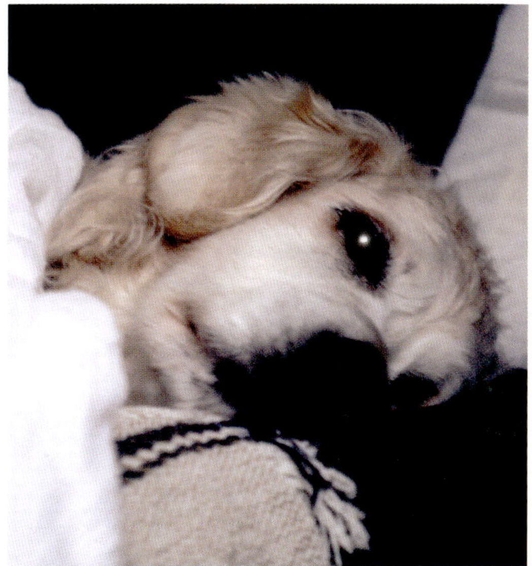

These pictures of Bella, the family pet, illustrated a humorous article by the author called, "Twenty Ways to be the Perfect Dog Owner"

Analysing the market

In the same way that you would analyse a magazine's pictures if you were just going to submit a selection of images, you need to do the same for the words if you are to write articles. Visit a large newsagent and pick up copies of magazines that deal with the subject matter your photographic stock could help illustrate.

Look at the magazine's contents page and identify any named staff writers, then go through the magazine searching for articles that they've written. The fewer staff-written pieces there are, the better the chance for freelance articles.

Study several issues to spot any trends. An article may look as though a freelance writer produced it, but it could be a freelance who writes regularly for the magazine. These freelances are almost like staff so the editor may give priority to their work. Your task is to try to identify the one-off articles.

Now calculate the average article length. Count how many words there are on ten lines, then divide this total by ten to obtain the average number of words per line. Count the number of lines in the article, and then multiply this by the average number of words per line. If all the features are about 1,000 words in length, writing a 2,000-word feature is a waste of your time and the editor's. If it's too long, the editor won't even read it. Your work has to fit the editor's requirements.

Take time to analyse the language used. Are the sentences long or short? How long are the words? Are they mostly two and three syllables or do they include complex terminology? Your contribution needs to be pitched at the same level.

Look at the magazine's adverts to get to know its average reader. The chances of your scuba diving article being of interest to readers of a magazine full of adverts for

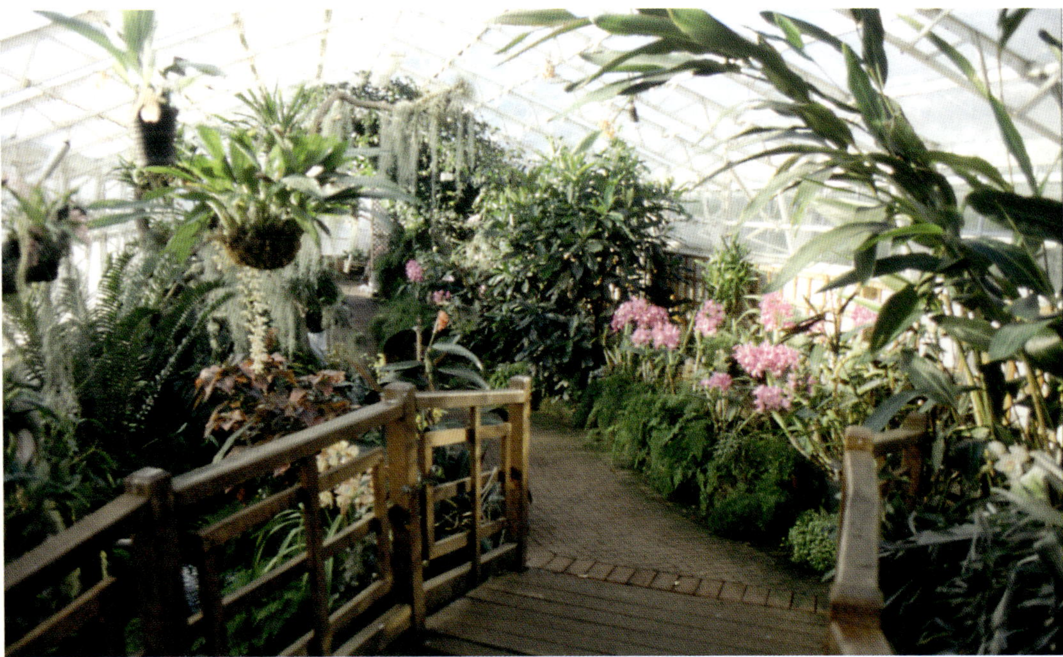

stairlifts, motorised scooters and walk-in baths are quite low.

Ask yourself what sort of readership the advertisers are aiming at. Are they mainly male or female? How old are they? Is money tight or can they afford to splash out?

A good way to confirm your analysis is to contact the magazine's advertisement department and ask for information about their advertising rates. Most will send a "media pack", which details these costs and gives a breakdown of the average reader's age, marital status, financial status and other interests. Don't use this as your only method of research though. You still need to read copies of the magazine to fully understand its aim.

Having studied a couple of issues of a magazine, you'll now have a better understanding of the types of article that they use and how long they like them to be. Also whether they include things like fact boxes or sidebars. These are the separate pieces of information used to supplement an article, such as the opening times and admis-sion prices of a tourist attraction, or the website addresses, telephone numbers or books that readers can look for to find out further information.

Writing and presenting a feature

The opening of your feature is the most important part. This is what will attract the editor to read on, and ultimately their readers too. A startling statement or quote is often a good way – look back at how this chapter started.

Use the first paragraph to indicate to the reader what the feature will be about and then use each subsequent paragraph to make a specific point. In my garden ideas feature, each paragraph dealt with one idea, each with its own photo for illustration. Your final paragraph should draw a conclusion to the article as a whole.

When you've completed your article don't send it off yet. Put it away for a couple of days and move onto your next idea. Returning to an article a few days later, it's

Orchid Greenhouse, Wisley, Surrey: this shot was used to illustrate an article about how the ideas to be found in gardens open to the public can be adapted to the home garden

amazing the number of improvements that can be made. Read it out loud, changing words that you stumble over, to ensure that they flow better.

Revision is an important process in writing. If an editor isn't interested in your words, then they won't be interested in your pictures.

Lay out your article professionally. Your work should be printed out in a simple font like Arial or Times New Roman. Fancy fonts don't improve the quality of your writing, but can infuriate an editor if they have to keep squinting to work out what the words are. Always double-space your work. Leave good margins – at least an inch – at the top and the bottom of the page, and the same amount on the right and left. In the header insert a page number and the title.

Give your article a front page, stating its title, your name, address and a telephone number or e-mail contact. You must also state a word count, but don't use the specific figure that your computer provides. Round to the nearest fifty. So a 1,022-word article would be stated as 1,000 words, whilst 1,028 would be stated as 1,050.

It is also important to state which rights you are offering. Usually this is First British Serial Rights (abbreviated to FBSR). This means that you are offering the publication the first right to publish it in the United Kingdom. Once it has been published you could offer Second British Serial Rights, although in practice if it's already been published in the UK then other magazines won't be interested. But it doesn't stop you offering First North American Serial Rights to an American magazine, because it's a different market.

Always enclose a stamped addressed envelope with your submission, with sufficient postage to cover the return weight of what you are sending. But don't submit your photographs with your article. Instead, enclose a selection of small prints or low-resolution digital images and clarify in a short covering letter which format the images are available in.

Only when the editor requests to see the original images should you submit them. Then supply them in the format and method the editor asks for. If they request digital images on a CD/DVD, don't even think about e-mailing them.

Record keeping

Keep a record of what you have submitted and to whom. As soon as you've posted it off, go back to working on your next idea. Don't sit and wait. You could wait for weeks, or months.

If your article is rejected don't panic. The editor hasn't rejected you personally. There are thousands of reasons why submissions are rejected.

The magazine may have already accepted a similar piece. This is common with seasonal subjects, so you need to be thinking about six months in advance of publication. Some Christmas issues are finalised in June!

Alternatively your work may not have been quite right for the magazine. That doesn't mean to say that it wouldn't suit a different magazine. Look around and amend your article to fit the style of another publication.

With some careful thought, it's possible to substantially improve your chances of selling your photographs by writing articles to go with them. Become that dream supplier of the complete words and picture package, and you too could see your stock photography being used time and time again.

Mounting an exhibition

by MALCOLM MacGREGOR

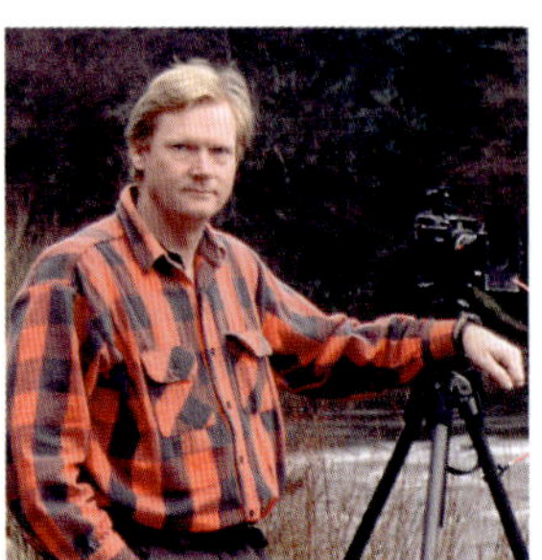

Exhibiting photographs is one of the most rewarding experiences in a photographer's career. Selling them at the same time is the icing on the cake.

There's an enormous satisfaction in showing and marketing your work. It's an opportunity to promote yourself and a good way to break into magazine and poster markets and book publishing. Mounting a show may even be the first time you look seriously at your work.

Of course there are risks. Is the venue right? What about costs? What do you do if nothing sells? The whole thing can seem daunting, but problems can be minimised through careful planning.

The planning

Planning an exhibition can take six months and much thought. For example, are you going to put on a solo show? It might be easier and more cost effective to team up with others who also have work to display – but make sure you like them and what they do.

Is the exhibition about self-promotion? Is it to make money or to break into or cre-ate a market? Is it to get commissions? It could be a combination, but make sure that everyone involved understands the aim. They will then feel part of the whole thing.

Then there's the venue. Unless you are very lucky you probably won't get into a gallery for a first-time show, so be prepared to start small and cosy. This is good, as it will build up confidence and let you make early mistakes without the whole world watching.

Look at a restaurant, hotel, coffee shop, library or business location. The important thing is that it's accessible, has space for photographs and people, and is aesthetic-ally pleasing. It also helps if the owner of the venue likes what you're doing.

Be clear as to the number of photo-graphs you can fit on the walls. And look at the lighting – this will probably need close attention in any location other than a gallery.

Now find a small team of helpers. It may be just your other half, or it could be the whole family. Do not attempt to do everything – pictures, opening night, food, drink, sales – on your own. It may be that the venue will allow its own staff to help out

Malcolm MacGregor is a landscape photographer who specialises in photographing the more remote regions of the world. He has held three exhibitions in London and two in Muscat, Oman. His first exhibition in the Troubadour Café in London was reviewed by the *British Journal of Photography* as having "succeeded in relating the raw energy of Scotland". His first exhibition in Muscat at Bait Muzna Gallery was reviewed in the *Oman Daily Observer* and *Middle East Photography Magazine*. He has sold over 100 photographs through his exhibitions. He has been featured in various photography magazines and has written and photographed his own book, *Wilderness Oman*. He is a Fellow of the Royal Photographic Society and the Royal Geographical Society.

WILDERNESS OMAN

An exhibition of landscape photographs from the Sultanate of Oman

by Malcolm MacGregor

PRIVATE VIEW

The Troubadour Art Gallery, 267 Old Brompton Road, London SW5

Tuesday 9th July 2002   7.30 - 9.30 p.m

Thursday 11th July 2002   6.00 - 8.00 p.m

Exhibition continues until 16th July 2002
12.00 - 3.00 p.m and 6.00 - 9.00 p.m

Ar Rub' al Khali, Oman © Malcolm MacGregor
Tel: 07867 970180 EMAIL Malcolm_Macgregor@btinternet.com

WESTSIDE 020 7434 0235

---

on the opening night, but this needs to be confirmed.

Next you have to decide the theme. Successful photographers generally carve out a niche for themselves – mine is the world of landscapes, yours may be people pictures. Remember that it helps the marketing if you have a theme rather than a selection of pretty pictures. Subjects that sell well are landscapes, flowers and photographs with "mood" or a distinctive style. The examples shown in this project have all sold well.

Confirm dates, timings and exhibition duration. For a private viewing the best days are Tuesday, Wednesday or Thursday. And so to the money. Check costs and be clear about who pays for what, as nothing sours relations more than squabbles over money. Similarly there's the question of who gets what from a sale. A gallery can take up to 50 per cent – other places should allow the photographer to keep most of the profit.

The marketing

You need to invest a certain sum to get yourself on the exhibition "ladder", but you also hope that sales will at least cover costs, so think carefully about who is likely to buy. Friends and family may well do so out of loyalty and others could follow. The important thing is to get the right people – and enough of them – into the room.

You will have your own guests, but to reach a wider audience try to get some press coverage. Write a press release, stating briefly who you are, what your pictures show and where and when the event is taking place. Next ring your local newspapers (it's unlikely you'll get coverage in a national, but if the event is controversial, you may just!) and ask who the information should be sent to. Attach a photo of your work and possibly a picture of yourself.

Remember you are selling yourself, the photographer, as much as the pictures, so if there's an interesting tale to tell, say so. You

An invitation card to one of the author's exhibitions. An A6 size card, printed with a photograph on the reverse

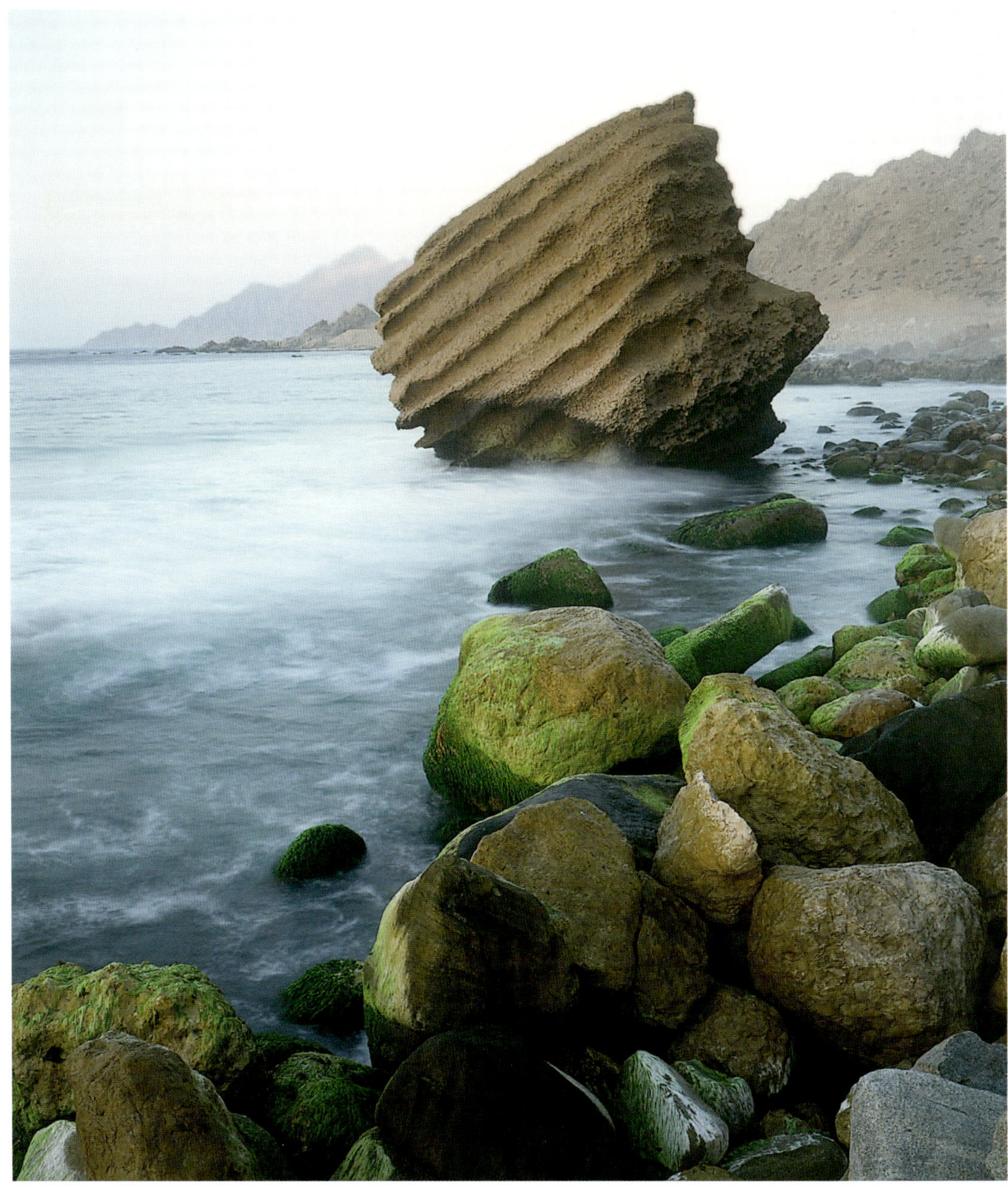

*Coast near Hadbin, Oman.
One of the pictures used
in the author's Wilderness
Oman exhibition*

may have been a coal miner who's branched out into photography. That's a good story, and even if they only come to see if your nails are filled with coal dust, at least you get them there.

Send details of the event to local radio stations and even the regional TV network – on a quiet news day they may just come. Look at other ways of getting free publicity, on websites and in giveaways, in "what's on" columns and in council events brochures. But remember you may have to contact them several months before the exhibition date as they always print in advance. Try to get publicity in photographic and trade magazines.

If the theme happens to be from a foreign country, contact the relevant embassy as they might help with promotion. Can you get a company with business interests over there to sponsor the exhibition, or will someone nearer to

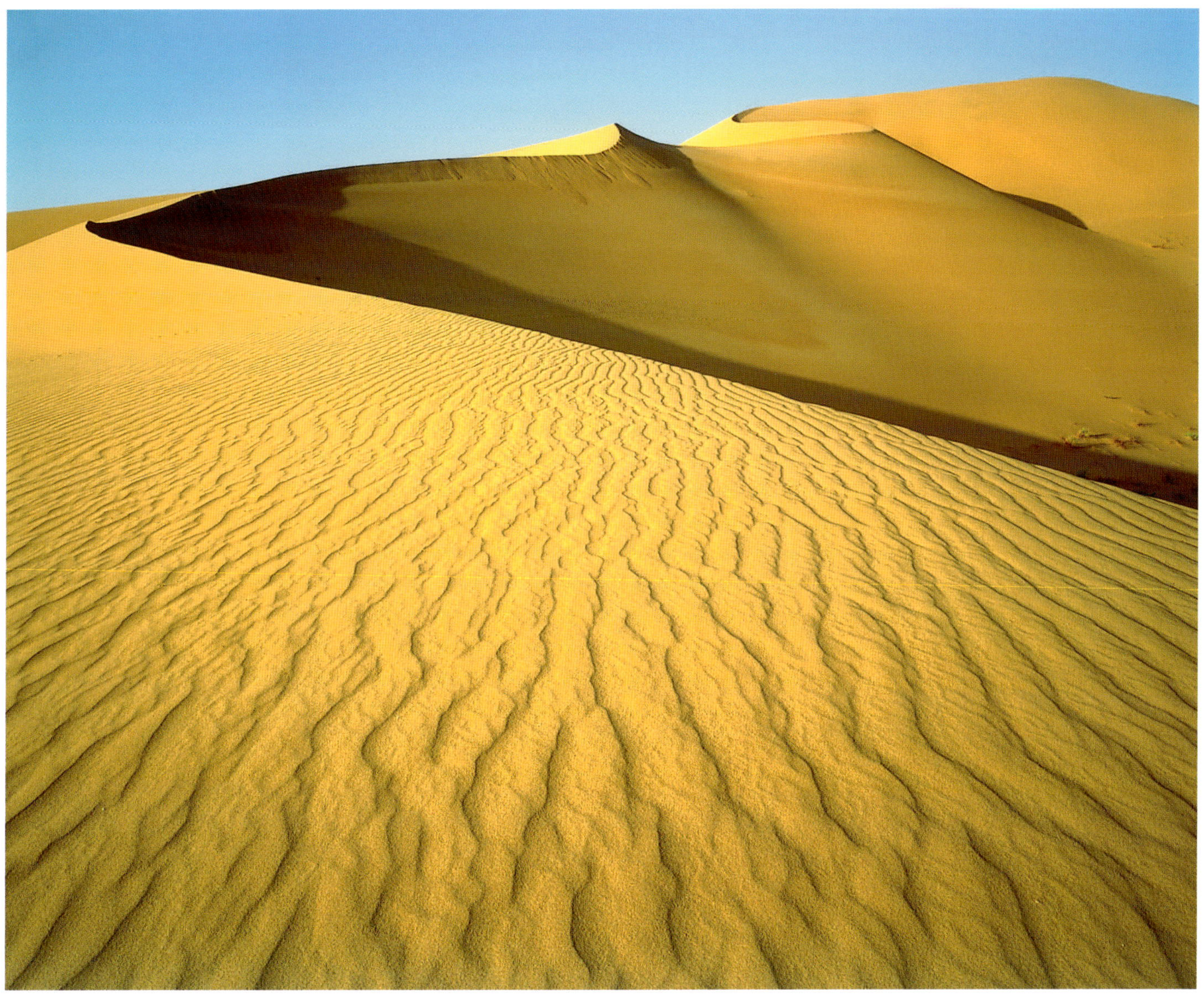

Dunes of the Empty Quarter, Oman

home put their name to the event?

Start with a bang and ask your guests to a private viewing. Evenings are better as most people can get there. A small party means you can schmooze those who've helped you and those that might, so have an invitation that sets the tone.

An A6 postcard-size card fits the bill (see the one I used for my exhibition "Wilderness Oman"). On one side is a photograph. On the other are details of the event. Design and wording are important, as is spelling, a telephone number, website and e-mail address. Include personal con-tact details and a contact for the venue.

Send these out in plenty of time because people's diaries are often full a month before.

The pictures

This is the crux of the exhibition. This is you making a critical selection from your work. It's about choosing your best and showing off your photographic flair.

This is what people have come to see, so it's worth visiting a number of other exhibi-

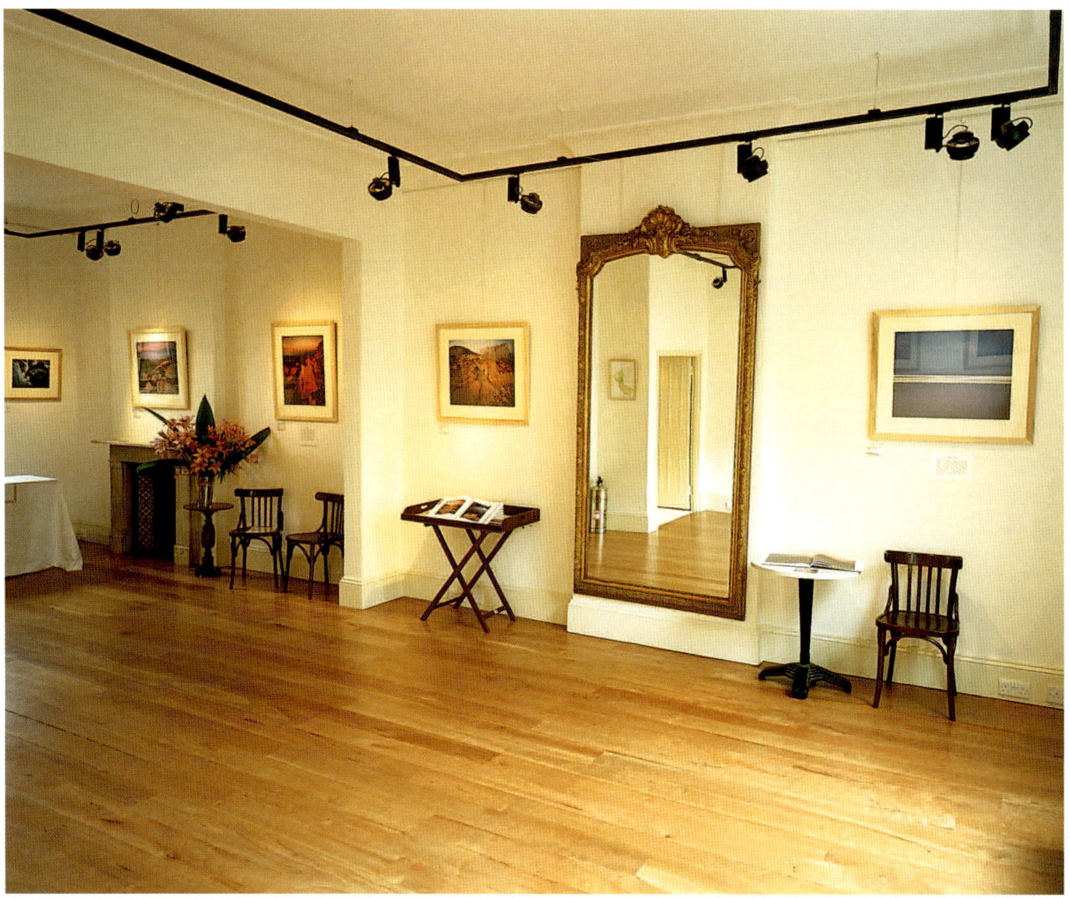

The Troubadour Gallery in London, where the author held his "Wilderness Oman" exhibition

tions to see what they sell and what looks good. The pictures must hang well together; there must be a consistency, from the size of the prints, to the mount-boards, frames and captioning.

There must be variety too, but if it's too cluttered people get confused and some photographs may be overshadowed by others. Make a plan for where the pictures will go. You can always adjust once you start hanging.

Be wary of exotic frames unless it really suits a particular photograph. The right frame should add to the picture and not overwhelm it. I use two sizes of prints only: 16x12in and 24x20in. This gives a choice of large or small. All photographs must be flawless and there must be no marks on frames. Make sure the wall colour doesn't clash with the frames or mounts.

Limiting the edition of a particular photograph is a good marketing tool. It makes each print special and adds to the rarity value. Anything up to 50 prints per photograph is the norm.

I like a limited edition of nine prints for each photograph and one artist's proof (for my personal use), rather like sculptors do with their work. Each limited edition print is then labelled 1/9, 2/9 and so on. But there's nothing to prevent you running another edition of the same picture in a different format.

Each should be signed and captioned with a soft lead pencil, either on the mount-board or on the back of the picture. Make sure the signature is legible because you never know who will see it once it's sold. Write a short caption (about 15 words) for each photograph, e.g. "Dunes of the

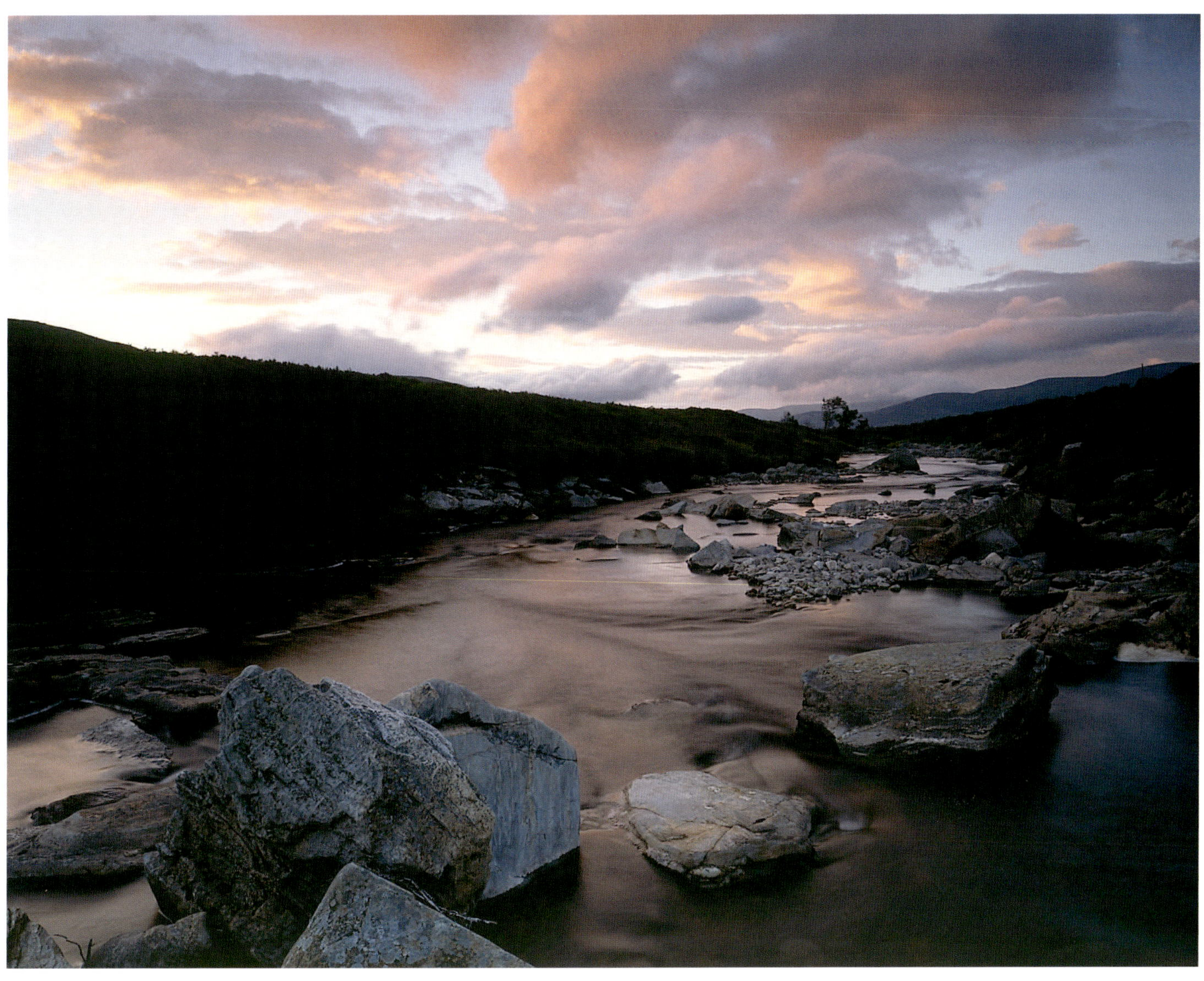

Dawn on the River Mark, Scotland

Empty Quarter, Oman. Limited Edition of 9 Prints".

Pricing is a difficult area. You want to sell but not undersell. £600 – £700 is quite normal for a 24x 20in framed print by a well-known photographer. But as a "beginner" you should consider the local market and assess your own value. So be realistic, but never reduce the price. With limited edition prints you can increase the price – for example by 20% each time three pictures are sold. The theory is that buyers are encouraged to get in early before the cost goes up.

Put the price of each picture at the bottom of the caption so people don't need to ask.

The private view

A full day is needed to set up and hang. It won't necessarily take that long, but once everything's under control you can relax and take a good look to see that things are straight.

If it's well organised you'll feel confident, so have a glass of wine and start to

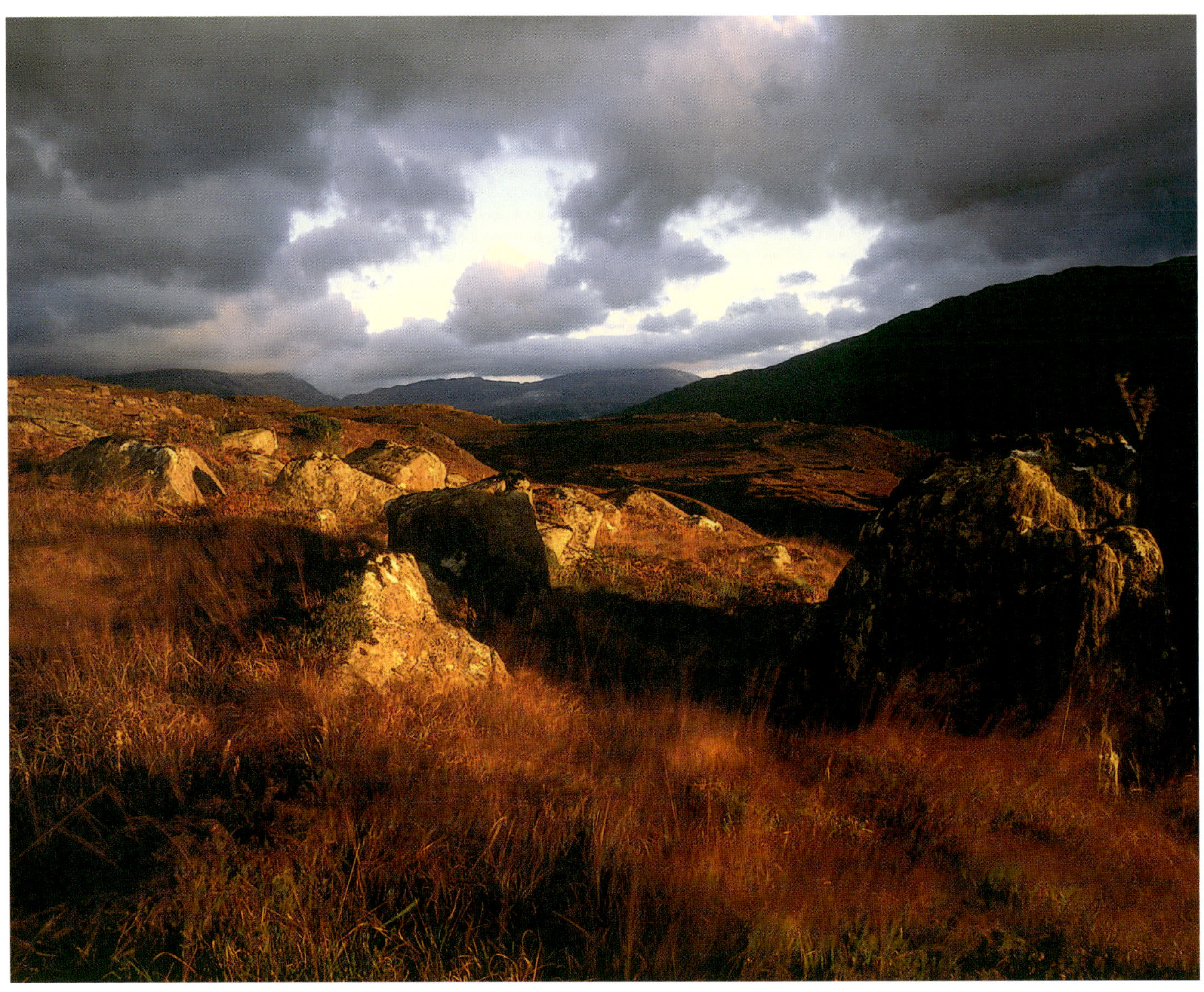

Evening Light on Quinag, Scotland

enjoy things. Make sure refreshments are plentiful and kept simple (and that someone else looks after this). But as sales grow, try not to overdose on the wine!

This is your show and months of planning have now come to fruition, with you centre stage – so don't hide in a corner but welcome visitors in. You may want to give a little speech, but if too nervous, ask someone who knows your work to do the honours. Have someone there who knows the photographs and something about you as a photographer to act as co-host and take orders. But remember that anyone who wants to buy will want to talk to you because you are the artist.

Have a notebook and pen handy for names and addresses to confirm a sale the next day. Make sure business cards are available. Some people will want to know not just about the photographs, but the camera, lenses, filters, camera, time of day – so have all these details to hand.

Look out for anyone from the media and make sure they're OK. They might ask searching questions, particularly if the exhibition is to be reviewed.

You will need to be alert for coming

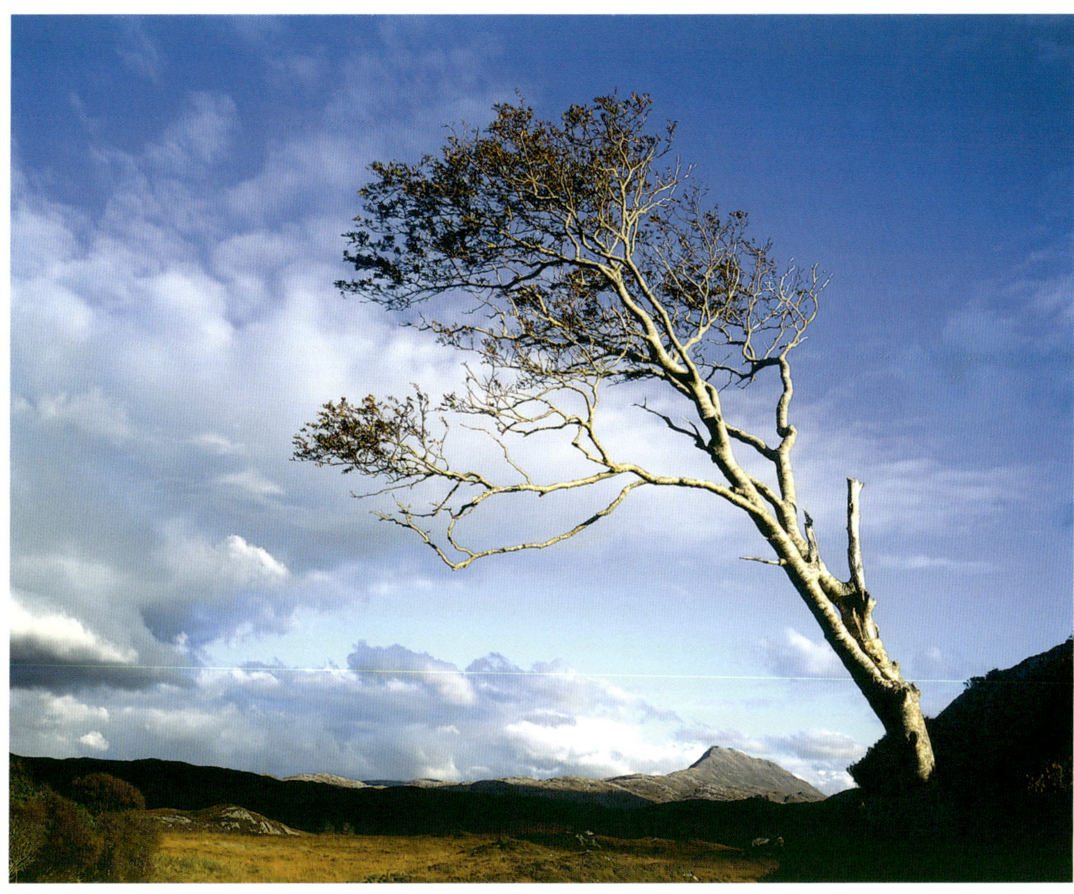

exhibition days. Be prepared to be around all the time, particularly at a weekend, because unless you're well known, it's unlikely a sale will be made without you. Some people who are interested in buying like a private guided tour of the exhibition, particularly if they develop a rapport with you. This should not be seen as a chore, but as a great sign.

Once the exhibition is over, it goes without saying that bills and letters must be dealt with quickly. Have a businesslike approach, but don't be a businessman. Orders for photographs should be processed, but remember they are works of art and shouldn't be rushed. Records need to be kept of who buys what, as they become potential customers for the next exhibition, and that's how you build up a following.

If articles are written about you, write and thank the author (assuming they are complimentary).

An exhibition is an excellent way to launch yourself into the fine art photography market or to improve your profile as a photographer. If you don't exhibit you may never be noticed. But it takes effort, forward planning and a commitment to succeed.

The first show is always the most difficult. Next time round you have experience of what sells and a track record to show to other venues. The good news is that it does get easier. When the costs and effort appear daunting, think of it as a personal investment in your quest to become a noted photographer.

Silver Birch in Glencanisp, Scotland

Producing a book

by SIMON JAMES

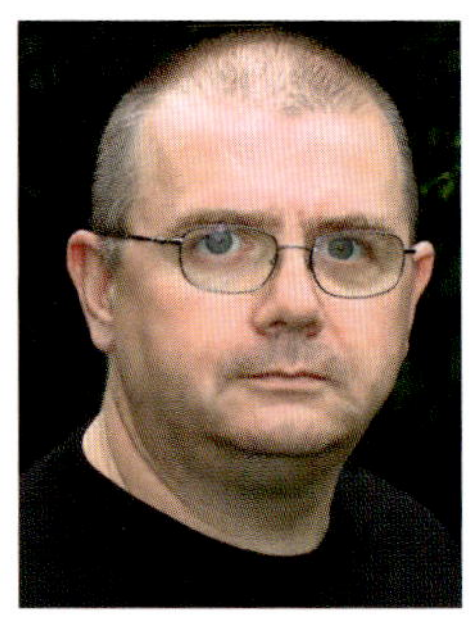

Almost every keen freelance secretly thinks their work would look good published in book form. In reality only a small number of photographers ever realise this ambition, the irony being that the failure is often more about the manner in which the attempt is made, than the publishing concept or quality of imagery submitted.

The simple truth is that publishing is big business, and like all businesses its primary requirement is to turn a profit. Books are commercial products, and to stand a chance of getting your book published it's imperative to adopt a businesslike approach throughout the process.

Is there a market?

Ask any publisher and you will immediately be told there's precious little profit in illustrated books. In fact this is a half-truth.

What they really mean is that there *is* a profit to be made from illustrated books, but that it's easier and much more profitable to produce a quarter of a million paperback copies of the latest chick-lit bestseller, printed on paper of a quality rather closer to that found on small, sometimes quilted, rolls in supermarkets.

Books that don't contain pictures don't require the expense of employing skilled picture editors and top-end book designers, getting high quality scans done by the repro house, buying in paper of sufficient quality to do justice to the images, buying time on six-colour presses, and all the other costs associated with top of the range illustrated publishing.

So publishers are acutely wary of taking on new illustrated book ideas from new authors, and potential new authors should arm themselves with an awareness of this prior to pitching to a publisher.

The good news, perhaps surprisingly, is that despite the above, it genuinely, honestly, and truthfully, can be done. And anyone can do it – you don't have to be a famous name to get into print. What is needed is a marketable idea, a realistic approach, good research skills, and the determination, commitment and ability to see it through.

The idea itself doesn't have to be hugely complex, or for that matter even highly original. Some would say the simpler the better. The only absolute necessity is that the idea jumps off the page on the commissioning

Simon James worked as an operating theatre paramedic until the age of 27, when he left to study photography as a mature student. His first book, *Signs of Life* (Cornerhouse Press), was published in 1992, and *Mind The Gap* (HarperCollins), an unauthorised geography of the London Underground, was published in 2001. He moved to London in 1996 to work full time as a portrait photographer, his pictures now being held in both the National Portrait Gallery and Imperial War Museum collections. As a writer he specialises in photography, travel and food. He is Contributing Editor to the *Royal Photographic Society Journal*, a regular contributor to the *British Journal of Photography* and has had work published in *The Daily Telegraph*, *The Sunday Times Magazine* and a number of other titles in Europe and the United States.

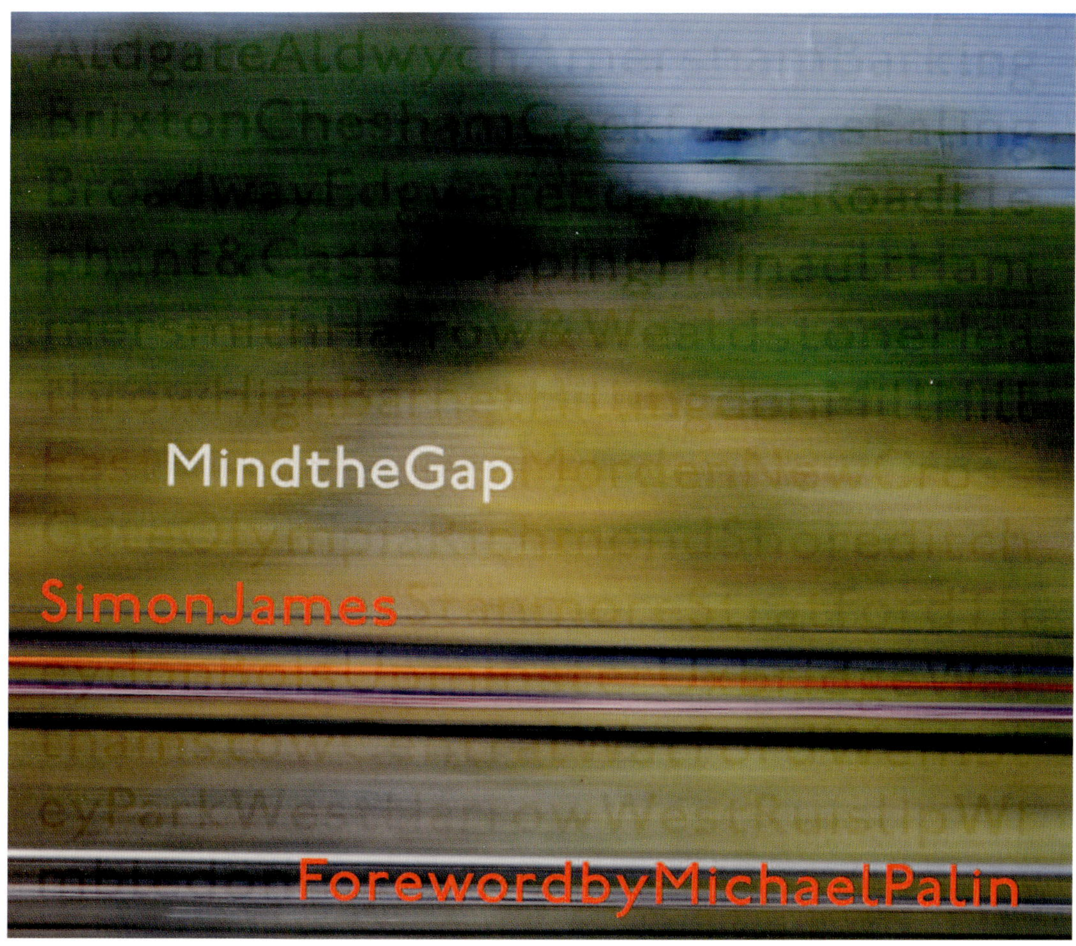

The cover of Simon James's highly succesful picture book on the London Underground, *Mind the Gap*

editor's desk, because at stage one it's going in there alone and won't have you on the other side of the desk to back it up.

The opening pitch has to be short, to the point, and good enough to convince the commissioning editor it will both sell easily in book form and fit comfortably within the range of books he or she produces.

The magic step into print is of course still a long way off, but if you can achieve that impact with your original pitch, the phone is rather more likely to ring.

Assessing the market

Considering the above, from the outset it's absolutely crucial to adopt a strategic approach to achieving a publishing contract. And, as ever, step one is always research. This takes several forms but begin, as dispassionately as possible, with a good long look at the idea itself. Is it really good enough? Or might it perhaps be better approached, or developed, from a slightly different angle?

The most important questions remain: "Who will buy this book?" and "Is this audience big enough to attract a publisher?"

It's also crucial to discover which company produces books in your chosen specialism, and having found them, to familiarise yourself with their list to ensure your concept fits with their current direction.

On the subject of the basic idea, it's worth mentioning that, while any original idea is worthy of consideration, certain subject areas are very much more difficult to break into. It's possible, for example, to

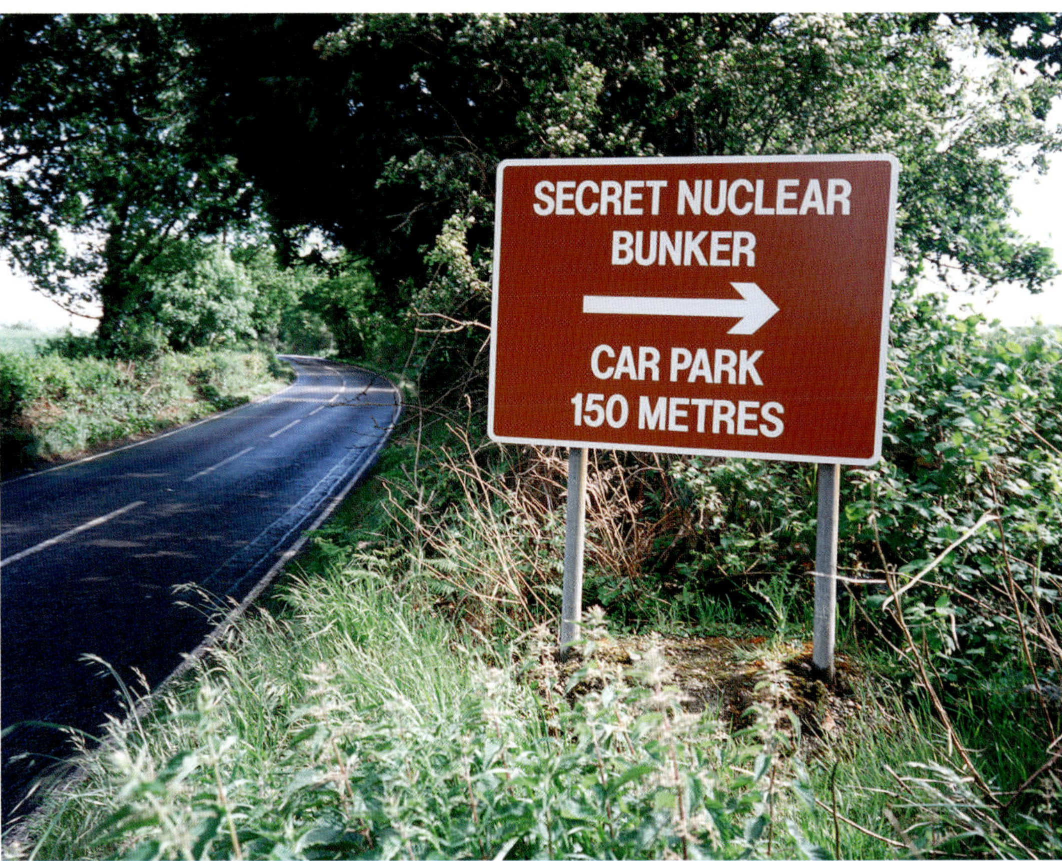

The secret's out! One of the illustrations from the author's book

produce a book of landscapes; but quite apart from the vast amount of library pictures now heavily marketed to publishers, well-established UK-based photographers regularly approach them with new ideas in this arena. It's more difficult for a newcomer to break in because the established figures have the crucial advantage of a track record, proving they can deliver highest-quality imagery, in the required form, to the required deadline.

Equally it's quite possible to get published as a photojournalist. But, on account of publishers' perception of how difficult photojournalism is to sell, this is by far and away the toughest arena in which to achieve book publication.

Probably the most successful route is to look for a subject that is quirky, rather than arty or earth-shattering, something that will appeal to as broad an audience as possible.

Perhaps a metaphorical hook from which witty, ironic, amusing photographs and captions can be hung. For if you get it right, and it's launched at the right time of year, such a book might just find its way onto bookshop tables at those times when customers are racking their brains for suitable presents for their friends and relatives. Such a publication has the potential to become that rare beast: a photographic book that generates a real income.

Having found the basics of an idea the next step is the research phase, the opening question being: "Has it been done before?"

A good way to find this out is to start with the major booksellers' websites. Amazon.co.uk, for example, not only include current titles on their website but often inform you when an out of print title is available from one of their used-bookseller partners. Google and other search engines are equally useful

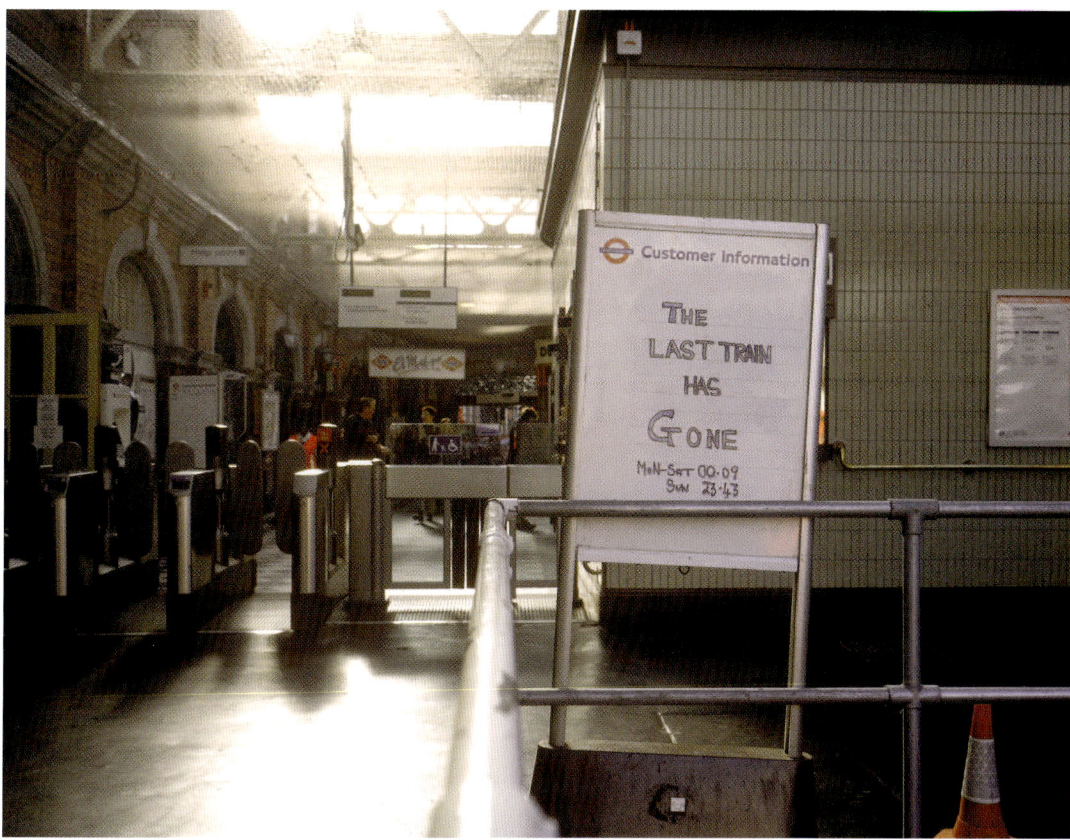

ports of call. But, perhaps surprisingly, an idea needn't necessarily be ditched even if research shows it's not original.

In my own case, standing on a London Underground platform one morning, it occurred to me that although three million people use the Tube every day, very few of them ever go to the ends of the lines. Gradually it dawned on me that three million was exactly the sort of audience size that might attract a publisher, and I began thinking about how one might produce a witty travelogue about journeys to the mysterious sounding places at the ends of the Underground lines.

There have, of course, been very many books centred around the Tube, but suddenly it seemed I might have tripped over a new angle on an old story. And so it proved – my second book, *Mind the Gap*, was accepted by a major publisher and went on to considerable success.

Planning the project

If, having researched your idea's potential in as detached a manner as you possibly can, you remain convinced it has legs, the next step is to begin planning it out. As with the initial idea, the plan itself doesn't need to be vast or complex, simply the broadest outline of how you see your series coming together.

How will it begin? How might it end? Do you envisage an introduction or essay at the beginning, and if so by whom? An introduction by a personality, if you can get one, is likely to enhance sales, but this needn't be something gone into in any depth at this stage.

At this stage the function of the plan is at least as much about clarifying the project in your own mind, as it is about persuading a publisher you're their next great discovery.

The last train ... another image from the book, providing a touch of humour

It's also about now that the picture making starts – initially again as a form of research – to see if the idea's apparent potential is really there when you finally pick up the camera. And then we come to picture making in earnest – working your way into the concept and watching it evolve as the series develops.

It's also important to emphasise that there's no real timescale to all this; quality is the essential criterion. People work at different rates on different projects, but as the series begins to grow you'll find it developing a momentum, and gradually begin to feel you have enough images to think about approaching publishers. Which brings us back to the pitch.

Making the pitch

The first thing to say about the pitch is it should be addressed to the commissioning editor by name. Anything addressed generically to "The Commissioning Editor" of your chosen publisher is unlikely ever to find the correct desk and will in all likelihood end up in the bin.

Despite our now inhabiting a world of electronic transmission, a formal pitch should still be sent in hard copy form. An e-mail, on a busy morning, is very much easier to delete and forget than a properly laid out, individually addressed, paper document. Publishers receive many hundreds of submissions every year and, in order to get yours read, it's absolutely paramount to maintain a professional approach.

One good source of reference on the publishing industry is the *Writers' and Artists' Yearbook*, although with potential photographic books there's no real substitute for legwork. Undoubtedly the best place to begin a shortlist of suitable publishers is the

shelves of major bookshops.

But before preparing your formal pitch be sure to check out the websites of publishers you are thinking of contacting. Often publishers will give details on their website of how and when they like to receive editorial submissions, as is the case for example with Phaidon Press and Dewi Lewis Publishing, both of whom publish photographic titles.

In cases where guidelines are stipulated it is crucial to follow them as close to the letter as possible, just as if you were applying for a job. Where no guidelines are given, begin with the briefest of letters introducing yourself, the idea, and why you are convinced this particular editor is exactly the person to publish it.

The actual pitch should be typed, not handwritten, on headed notepaper giving clear contact details, and sent in an envelope large enough for it to arrive unfolded on the recipient's desk.

It should take the following form: Head up the sheet with a working title for the project, labelled "working title" to indicate you anticipate and are prepared to work with editorial input. Beneath the working title should be a paragraph, or at the most two, headed "synopsis". Here you describe what the book is about including, if it's a well-travelled subject, the unique selling point of your idea and how it differs from previous publications, followed by a brief outline of the proposed audience.

In other words the pitch should, in the shortest manner possible, describe the concept and who will buy the finished book on publication. You may also wish to include a brief CV telling the proposed editor a bit about yourself, and a stamped addressed return envelope for them to acknowledge receipt of your submission.

Neither the pitch, nor the letter, nor the

CV, should cover more than a single side of A4, and it is most unlikely they will be returned.

The final element of the pitch is sample images. A good number to enclose is 12–15, which should be enough to provide an outline of the concept in illustrated form, as well as offering the editor an inkling of how you personally see through the camera.

Again the issue of the businesslike approach comes to the fore when considering how to present the images. No matter how they were produced – on digital, negative or transparency – the images included within the initial pitch should be of a suitable size for their quality to be appreciated, yet for all that disposable. The optimum is A4-sized laser copies or inkjets, large enough to create impact and assure quality for future reproduction, yet cheap enough to produce not to require return.

Never, ever, send unique original images when pitching for publication.

Commissioning editors are very busy indeed and showing the courtesy of pitching in disposable form is one of the small ways in which you announce yourself to be adopting a professional approach to an entirely professional issue.

The idea is the key

In concluding it's important to emphasise that, while comparatively few photographers make huge income from book publication itself, a published book, managed properly, is one of the best PR vehicles a photographer can have. The guidelines above deliberately pull no punches and determinedly tell it how it is.

But the most important issue always remains the idea. If the concept is good enough, you adopt a professional enough approach, and you develop it to it's best advantage, your name is very likely to appear on those bookshop shelves.

About the BFP

Founded in 1965, the Bureau of Freelance Photographers is today the foremost body for the freelance photographer. It has a worldwide membership, comprising not only full-time freelances, but also serious amateur and semi-professional photographers. Being primarily a service organisation, membership of the Bureau is open to anyone with an interest in freelance photography.

The most important service offered to members is the *Market Newsletter*, a monthly report on the state of the freelance market. A well-researched and highly authoritative publication, the *Newsletter* keeps freelances in touch with the market for freelance work, mainly by giving information on the type of photography currently being sought by a wide range of publications and other outlets. It gives full details of new magazines and their editorial requirements, and generally reports on what is happening in the publishing world and how this is likely to affect the freelance photographer.

The *Newsletter* also includes in-depth interviews with editors, profiles of successful freelances, examples of successful pictures, and other general features to help freelances in understanding and approaching the marketplace.

In addition, members receive *The Freelance Photographer's Market Handbook* every year as it is published. While the *Newsletter* keeps members up-to-date with current picture requirements, the 250-page *Handbook* provides an overview of market requirements, listing the continuing needs of magazines, book publishers, card and calendar publishers, and other markets for freelance photography.

Other services provided to members for the modest annual subscription include:

● Advisory Service. Individual advice on all aspects of freelancing is available to members.

● Mediation Service. The Bureau tries to protect its members' interests in every way it can. In particular, it is often able to assist individual members in recovering unpaid fees and in settling copyright or other disputes.

● Exclusive items and special offers. The Bureau regularly offers books and other useful items to members, usually at discount prices.

● In the Services section of this *Handbook* can be found a number of companies providing special discounts to BFP members on production of a current membership card. Amongst various services members can obtain comprehensive photographic insurance cover at competitive rates.

For further details and an application form, write to Bureau of Freelance Photographers, Focus House, 497 Green Lanes, London N13 4BP, telephone 020 8882 3315, e-mail mail@thebfp.com, or visit the BFP website at www.thebfp.com.